WITH A FLY'S EYE, WHALE'S WIT, AND WOMAN'S HEART

ANIMALS AND WOMEN

Published in the United States by Cleis Press, P.O. Box 8933, Pittsburgh, Pennsylvania 15221, and P.O. Box 14684, San Francisco, California 94114.
Printed in the United States.
Cover art: Cecilia Brunazzi
Typesetting: CalGraphics
Logo art: Juana Alicia
First Edition.
10 9 8 7 6 5 4 3 2

Library of Congress Cataloging-in-Publication Data
With a fly's eye, whales' wit, and woman's heart : relationships between animals and women / edited by Theresa Corrigan and Stephanie T. Hoppe. — 1st ed.
   p.   cm.
   ISBN 0-939416-24-7 : $24.95. — ISBN 0-939416-25-5 (pbk.): $9.95
   1. American literature—Women authors. 2. Women and animals—
Literary collections. 3. American literature—20th century.
   I. Corrigan, Theresa, 1949- . II. Hoppe, Stephanie T.
PS509.W62W58   1989
810.8'0352042—dc20   89-7089
                                                                      CIP

Every possible effort has been made to ensure that permission has been granted for use of the material printed herein: *Gloria Anzaldúa:* from *Borderlands/La Frontera* by Gloria Anzaldúa pp. 148-152 © 1987 by Gloria Anzaldúa. Reprinted by permission of Spinsters/Aunt Lute Book Company, P. O. Box 410687, San Francisco, CA 94941. *Margaret Atwood:* from SELECTED POEMS II: POEMS SELECTED AND NEW, 1976-1986 by Margaret Atwood. Copyright © 1987 by Margaret Atwood. Reprinted by permission of Houghton Mifflin Company. Copyright © Margaret Atwood 1986 (Toronto: Oxford University Press Canada, 1986); reprinted by permission of the publisher. *Hope Sawyer Buyukmihci:* From UNEXPECTED TREASURE by Hope Sawyer Buyukmihci. Copyright © 1968 by Hope Sawyer Buyukmihci. Reprinted by permission of the publisher, M. Evans and Company, Inc., New York. From *The Hour of the Beaver* © Hope Sawyer Buyukmihci 1971. Chicago: Rand McNally & Co., 1971. Reprinted by permission of the author. *Sally Carrighar:* from HOME TO THE WILDERNESS by Sally Carrighar. Copyright 1944 by Sally Carrighar. Copyright © renewed 1973 by I.C.E. Limited. Reprinted by permission of Houghton Mifflin Company. *Joan Dobbie:* "Still Another Road Kill" © Joan Dobbie 1984; reprinted by permission of the author. First appeared in *Ariel III*, Triton College, 1984. *Judy Grahn:* from *Mundane's World*, copyright © 1988 by Judy Grahn, published by The Crossing Press, Freedom CA 95019. *Stephanie T. Hoppe:* "What the Cat Brought In" © Stephanie T. Hoppe 1986. A different version of this story appeared in *BEYOND: Science Fiction & Fantasy*, no. 3, January 1986. *Natalie Kusz:* "Small Purchase" © Natalie Kusz 1989; reprinted by permission of the author. First appeared in *The Threepenny Review*, vol. x, no. 1, Spring 1989. *Aileen La Tourette:* from *Cry Wolf* copyright © Aileen La Tourette 1986. Published by Virago Press 1986. *Ursula K. Le Guin:* "May's Lion" Copyright © 1983 by Ursula K. Le Guin; reprinted by permission of the author and the author's agent, Virginia Kidd. First appeared in *The Little Magazine*, Vol. 14, No's 1 and 2 (1983). *Cris Mazza:* "Attack at Dawn" © 1984 Midway Review; reprinted by permission of the author. First appeared in *Midway Review*, 6, 1984. *Rochelle Natt:* "Mrs. Schultz Walks Suzie" © Rochelle Natt 1988. *Mary TallMountain:* "Meditation on a Cat" © Mary TallMountain 1983; reprinted by permission of the author. First appeared in CATS Magazine, April 1983.

WITH A FLY'S EYE, WHALE'S WIT, AND WOMAN'S HEART

ANIMALS AND WOMEN

EDITED BY THERESA CORRIGAN AND STEPHANIE HOPPE

Cleis Press
SAN FRANCISCO • PITTSBURGH

Contents

Introduction

I. Cat! Tell Me

II. The most difficult task the birds demand is that we learn to be equal to them, to feel our way into an intelligence that is different from our own.

Introduction

This is a book not just by women or about animals, though all of the pieces in it are both, but about relationships between animals and women, examinations of the realities and the possibilities of our dealings with members of other species and theirs with us.

In these pages you will meet women of all ages and conditions and animals of many species, dogs and cats, spiders and crabs. Also Max, the one-eyed fish who lives with a one-eyed woman, and the orphaned elephant "71" and the woman who mothers her. A woman who believes she may be a goat and the goat who thinks she may be right. An alien named Leyla presently living in New York, a rooster named Clarence, and Cinderella Dober-Mutt — that fearless old tart, Leader of the Gang of Rebels. A foursome of spiders in a garden. A solitary crab. Harriet the rabbit and Harriet Baboon. An old, old woman in search of a last dog.

You will be asked to consider what a cat might say if she took to speaking English, what cows think of passing humans, what role a person might find for herself in a family of beavers; what death is to the mountain lion seeking company in his dying, to a deer hit by a poet's car, and to the millions of animals used every year in testing consumer products.

To these stories — "stories" in a wide sense, the sense in which all writings that give shape to perceptions are stories — the contributors to this book bring all the tools of mind and word across a range of perspectives and genres: fiction, poetry, reminiscence, interview, political and historical analysis. Their answers — the book in your hands — are both incomplete and provisional, and we are even now working on a second, companion, volume.

But we do not expect it either to suffice. While Earth endures, how can there be any end to the company of animals and of women? As editors, the two of us are grateful to have been given, and to be able to share with you, these glimpses and visions of the perhaps fleeting, but surely immortal, grace of particular actual living beings.

Theresa Corrigan and Stephanie T. Hoppe

I.
Cat! Tell me...

What the Cat Brought In
Stephanie T. Hoppe

Was it only yesterday? It was, yes, and afternoon, late at that when my cat first spoke to me.

"The fog is coming in early," she said. "And look how thick it is."

In itself the remark was unexceptionable and I grunted only, the wordless small noise one makes to acknowledge people talking. But this wasn't "people." I stopped writing and looked up at the cat where she sat on the arm of the chair opposite mine, crouching sphinx-wise on that narrow perch, her yellow eyes wide and glossy, fixed on me.

"The fog — " she began again deliberately. I interrupted her.

"Yes, it's early, I heard you the first time."

"In that case you should have made a proper reply." She flattened her ears a little, taking on a mean look. "Surely that is the way of it — of this talking. Talk must be reciprocal. Words cry out for more words."

I pushed away paper and pencil. I wasn't sure I wanted even to begin to think how it came about she suddenly could talk — but certainly I could not work while she did. Nor could I be still. I went to the kitchen, set water on the stove and stood hunched over it though I knew it could not then boil. The cat spoke at my back, conversationally.

"Now we're in here you could get my dinner."

I could not but hear her. Words are what I never can resist, not in any form. Signs, labels, warnings, instructions: every word I encounter I read. I hear every whisper, meant for me or not. And of course it is my chosen work to turn all existence into words. I did not look at the cat. "It's only a little after four," I muttered. "Not time for dinner."

"You won't ever get me trained to a schedule," she said. "I know how you try but I will always want my dinner when I think of it, whatever the time."

I have always kept cats, a touch, so I liked to think, of untamed nature, that by contrast sets off the homeyness of a house. Small and compact as cats are, self-centeredly aloof and mostly asleep, they seem a conveniently slight touch of wildness.

A cat that talked would be something altogether different. There could be no peace in a house with a cat that talked. I felt myself on a brink; I dared no words of my own now, from fear of what might follow.

The water boiled. I poured it, gulped the coffee too hot and scalded my mouth, all the while feeling the cat's gaze on me, her silence precarious. I muttered at my cup as I put it down. "We need a few things from the store." I headed for the front door.

"Goodby, then," the cat called after me politely, and I shuddered. Just in itself the cat's voice was unnerving, lacking expression, the hissing of sibilants prolonged; the anatomical arrangements for voice in cats must be far from ideal. And what if the plants and furniture now also took to talking to me? My everyday life would turn into an unending round of formalities. I would never get any work done.

For the moment I thought only of escaping. I fled the neighborhood, slowing only when I came to streets busy with people. I stared into shops scarcely seeing, choosing the most crowded, patient with my own kind as I had never been, with their noise and their demands for attention — I even felt grateful. Out among people I could not maintain my belief that my cat had spoken to me and thereby chased me from the house. It could not be. I stopped short in a busy passageway, turned right around against the traffic and went home.

As I set my purchases down on the table in the kitchen the cat materialized beside them. She surveyed what I had bought, with an air of disdain I had to admit was not unwarranted — here was nothing we needed, nothing with any use beyond delaying this moment . . . that was now come. She lifted her gaze to my face.

"Are you going to sit on these things or do I have to do it?"

Instantly I was diverted. "I always wanted to ask you!" I exclaimed, thinking how every object brought into the house or moved from its usual place — a jacket not hung up, a letter or postcard left lying about — would soon be coated with a thin layer of soft shed hair; if indeed the cat was not herself still present, curled up asleep, however precarious or anomalous the place. Many times I had wondered if there was not some larger significance to this often exasperating behavior — if the objects she sat on were not altered also in unseen ways, made more certain or integrated better into reality.

Certainly nothing holds together of itself. I had speculated that cats might be a first line of defense for the world against entropy — that not the twelve just persons of legend but a cat, or all cats, might underlie the physicist's discovery I read of that the universe was not after all running down to its end.

"Cat! Tell me — why do you sit on everything?" Now let her talk, I thought.

She rose twitching her tail and walked back and forth under my hand where I had been scratching her the while, apparently inadequately.

"Well?" I asked.

Could she even know? If she did anything, she did it more sleeping than waking. It might be no more than the merely physical interaction of air and cat fur in magnetic or gravity fields. Action and reaction: the necessary and natural counterforce to the inherent contrariness in things. I looked her over with a new eye, the lines and whorls of her fur. She grumbled at me.

"You bring too many things into the house. You can't distinguish between what is real and what is illusory and what you merely desire."

I shook my head. "We're talking about you. About what it is that you do — you and other cats, I suppose?"

She butted her head against my hand, which had fallen still. "I know nothing about other cats. Larger things. The world. If there is a world beyond this house and yard." She paused, then corrected herself. "And the yards for two — no, three — houses to the west. And one diagonally in back. The other adjacent yards have dogs. I do not concern myself with dogs' yards. I doubt if a dog can keep a yard real."

I dismissed dogs also, for the moment. "Schools of philosophy have been built on notions like these," I said. "The notion that, say, beyond what we know or think we know there is nothing. Or, when we aren't attending, intermittently — "

"Philosophy!" she interrupted. "I have precious little time for philosophy!" She walked right out from under my hand, the assurance of a giant in her stride. I stared after her: little soft creature, seemingly no more than a cloud of calico fur. I could pick her up in my two hands and hardly feel the weight.

"Nothing lasts long of itself, you know!" She turned and her eyes bored into mine a lengthening moment and I thought — but she bent her head, veiling her gaze. I took a deep breath and straightened my shoulders.

"No doubt you work very hard." The sound of my own voice steadied me. "Lucky for you it's mostly work you can do while you sleep."

She lifted her right paw, licked it meticulously, held it out to observe the effect. She was, after all, a cat. She might not be able to joke, particularly about herself, but she could be embarrassed. I recovered more of my sense of myself. Whatever was going on — if it was real — was surely only between the two of us. I could stand it if she could! Stretching my arm across the distance she had put between us, I flicked the fur of her ruff with one fingertip.

"I'll get your dinner for you now," I offered, magnanimous.

"All right," she said, still intent on her paw. I grunted. This had gone on long enough. I would feed her and then I would get back to work. I fetched a can of cat food, spooned a portion into her dish on the floor. She jumped down beside me.

"I prefer the other brand — the cans with that complicated writing on the label. You never buy those any more."

"*I* don't like that brand! It smells bad — smells up the house." The future gaped in my mind, horribly, interminable petty squabbles with her. "Anyway, this is what's open. Do you want some or not?"

"Oh. . .very well."

She took a bite of the food with her curved white teeth — huntress's teeth. And I watched, absorbed anew. How cats fascinated me! And what a chance it was to talk with one! I put off the thought of work.

"If I were not the person who feeds you, who lets you in and out of the house," I began reflectingly. "If I were small, say the size of a mouse, what would you think of me then?"

"I would eat you," she said thickly, her mouth full.

"So." I stood up, offended. "You care nothing for me. After all these years that I have loved you."

She swallowed and spoke more clearly. "You are what you are. If you were altered in any detail you would not be what you are. . .I don't think — "

She stared at her food, or rather at a vacant place in the air somewhere between her face and her food. Then abruptly she lowered her head and took another bite and another, quickly, until she had finished the bowl. Still she was silent. I asked if she would like to go outside. She moved without a word toward the back door. I opened it for her and shut it again behind her.

Now I could work.

But I could not. I could not make the story I was writing come to words. I could see it in my mind, a sort of glow but without shape, uncertain and shifting. I tried to draw it down to paper, to fix its form, but each stroke I set with my pencil lay only lifeless beside the next, clumsy markings that clouded over my bright vision. I had to give it up, turn to something else.

I remembered the cat only hours later when I was getting ready for bed. I opened the back door and she scuttled in chattering.

"The fog!" she cried. "The fog is so thick tonight! I hardly got things safely into night at all. I think I may have lost one of the neighbors' yards. I just hope our yard makes it through to dawn!"

Startled, I peered past her into the night. The back of the yard roared — the trees, that would be, the wind blowing them about. I knew they were there but I could not quite make them out behind the clumps and streamers of mist that gleamed dully in the night light of the city. The fog always comes through these hills with a strong wind.

Perhaps it was unusually thick and low, but it was still only fog. And the cat's words were only words and nothing to me if I did not heed them. Shutting the door I told her, "That's the weather for you any time of year in our city. Will you be quiet now and go to sleep? And let me sleep?"

And she let me go, muttering and grumbling but nothing I could make out.

In the morning she was full of words but I stood firm against them. When she had drunk her dish of milk I insisted she go out, cold and gray as the morning was, the fog thicker than ever. I was going to work. Perhaps, as she claimed, the work she did kept the real world real, at least that part of it where I was. I would grant the point. Let her see to it then. And leave me to my own work of teasing some semblance of reality out of the wisps and dreams of my imaginings.

As sometimes happened, the night's sleep had focused my mind.

Now I slipped easily into the story I had been writing — or rather it flowed out from me, strong and full; what drives more than is driven, this process whereby a story adds word to phrase to page until, apparently just of itself, it comes alive. And if it fed upon my life, I was only willing.

At the kitchen door the cat howled. When finally I noticed her noise I realized it had been going on for some time. Just the animal noise of her I might have continued to ignore but against words, once I heard them, my words broke.

"Let me in!" she cried again and again. "Let me in!"

And I did.

She was through the doorway in a flash, up on the kitchen table, shaking and quivering, her fur flying every which way, her yellow eyes wide and wild-looking. Catching her alarm I slammed the door.

"What is it!"

"Look for yourself! Outside!"

I glanced at a window. Fog — but somehow I could not keep my gaze steady on that gray featurelessness, could not see anything at all through it; could even think there was not anything beyond it.

"It's all these words!" the cat hissed. "Language! Ever since I started talking all my attention has run off into abstractions and symbolic manipulations. I have lost my capacity for reality! And now look at the result."

At the corner of my eye a wall heaved, started to dissolve, turn foggy. Fear coiled like a cold fog within me.

"No," I said. "No, it can't be."

"But it is. We're lost, and I don't know how much else. And I can't undo it."

In that moment I believed her. But had we then no chance? I thought of one, a small one, nothing to hang all existence on, not even the existence of a house and four, or was it five, back yards.

I had to try. I hurried to the living room keeping my gaze on the floor, well away from the windows and walls, not lifting my eyes until I could fix them again on these pages.

The cat followed on my heels. I heard her small quick padding. I shut it out — I shut out everything and threw myself into my story. Where of course she also was but only as I wrote.

For hours now the cat has not said a word. She's sleeping, a warm living presence pressed against me — the last warmth left perhaps anywhere.

I'm afraid. It's going to be a near thing. If I can do it at all. My fingers are stiff with cold but I'm still writing, like never before. Terrible thoughts swarm at the edge of my mind, distracting me from my work, desperate though it is. I think that physicist I read of is being disproved, that all may be ending, the universe winding down and dissolving into a cool gray fog. . . .

Can it be? And can the outcome hinge on me? I have to assume so, act on that assumption, make the attempt.

I'm so cold! I feel so very tired! But if the cat will sleep on, warm in my lap. . . if the story will come. . . . I've got it now, I think I have, a few more words, yes —

And now the rest is up to you.

Cows

Jean Anaporte-Easton

At the beginning of the hill I walk each morning, cows
with furry brown bodies and white swirled faces
regard me. They stare and stare.
I wave, call out, salute apart from the group
one calf more determined and truculent
in his staring: "You have a muddy face."
To the adults: "Your baby has a muddy face."
They stare and stare. Moving on
I see over my shoulder that the white
heads have moved along the line of my
.motion. I wish to shout again, but I'm opposite
the lighted barn. Do the cows connect me
with the people in there pulling down hay,
mashing oats and bran? Or do they see another
kind of being moving up and down the road
waving and clomping black hooves?
When I return, they are still in the same place,
still looking toward me, still seeming dubious
and wondering. Either I am so magnificent
a phenomenon they have been standing staring
these thirty minutes at the spot where last
they glimpsed me, or, there has been no point
in moving, and, here I come again, full
of wasted energy.

Her Days at Beetle Rock
Sally Carrighar

Sally Carrighar's experience with a flock of linnets and a mouse who sang while she was convalescing from an illness led her to what became her life's work, nature writing of a very particular kind in which, while she portrayed the overall relationships of animals in their environment, she devoted most attention to individual creatures. She wished, she said, to show chiefly "what was interesting to the creatures themselves." She spent portions of four years in the late 1930's observing the wildlife at Sequoia National Park in the Sierra Nevada of California. She wrote about her experiences there in her autobiography, Home to the Wilderness.

During the long stay at Sequoia, from snow to snow, the plan was to both watch and write, and therefore I needed to have the birds and animals at my cabin instead of around the Rock. They were the same species at both places; it was only preferable to get a group of them to assemble here.

I had advice from my tutors. A range lick, a large cake of salt used in pastures for cattle, is one of the best attractions, they said, and it proved to be true. The mammals all licked it and as it became smaller the deer tried to eat it. And water: I sank a dishpan in the ground with a rock placed to slope into it; when the deer lowered the water level small mammals and birds could still reach it to drink. About food, the best, I heard, is a surplus supply of what the creatures gather themselves. Take a shopping bag as you walk through the woods and gather berries, acorns, pine cones and staghorn lichen that wind has blown off the trees, and also the seedheads of flowers and grasses. These might have been enough to convince the wild ones that they would find friendliness at this cabin, but some other natural foods were considered permissible: raisins, carrots, peanuts and sunflower seeds. I took up one hundred pounds of those and sent for more. All processed foods, including cake, candy and chocolate cookies are indigestible in wild stomachs. I was told not to throw out table scraps nor especially uncooked rice, which swells in a small stomach and causes the death of the bird or animal. Their instinct is not a good guide. They will eat foods that will harm them.

The biologists had another stern warning: never give what would be more than one meal a day. Otherwise the animals will get out of the habit of hunting for food themselves and the young ones may never learn and will starve when one is gone. If one wants them as friends it is important to *be* a good friend.

I put out the food in the morning, but then I wanted my wild guests to stay all day. How to persuade them? First of course one must be reassuring. When I was on their own level they seemed to feel safer. They apparently sensed that a human being who sits on the ground, leaning in a relaxed way against a tree, is in no position to suddenly leap and attack. And what does one do while sitting there? I have a conviction that birds and animals often are bored, or at least they enjoy anything that is harmless but new and stimulating. They seemed to be fascinated by a paper pinwheel on a stick stuck in the ground; as they watched it whirling they came in closer and closer. They appeared to be interested in any continuous small motion that wasn't threatening. John Muir used to twirl his cap on a stick; I crocheted. They had confidence in that monotonous side-to-side weaving of fingers whereas knitting seemed slightly alarming — the finger which kept darting forward (as I did it) was too much like a strike. For a while I carved little figures in Ivory soap, of the birds and animals themselves, shellacked later, and they watched that. I learned not to sit still at the cabin, as I'd learned with the linnets, but always to move in smooth ways. It is amazing how many aggressive motions one finds in oneself by observing their effect on animals: human beings walk, drop into a chair as we say, get up, reach for things, put things down, turn our heads, gesture, all more abruptly than necessary and that makes us startling.

I talked to the birds and animals and I talked sense, in a normal voice, not the high-pitched baby talk that is one's impulse. I would say to a chipmunk, "You whirl so fast you are just a brown blur." Or to a very shy grouse, "Have you thought of taking a dustbath? Look here where the earth is so fine and dry." I knew they did not understand the words, but to such sensitive creatures a tone may convey more than we realize. I am sure that I would have made a poorer impression with a deliberate stream of talk, planned and purposeful, for they would recognize such artificiality. It all had to come out naturally, from whatever I felt at the moment. For in making friends with the wild ones, I found, it is necessary to be absolutely sincere. I had to act in a friendly way for no other reason but that I cared about these companions; to seem like a friend because I wanted them to come near so I could watch them and write a book about them would never have been enough. It seemed that they had to feel a true sense of warmth, not sentimentality but concern. On the days when my thoughts were absorbed in some writing problem they went away.

Often I sang. Nothing as rousing as *The Star-Spangled Banner*, be assured; I sang the lullabies I used to sing to my dolls and, better, hummed little random songs, thinking of them as subsongs. These seemed to provide the right atmosphere and helped to keep me in the right mood, for a consistently gentle mood is important if the big human animal is to inspire confidence. Consistent moods are not always typical of human beings. Letters don't come or they come with distressing news, or one has had a disturbing dream, or is catching a cold, or may have eaten too many onions last night — or just feels out of phase. Let that happen too many times and the birds and animals no longer trust us.

They did come to my cabin and finally stayed most of the time. When I opened the door in the morning there they were waiting, about thirty of them, a lovely sight. The tails of the squirrels and chipmunks would twitch, the birds flash their wings, and the ears of the deer turn my way with subtle flickering motions as I began to talk. Before thinking of breakfast I fed them all, the seeds, nuts and fruits from the tin cracker boxes kept in the cabin and whatever I'd gathered the previous afternoon. Since I didn't put out any food for their meal at the end of the day, most of them disappeared then to get their own supper, and that was the time when I went for walks in the forest, incidentally gathering food for them.

The next morning they would have come for it: four kinds of squirrels — a chickaree and gray, golden-mantled and digger squirrels; two deer mice that soon moved into the cabin with me; a magnificent four-point buck and a little spike buck and a pregnant doe until she left to have her fawn in the deer's meadow. To the deer I fed carrots mostly, and the big buck became so tame that he would let me come to him with my offering even when he was lying down. He lay for hours each day under a very large sugar pine near the cabin. Among its roots lived a pair of chipmunks and their young and as soon as they heard the door open they whisked up out of their hole. No lizards came; they stayed on the Rock. Late one afternoon a coyote passed and I was glad that my small friends had disappeared by then. And I was well satisfied that the bears left at dawn. A mother and cubs came every night — to the garbage can, not because I was friendly. I watched them at various times away from the cabin but I didn't feel much affinity for them.

The birds greeting me every day were even more numerous than the mammals but did not stay as continually. In the early part of the summer at least, they had nests to build, eggs to brood and young to feed but fortunately for me most of the nearest trees were bird-size, not the tallest, and there were bushes as well — homesites and perches for almost every bird taste. With us much of the time were a Steller's jay and a robin, a very shy female grouse and the male who was hoping to mate with her, a splendid red-shafted flicker, coming down in a power-dive to pick up ants on the ground; and besides the flicker, really a woodpecker, there were two others: the white-headed which was tame and bored away in the closest trees for his insects, and farther out and up, one of the stunning pileated woodpeckers, black, white and red and almost as large as a crow. He was not only big and colorful but his constant loud hammering at the trees kept reminding us that he was there.

Our associates with the prettiest songs were the smaller birds. Every bush and young tree seemed alive with them, fluttering about in their delicate way among the splinters of sunlight along the waxy evergreen needles. Two whose territories adjoined and who therefore did a great deal of arguing in songs liquid and urgently sweet were male ruby-crowned kinglets. Their songs were amazingly loud for such tiny birds and so musical I wondered whether the rest of our group, as well as I, weren't enjoying them. A junco jingled his cheerful gold trill while the wood pewee, with his two falling notes, seemed to say, "It's not quite as good as all that." But the pewee lightened his song during the times when he watched his mate as she built their nest and he stood by, singing encouragement. The red-breasted nuthatch, working over the sugar pine for his insects, kept blowing his one little trumpet note. Less vocal but interesting was the brown creeper at the same task, skillfully turning his white throat-shine into the cracks. Others among us were a warbling vireo who sang almost all the time, a tame yellow and black western tanager, chickadees, purple finches endearingly like the linnets in color and song — and still more.

The songs were fewer as summer wore on but there were always birds' voices around us, twittering and chirping. Dr. W. H. Thorpe in his fascinating book, *Bird-Song*, lists ten different kinds of calls. Two which are opposite in effect he describes as pleasure calls and distress calls. Neither is always literally a "call," that is, with a "come here" meaning. My own thought is that a pleasure call, which is sometimes like a little song, might be the equivalent of our humming or whistling when we are feeling contented. In birds it is most typical of the young. Distress calls do not always mean that a bird is endangered. They may be heard when a bird is cold or hungry or they may be what Konrad Lorenz has defined charmingly as "the peeping of loneliness" of young ducks, geese, and swans. Dr. Thorpe remarks on how even man can recognize cheerfulness in the bird sounds that rise in pitch, the pleasure calls; and the ones that descend as sad or pathetic.

Among the insect-eaters the only birds that came to the cabin for food were those that liked ants, but all came for the drinking water, and to splash in it and to take dust baths on the ground where human feet had made a powder of fallen evergreen needles. For a long time we didn't have any predators there, no weasels, pine martens, foxes, coyotes, wildcats, cougars (which were sometimes near but secretive), not the rare wolverines, or bears in the daytime. Nor did hawks or owls come at first. I watched most of those hunters at other places, but what I saw intimately at the cabin was not a complete picture of the wildlife in this high wilderness. However, one could visualize the predators by observing the prey's instinctive caution. And in this, only the start of a long association with birds and animals, I had to come to terms in my own mind with nature's hunters-and-hunted system. How to accept it? How could one not be repelled by it?

At least one must recognize that the beauty of the wild creatures, the vitality and alertness that allow them to flee or attack *in an instant*, are due to the hunted-hunter relationships. Potential victims must never forget the dangers, otherwise they won't live, and their enemies must be keenly aware at all times of chances to strike, otherwise they don't eat. A cruel arrangement? Yes, from the human point of view but animals that have virtually no enemies and subsist on food as easy to get as green leaves are apt to become sluggish and even ill-tempered. And of the various kinds of squirrels, the ground squir-rels, which have the easiest, if somewhat vulnerable life, are the dullest and least attractive (except for the golden-mantled). It is some-thing for human beings to think about. We have succeeded in mak-ing our lives almost safe. Will our own vitality and alertness survive the lack of physical challenges?

But impersonal and fast though most animal hunting may be, no creature is ever a willing victim, and by one means or another nature gives most of the prey a fair opportunity to escape. A mother bird on a nest brooding eggs or young is at risk, and to help keep her in-conspicuous most female birds have dark or dull colors. And camouflage is a well-known protection, saving many a spotted fawn and speckled nestling long before it was saving soldiers. Others who might become victims are very swift, faster if they are in good health than their hunters; deer, caribou, and antelope all escape in that way — but they also need to sense keenly the approach of an enemy. Some prey avoid capture by stillness and others by making themselves inaccessible to most predators. All those skills were evi-dent in the animals at the cabin. And I had to learn one defense that may apply only to human beings.

In each stay at Sequoia I had observed the torn-eared buck and had seen how all other deer would give way to him. The particular herd that browsed around Beetle Rock numbered twenty or thirty animals. The leader had probably got the injury to his ear in fighting other deer to assert his right to first choice of the does. In such com-bats he would have proved his supremacy — but a herd leader is more than the strongest individual. These leaders are sometimes referred to by men as the master bucks, but once they have won their harem they aren't masters in the sense of having power over the rest of the herd. They are leaders in the true meaning of being guides. They make decisions about when the herd should start down to the lowlands for winter, when to come back to the mountains in the spring, when and where to move if there are human hunters the deer need to avoid. They are the sages, the wise men as long as their faculties are still functioning. Whenever I'd seen the torn-eared buck with the others, he had been the one most alert and the others watched him for signs that he was aware of danger. Anybody could read his warnings: the sudden tensing of muscles, the stiff movement of legs if he took any steps, the head flung up, the expanded nostrils to reach for a scent, and above all his mobile ears, now pointing in unison to the source of his dread. At these signals all other deer stopped whatever they had been doing and now also tense were ready to bound away.

On my third summer he still was the leader; the others deferred to him as they had before. But I thought I could detect a little falling off of his caution. A slight sway in his back and less majestic carriage of head suggested that he was showing the first indications of age. The very fact that he spent so much time at the cabin seemed like a slackening of his sense of responsibility. But he was still magnificent and I learned how all other creatures, not just the deer, depended on his alertness to warn them.

As he lay under the sugar pine he was like an instrument finely tuned to pick up distant signals. Often swinging his head, he was apparently testing scents, but his ears were his chief antennae, the tear in one not being serious. Large ears, as the species name, mule deer, suggests, they moved independently — unless the buck heard suspicious sounds, when they pointed together. At other times one ear might turn to the stream below while the other attended to sounds from behind the cabin; or one caught a sound from the right and the other one from the left. They never were still. They were scanning the whole horizon continually and flickering with the most delicate nuances of motion, most of the time responding to sounds that did not reach my ears at all. I tried to imagine how it would be to have that apprehension of everything that was happening within the very wide range of the buck's hearing, to know so many things that would be out of one's sight. Was he aware of a chipmunk's cracking a seed in its underground burrow, of the small weird hum of the bear cubs while they were nursing on the ledge of the Rock, of all the whisper songs of bird mothers, of a squirrel's lapping of water below at the stream — and if it had been a louder lapping would the buck have suspected a coyote or cougar? Perhaps that was why he was sometimes up on his feet in an instant, his nostrils quivering as they reached for a scent and his ears focused together, so exactly that one knew the precise spot from which the sound came.

And did the buck distinguish between the bright sharpness of wind in the oak trees (to a human being sounding like taffeta rustling) and the overhead murmuring of the wind in the firs, pines, cedars and tall sequoias? When the wind eased away the sound seemed to drop in pitch, bringing to human ears the suggestion of sadness that Dr. Thorpe detected in the falling of pitch in bird calls. The wind in evergreen trees is often described as a sighing; so it seems to us and I can believe that it had the same emotional tone for the buck, since these impressions seem to be universal. And did the buck, that summer, have an instinctive sense of his own down-going? The next year, my fourth and last summer there, the buck remembered that I had previously been occupying that cabin, and he came again to lie under the sugar pine. But one day when I had laid some food on a flat stone and the buck was eating it, another buck came around from behind the cabin, a younger, stronger deer, imperious in his manner. And the torn-eared buck stepped away to give a new leader the food. I wept.

During the longer summer when he was still unquestionably the leader, he had a friend who stayed all the time near him, not the pregnant doe and the spike buck who came and went, but a female grouse. It was one of those curious relationships between members of different species that occur now and then, for example with badgers which are likely to invite a fox or coyote to share their burrows, after which the two animals may become almost inseparable. It could be said that the grouse always rested beside the deer because she was relying on his alertness and undoubtedly that was one of her reasons. But she could have been farther away, among the other birds and animals, and have noted his actions just as the rest of them did. The buck, for his part, often watched her. It seemed obvious that the two were aware of each other.

I don't know how many days she had been there before I discovered her. She stayed on the far side of the buck and was shadow-colored, but she was a large bird, about the size of a pheasant without the long tail, and I think the real reason I didn't see her was that she had a stillness so complete, it was like a disguise. It was an uncanny talent. Few birds except mothers on nests are absolutely quiet for long, but once after a red-tailed hawk had flown over I watched the grouse and for eighteen minutes she did not even wink. Her eyes were remote, as if in consciousness she had removed herself and by that means avoided any intensity of emotion that might attract notice. And when she finally came forward her walk was so smooth and quiet, even then it appeared like stillness. She placed each foot in exactly the center line of her body and being thus always in perfect balance, she could stop at any point in her progress. I tried that and found that a human being can't do it without making adjustments to redistribute his weight.

Insects furnished part of the grouse's food. In taking them off the ground she didn't peck here and there jerkily as a hen does; she waited until the insect was under her throat and she could reach for it with the least possible movement. Poise and calmness spread out from her. It spread to myself. Stillness, I told myself as I watched her, is beautiful.

In the early part of the season she was a little lame, and from the amount of time she spent in the sunshine, lying with one leg extended beyond her wing, I thought that it probably ached. Of all the birds and animals she was the most shy about trusting me. I thought that the lameness, due perhaps to a recent attack by some predator, might have made her more than normally wary, and believing that it would help her to regain confidence if she accepted my friendliness, I made a special effort to get her to eat from my hand. I knew she liked peanuts because she would pick them up off the ground but she wouldn't come nearer than four or five feet. Finally one day, when her friend the buck was not there, she did come and very cautiously took a nut from the offered handful. Just then the buck walked around the side of the cabin. "Oh, don't disturb her now!" I said impulsively. At those words, which of course he didn't understand literally, the buck stopped completely; he even held one front hoof off the ground until the grouse had finished the nuts and moved away. As he walked to the sugar pine then I noticed for the first time that he avoided stepping on flowers. Even his hind feet avoided them. One is in a different world with wild creatures, one of infinitely fine sensibility.

For all her shyness the grouse actually was a forceful bird. Her strength was shown with our little tree squirrel, the chickaree. When nothing else was absorbing his electric energy he would tease her. Darting around her and chirring in a voice that was meant to be taunting but actually was pleasant, he kept trying to get a reaction. She would seem not to be aware of him till he came in too far, when her feathers would rise and her eyes flash with anger. Ordinarily he would retreat. This went on day after day.

Once when he was not there the grouse had a dust bath. There probably were some mites on her skin, for extending her feathers widely, she threw dust with her feet all through her plumage, onto her back, wings, sides, down to the base of the feathers. Fluffed out widely, she waited a bit to let the dust smother the mites. The chickaree had seen her. He raced down his tree and began jumping around her, dashing up to her face and back as if he really intended to nip her. Suddenly when he was close she hissed and gave an immense shake that covered the squirrel with dust. With a shrill protest he ran back up the tree.

He was always in motion. Like other chickarees thereabouts he had a territory, his consisting of seven trees, and he patrolled them constantly to be certain that no one intruded. It was breath-stopping to see him leaping from tree to tree on branches so high in the sky. Sometimes the gap was many times his own length — he would surely fall! He had a chickaree friend that he allowed to come into his territory and the two chased each other in games of tag, taking chances greater than ever — a brilliant performance and actually good practice for their defense against predators. Sensibility was the buck's defense, stillness the grouse's, but the chickaree's was speed. Swiftly he could be off the ground, avoiding coyotes, foxes, snakes and other hunters, and up in his tree he could dash through the foliage so fast that even the hawks and owls were handicapped unless they could catch him asleep. He could be noisy and was, with always a sweet liquid voice; he could be much more conspicuous than most prey, and yet part of his liveliness was no doubt due to temperament as much as to assumed safety.

I had a personal reason to remember his bold courage for a long time — a startling experience but I respected his bravery for I could have caught his tail and in anger hurled him against a tree. The cabin was in his territory of seven trees and he felt that he owned the ground space in front of the door. But two other chickarees came for nuts, and to avoid fights I worked out three miniature territories on which to feed them. These were flat rocks, two placed near the corners of the cabin and one in front. Very quickly the three squirrels learned that they would receive a nut only on their own rocks and amusingly all three would come, often at the same time, and sit each on his rock and call if I was inside. I would come out then and toss them their nuts. This had gone on for weeks; I knew the squirrels apart and none had ever gone to any but his particular stone. Our chickaree had the one in front. But one morning one of the other squirrels went to his rock and sat on it and called. Absentmindedly I threw him the peanut to which he was not entitled. At that instant our chickaree arrived.

I have told that much of the story to several biologists and asked what they would have expected to happen. All said that the rightful owner of the rock would attack the trespasser. But he didn't. He attacked me. In his fury he climbed my body as fast as if it had been a tree and ran out on my arm and dug his claws into my wrist so deeply that the scars lasted for many months. This transferring of anger from his intruding neighbor to me seemed to reveal a surprising degree of intelligence and moreover a delicacy of feeling — outrage that I could not be trusted, that I had betrayed an accepted agreement.

This was but one of many proofs that birds and animals have a very strong sense of fairness.

I had offended the wilderness code and again offended it with nearly disastrous consequences. For I stared into a pair of wild eyes, which is not permissible. Wild eyes can put us in touch with our primitive selves, with unsuspected strength. We feel a hint of the energy displayed by the flying, bounding, leaping, climbing, searching creatures who seem so incredibly tireless. So there are the eyes, telling us that we once were as they are. But their eyes do not look directly, inquisitively into others'. They look across yours and glance away, and glance back. But if we look straight at them the birds and animals quickly become restless and then either attack or leave. The bear attacked.

At the time I was writing a story about a black bear mother and her two cubs that I had been watching frequently. Because mother bears are quick to anger, I had not gone as close to them as I wished. I had wanted to study their faces, to try to see whether I could get any feeling of what a bear's consciousness was like — dull and lazy or sharp and suspicious, inquisitive, tolerant, or sometimes seeming like the big brown bears of Alaska who don't eat human beings but tear them to pieces savagely? These Sequoia black bears were supposed to be harmless unless provoked, but with irritability quick to rise. I was immensely curious.

One evening at dusk I was heating two saucepans of water on the cookstove outside the cabin. As I waited I watched two exquisite young deer mice who came out of their hole at the base of the sugar pine. These are beautiful little creatures, deer-brown above, white below, with white feet and furry tails — in no way like house mice, though of course I felt tender towards all mice since it was the song of one that really had sent me here.

The two mice under the tree probably wanted to run about looking for seeds, but if they ventured so far apart as twelve inches they rushed back together again, clinging like two little maidens. Then I happened to raise my eyes. From around the side of the tree was peering the face of a large male bear — in the cinnamon phase, and those cinnamon bears are supposed to be surly, perhaps because other bears shun them, as animals often do avoid one who is an odd color.

My only thought was, here is a bear's face, less than eight feet away, a fine chance to study him. I was staring, of course — with the bold, aggressive looking of human beings. I knew better but I continued to stare.

He was attacking! Half rising to give himself height, he had hurled himself towards me. Grasping the pans of hot water, I threw them full in his face and rushed for the door. I fell going up the steps with the bear close behind, enraged now, but I tumbled inside and banged the door shut with only a second or two to spare, for he fell against it. The lock had the old-fashioned wrought-iron type of latch and marvelously the bar did fall into its notch. That very small piece of mechanism was now my security.

Or so I thought for the first few minutes. But the bear began ploughing around the outside of the cabin, apparently pitching himself against the walls, for it sounded as if some heavy body had struck them. I sat on the edge of the bed, huddled into my fear. One hour, two hours, three hours passed. I was remembering how I had heard that on occasion when visitors went away leaving bears' favorite food, the bears had tipped over the flimsy cabins to get it — not often, but it had happened.

The bear kept up his siege of the cabin all night. I could hear his snorts. I didn't sleep of course. And when the early light came it showed the bear standing up with his front paws on one of the windowsills. He was looking in and on his face was a viciousness I had not dreamed existed. My heart simply caved in with fright.

He didn't try to get in through the window and soon, when the park attendants came to bring firewood and collect garbage, he left. I had a respite from fear and, stilling a slight hysteria, fell asleep.

When I went out for breakfast the bear was there, perhaps fifty yards away down the slope in front of the cabin. He had been watching the door and then he watched me as I moved around the stove. I cooked no bacon or anything else that would smell delicious and the breakfast I did make I carried inside to eat. I had to get away from that cinnamon-brown face and its look of threatening anger.

The park rangers had been in the habit of coming around every few days, being interested in my group of wild companions and the writing about them. One dropped by that morning. The bear was still there. I described what had happened and the ranger apparently took it rather seriously. He especially didn't like the bear's staying. He helped me to make some piles of rocks here and there, on each side of the cabin and on the steps. In an emergency I could throw them and perhaps gain a head start. He said that he would return in the evening.

He came and learned that the bear had not left all day. The bear had moved back and forth on the slope a few times but not very far away. He was always in sight and continued to keep his eyes on me and the cabin. The ranger thought I should stay somewhere else for a week or so, but if I did wouldn't my creatures disperse? I said I did not want to leave. The ranger did not think the bear could tip over this cabin, or at least so he assured me.

For three weeks the situation continued. Sometimes the bear would leave for a few hours, probably to get something to eat, but he was there most of the time and always from late afternoon on. The men tried to lure him away but were not successful. Meanwhile he had begun coming in closer. Sometimes he was only thirty or forty feet away.

During those weeks a curious thing happened. I regressed to a very primitive instinct, an imperative need for something solid and strong touching my back. It would be an animal's way of insuring that an enemy could not approach from behind. Ordinarily human beings don't have it, perhaps never have had it, and yet there it was, a sensation as physical as intense thirst but very different. We have no other sensory feelings to which I can compare it, but it was absolutely irresistible. I *had* to sit with my back touching the wall and for as long as the bear stayed I did, though I tried to argue myself into believing that I was no safer there. When I could feel the wall the sensation ceased but if I leaned away even as much as an inch it returned instantly.

I called it the need for a "shelter-touch."

As the weeks went by the park authorities expressed some alarm. Everyone knew what was happening. Other park visitors came to see the bear, though they stayed pretty well back. I ate my simple non-fragrant meals, got my bucket of water each day, and fed the birds and animals, although I was too tense to be an easy companion with them. Then early one evening two of the rangers called. They said it had been decided that there was too much risk in allowing this to go on any longer. The next day they were going to shoot the bear, or else try to trap him and take him away to some distant part of the park.

I have seldom felt more humiliated. I, friend of wildlife, believing myself a naturalist by now, couldn't handle myself in a wilderness. No other visitors had had any trouble with bears that year, although sometimes they did. But I, the expert as I assumed, was going to cost the bear his life, for that, I believed, was the rangers' intention. I felt very sick about it.

The rangers left. As they said goodnight we looked for the bear. He was not in sight. It was only dusk but I began to get ready for bed and had taken off my dress when the voice of a stranger called from behind my cabin, "Your enemy's out in front."

I don't know what happened. Was a cupful of adrenalin released into my blood? The weeks' tension broke and I was simply beset with fury! Flinging open the door I dashed out in my slip and snatching up handfuls of rocks from the step I tore after the bear. I screamed at him, words I hadn't even realized that I knew, and was hurling rocks at his face and hitting him too, for he was less than ten feet away. He reared, but not with rage this time, with stunned surprise, quickly let himself down on all fours and ran away fast down the slope. Trembling I pulled myself together and went back into the cabin.

The bear never returned. The rangers did not dispose of him and I settled down to absorb my lessons.

First of course, one must not stare at any wild animal, a stare being an invasion of privacy, rudeness they will not tolerate. But second, an overpowering sense of outrage can be a defense in some circumstances. The bear had threatened too long and my fear had turned into its opposite. But one shouldn't depend on outrage to save one's life. I am sure it would have to be genuine; no phony attitude ever works with an animal and the excess adrenalin really would have to be in one's blood, perhaps emitting an odor. There would be some occasions, with a bull moose in the belligerent rutting season, I think, when humility might work better. But best, try to achieve something like the wild ones' alertness and not to get into these tight situations. If I had not stared and had gone quietly, unobtrusively into the cabin when I first saw the bear, I feel sure there would not have been any incident. And I still think that the wilderness is a very good society.

Many people assume that the true state of nature is anarchy. That was not what I found, at Beetle Rock or in more remote congregations of wildlife. There were dramas, some very sad, and occasionally I was in danger, but what impressed me more were the stability and the sanity. They seemed almost spectacular. After all the giddy and irresponsible people I had known in the human world, here in the wilderness there was a code of behavior so well understood and so well respected that the laws could be depended on not to be broken. There was always the need for alertness, required by the hunted-hunter relationships, but otherwise birds and animals knew just what to expect of each other. They could be sure their associates, whether of their own or different species, would act in dependable ways. If something ought to be done, it was done. What is, in the literal sense, integrity — "reliable adherence to a code of behavior" — was almost infallible.

There were contests for mates but once a pair-bond was established it was accepted as final, both by the couple and by anyone else who might covet either of them. It might last for a lifetime — a pact usually preceded by a rather long courtship as in the case of geese or, elsewhere, wolves. Or it might be the species rule that it only would be for the raising of one brood or litter; but the devotion and loyalty during that time was absolute and so was the sense of responsibility for the young on the part of one or both parents. Most parents wore themselves to a ragged extremity of fatigue by the time the young were grown but they never shirked the task — not even though the fatigue, exposing them to disease and predators, might mean that they would live only a tenth of their possible lifetimes, as is the usual case with wild birds.

Sometimes there were deviations, but on the lenient side. A female cougar, having her own territory, would allow another cougar to trespass if she had young to feed. An unmated female bird would sometimes assist a mother; and mothers would often baby-sit for each other.

A bird or animal could lay claim to a homesite simply by moving into it, but he would not do that if it already belonged to another. On the edges of his property there might be disputes over boundary lines, sometimes with a "showing of fists," but there were no deadly fights on that issue. The wild ones are masters of compromise. As soon as ownership of the site, the plot of ground or the niche in a tree, had been established, the home itself, the burrow or nest, belonged without any question to the one who had dug or built it — unless the owner left or died. In that case a new owner was quick to move in, suggesting that others had been aware of the home's advantages all along.

It seemed remarkable to me that a more powerful bird or animal, or one higher in rank, never tried to take a desirable home or mate just because he was stronger or was superior in a hierarchy. The weaker or humbler one might be expected to give way on a path or at food or drink, but his family and home were inviolable, his without argument.

About food there did not seem to be any intense possessiveness. The remains of a kill the predator no longer wanted was community property — it could be eaten by anyone. While the hunter was first enjoying his meal there would usually be a circle of lesser creatures standing around waiting to have their chance, and if they darted in for a bite ahead of time, the owner of the catch might growl a little but he would not attack. One day our chickaree cut off eighteen cones from a tall tree in about as many seconds, let them fall to the ground and then raced down the tree to bury them. Meanwhile a digger squirrel, not able to get his own cones by climbing, began pulling some of the chickaree's into his burrow. The chickaree didn't waste time in more than a brief sputtered objection. He got busy and buried the rest of his cones, first giving each one his lick sign which said, "This cone is mine." They would still be there in the ground when he dug them up in the winter.

And water: it often happened that two would meet at a rain pool or the drinking pan at the cabin. If there was a little personal friction between them, as sometimes there was between the robin and jay, they argued a bit about which should drink first but they never injured each other. It was much more typical for thirsty creatures to wait without bluster, because there was a well understood — and observed — custom of taking turns.

Tempers never seemed to be short. Once I was watching a mourning dove and a sparrow, perched a few inches apart on a branch, when the sparrow left the branch and, clamping his beak on one of the dove's tail feathers, hung from it and with a reverse wing-beat tried to pull it out. That was the nest-building season and no doubt he wanted it for his lining. The dove, though keeping her balance with difficulty, did not protest, not even when the sparrow tried to get a feather again a few moments later. It wouldn't come out, so he flew away and she settled back into a dove's usually peaceful emotions.

If there was a contest, as between bucks over a doe, the one who was losing would turn away, leave, and that was the end of it; and a wolf, sensing defeat in a fight, exposes his jugular vein to the victor's teeth, the victor in that case being "honor-bound" not to harm him. I think of those animal contests sometimes in watching a tennis match and seeing the winner run up to the net to offer his hand to the loser. The tradition goes back a long way.

The deer and wolf rituals are only two of many inherited forms of behavior which prevent members of the same species from killing each other. Around Beetle Rock, as in other wildlife communities, many and various species could be observed, all with different habits and needs but living in close association. Aside from the prey-predator situations, were there not countless conflicting requirements that would precipitate fights? The issues were there but almost always were solved with tolerance. The powerful did not assert their superiority with any unpleasant display of strength, and the weaker or smaller ones never showed any resentment in yielding.

Late in June of the long summer our little company were enjoying a sunny morning, the birds singing, the mammals scampering about, when tragedy struck. The female grouse was there and the cock, who had been booming for her, approached through the surrounding bushes. He was conspicuous in his courtship finery, bright yellow throat sacs, orange crests over his eyes. In less time than it takes to read this sentence then he was up and away through the sky in a goshawk's talons. The goshawk must have concealed himself in a thick clump of foliage and he came down from the tree like a shot — a "bullet hawk," he is sometimes called. There was no sound; one moment the cock was there and the next he was gone.

The door of the cabin was open, and in a wave of terror all the rest of the creatures including the birds swept in. Many had been inside at other times and now they found safety here. Any small previous irritations were forgotten; the jay and robin were eating and drinking without competition, the chickaree and the digger squirrel picking up nuts side by side, and the female grouse and the golden-mantled squirrel, who had sometimes shown jealousy when I had fed her, were all harmonious now. Feeling safe under the roof, they didn't attempt to hide, but walked and hopped about. I had scattered food on the floor and their fright quieted as they began to eat. Even the torn-eared buck, lonely perhaps, tried to come in although he had not been in danger. He had his forefeet up on the sill when one of the rangers walked by. Amused, he told me that I must keep the deer out for if he did enter he would probably panic and jumping about he might break a leg. We put a bench in the doorway.

I sat there among the refugees, a dozen within arm's reach and two on my lap. It had not occurred to me that I would create an emergency by assembling this group at the cabin. There would have been no such concentration of prey otherwise and I felt guilty about the loss of the cock, although I did realize that in his erotic mood he might have been careless about displaying in some other place. What worried me more was the future. It seemed hideously possible that the goshawk would keep coming back and one by one would pick off my birds and animals. But that didn't happen because it was their own impulse to spend every day inside. I fed them there and brought in the drinking water and salt lick; later on in the afternoon they would go out to do their own foraging. The goshawk did return and sat in the tree near the door several times but then he apparently realized that there was no longer a gathering of available prey and stopped coming.

It was a sweet experience to have all these birds and animals in the cabin with me. They seemed as much at ease here as anywhere else. When they had finished eating they would relax, some would sleep, the birds perched on the two-by-fours that braced the walls.

One day when I was looking around at them with satisfaction and out through the door to the wider green walls beyond, I thought, suddenly, This is a home I have come to. I know now what home means to most people, not only walls but a shelter-touch for the heart and mind. Here I have found it, home at last — and with all these delightful children.

Mice Born Over and Over Again

Judy Grahn

A Fly Is Born with Little to Do

In the middle of the morning of a midsummer festival a fly has been born with little to do. Several hundred feet from a human procession which has been forming and now is waiting a fly is drying himself off inside a stable where it is not unusual for many creatures to be born with great irregularity and abundance. While the leaves of an oak tree may be born with regularity, and even ants and beetles may be born with regularity, this is not so true of creatures born inside a stable.

Wiping his face with new found feet and waiting for his wings to dry a copper green fly has begun another phase of life inside a stable in a stiffening pile of dung produced by a proud donkey who had several days before lost and won a noisy argument with a woman of the Bee clan. This same donkey had returned to the stable thirsty, dusty and bad tempered and had at the last moment stepped into the pile of dung burying the fly mother's new laid pocket of eggs down deep deep inside the pile and making the first struggle of the pallid maggot difficult though still possible.

With a wriggly determination and willful movement the maggot had emerged from the donkey pile and rolled forward down its long blind body to the shadows of the stable floor joining the stable wall. Now days later from the woody shadows he has emerged transfigured from a wriggly determined and willful maggot to a brilliant fly with green and blue armored heavy coat and light transparent drying wings, learning to walk around and wash his face and after a while dive into the welcoming waves of hot midsummer air.

Elsewhere in the stable other creatures have also been recently born of no concern to the fly and in addition of no concern is a girl squatting with prominent hair and reaching the fingers of one human hand into a hole in the straw pile nearby to where a donkey is impatiently standing swatting its tail and occasionally shitting.

She was squatting, wearing a plain white work dress of the Tortoise clan, a dress she did not like not even with the yellow trim. She thought it was very dull and much preferred bright red and orange or even blue, however plain white with narrow yellow trim is how the Tortoise clan approached its festival dressing.

"My mother is so interested in clothes," she thought. "You'd think she could do something about this."

She did not remember at that moment the first years of their living in the city of Mundane that her mother Gedda hid at home or out in the countryside as long as possible during festivals covering her skin with long sleeves and heavy makeup so the fewest possible numbers of people will notice her tattoos of origin and strangeness. Only on later festival occasions has Gedda come to know the people of the Tortoise clan well enough to have gotten to be proud of her own place in the procession, of her white festival dress and sometimes of her own origin.

Margedda stuck a copper comb deeper into the tower of her hair, a comb she had taken for this special occasion although here she was not going to the festival instead crouching in the stable where a fly has just now been born of a cocoon at the opposite wall and an unseen tall white-chested owl sleeps in the shade of the overhead rafters. Deep under the straw where Margedda's fingers probe a mama mouse watches with brittle black eyes of her very own. She now has nine babies left of thirteen in this second litter to watch over and they had recently begun twittering revealing their positions to the ears of a waiting raftered owl under the straw.

Coming to her maturity only a few months ago, on both occasions the mama mouse had three men mice in the stable to choose from at the time of the mating. Two of these had been so attracted to fighting and chasing each other that she ignored them altogether, mating a variety of times instead with the more placid excitedly squealing third one.

Inside the stable where a copper green fly has recently emerged is Margedda a heavy set rapidly maturing girl with a round face and little eyes which no one at first notices because of her labyrinthian hair being so prominent. She has thrust the fingers of one wriggling hand deep into a hole in the straw and her tiny round eyes are closely watching the hooves of a restless donkey coming closer to her.

She is more concerned with what she is doing than with anything gathering outside in a courtyard and after noticing her reddish towering hair anyone would then notice that she has a small slatted birdcage hung from the wrist of her one free hand lifted high in the air as she is squatting. Anyone would see next that inside the tan slatted cage that hangs from her thick and sturdy wrist is a fluffy small gray ball of owl, fluffy with unhappiness and hunger, with eyes clamped tightly shut so you cannot see their color or their expression. For this fluffy unhappy reason Margedda searches deep in the straw for mouse babies and is not attending the festival, in fact has disappeared from the watchful control of her mother Gedda.

Two Who Watch Out for Each Other

If a fly is created by odors it is also true that what is created creates in its own turn. Once a form is created it creates other forms and not just those like itself, often it creates other forms unlike itself in order to give itself limits, company and composition. As the bright eyes of a mama mouse watch from the mounds of straw on the floor of the stable, so a white-chested owl dreams on a rafter near the roof of the stable. The two are related especially in the time they spend thinking about each other. The mama mouse thinks about the owl dreaming on its rafter above herself and her large family about thirty percent of the time, more thought than she often has time to give to her grown children although they will soon number in dozens. Since the owl thinks about the mouse and her children about seventy percent of the time, together they are thinking about each other one hundred percent of the time.

Living together as they so often do in the stable, the owl sits working on a beam near the ceiling while the mouse works below gathering goods into collections keeping them stored in a number of places. The two watch out for each other. The owl watches out of her huge flat eyes below her for the least motion or displaced shadow and the mouse watches out of her little round eyes above her for the similar motions, and she also watches the floor for any changes in the shadows of intent dropping. While the two were watching out so closely for each other they have forgotten to watch for a third entity who has appeared in the form of an immense, chubby determined stalking person named Margedda.

Trying to be unlike her own mother Margedda was determined never to cover her tattoos or be happy with a plain white dress of effort and gratitude, and never to go stalking in the woods or wild meadows for secret joy and not for mushrooms as her mother did. Instead she would stalk crouching in the stable, and she determined as she did this never to like farming as her mother had finally learned to like farming, bending and stooping, squatting and hauling, but rather to be a wild dancer and a gatherer of dreams and predictions. And today she would squat in order to be a gatherer of mice and other delicacies to take care of the baby owl her mother's lover Jon had brought her from the river.

"His mother is obviously dead," Blueberry Jon had said. "This little baby needs a patient person to take care of him." And for this task of patient care she must be wily. And she must grow up to be a wily woman.

For her part the mama mouse has already grown up to be a wily woman. The little present-minded children that she had trained ran around the edges of the objects in the stable as she herself did growing large and thickly furred while the little absent-minded children she forgot or decided not to train ran across the middle of the designated spaces directly one by one into the course of the owl's shadow of intent and rapidly dropping flight and nails and beak and stomach.

Because of her habits of trembling without moving the mouse has taught the owl to do a great deal of sitting and of dreaming it would not otherwise be doing. Because the mama mouse has habits of working at night the owl has been given plenty of night vision and silent, rapidly dropping flight in order to fall down on her from above. Falling down on a mouse from above is something the owl has practiced a great deal involving air currents and the precision of foot muscle releasing and gravitational diving. And because of this dropping flight of owls the mouse keeps always to the edges of the objects of her environment in the stable or anywhere, moving always in geometric lines as though drawing pictures of a space by running all around its parameters. For their part the owls have learned to think of other things extensively with their big eyes open for otherwise the waiting is all too boring. Waiting for a mouse to move within a given space so you can suddenly drop down on it from above is boring, even apparently paralyzing unless you are excellent at finding other things to ponder.

For a mouse to have so many babies at a time as she loves to do she must have someone to give some of them over to and for this reason her kind have thought up the family of owls and dreamed them into existence. With their bright mouse eyes gleaming and jerking they dreamed and thought them up, with their noses pointed into a circle of each other around the scattered grain pile, the sharp whiskered noses of the mama mice and the imitative smaller noses of the children mice and the jowlfaced noses of the men mice. They thought them up, the few birds who do not live at all like mice at the scattered grain pile but who rather live on the succulent bodies of mice and who constantly ponder the smell and the feel and the possible every movement of mice.

Though most birds live on grain and fruits and twitter and play and tremble and live somewhat like mice a few birds do not do this, they do not twitter or quiver but perch and hover for long periods, sitting in the rafters or the tree limbs hour upon hour of their lives worshipping mice and pondering the subjects related to waiting for mice and how and just exactly when to drop down from above onto the sweet grainy bodies of mice. They do not do much more than this, and because of it the mice can produce plenty of hot little pink children knowing there will never be too many, and knowing that now there can also be great feathered creatures with large dreaming eyes who can never be disconnected from mice. For their part owls give a mouse more than one thing at a time to think about, so it is never boring to be a mouse. It is very exciting to be a mouse, so exciting she trembles and quivers continually from having different possible events to think about and different places to go that she might not come back from.

Smelling and Feeling Are Not the Same as Drinking
Standing on the floor of the stable with all eight lenses of his eyes the drying fly is beginning to see in all directions, and everything is beginning to be interesting to imagine taking off and landing on. In particular dark shiny surfaces like pools of liquid substance are interesting to imagine and for his first landing the fly has decided on the large visible eye of a donkey. Taking off however shortly he has found that the surface of a donkey's eye is not good for a landing, being guarded by heavy blinking, and moreover is not good in any case for drinking, being more solidly constructed and less giving

than its first appearance. Knocked away by the blinking back to the floor at least the fly feels he has made his first imaginative landing.

Not learning from the first disappointment is one of the fly's primary characteristics, so that he must try to land on the donkey's eye forty-one more times before attempting some other imagining. Launching his new body into the heavily holding air he has been waved away vigorously from the face of the little girl with the prominent hair using one free hand that had been a moment before groping for mice and has zoomed out of the stable door into the hot air over the street.

There are four major streets in the city altogether just as there are four clans and four great houses. The street over which the fly is now maneuvering leads from the stables of the Lion clan past the now quiet steamy baths for humans past many connected houses with shuttered windows to a busy bakery with open doorways tended by people wearing white dresses with yellow trim from the big farming Tortoise clan, the clan of provision.

In preparation for the festival smells from the bakery suggest warm puddles of edible matter toward which the fly buzzes in a zig zag course with occasional pauses. Thick with smells of hot wet grain, people in the doorways of the bakery are guarding it with fans waving that are frightening to a young fly not so used to being batted about. Trying one hundred and twenty-three times to get into the bakery the fly is too recent in his body to make full use of his physical knowledge of aerial acrobatics necessary to bypass fans that long ago his ancestors had arranged for his inheritance.

Spiralling high into the sky for a change of air the fly can see if he is looking that there are four wider streets in the city altogether and four large freestanding buildings among the close cluster of living buildings attached each to the other. The city is united into four clans; all of them are of different numbers. The proportions of the numbers of people in each clan are that the Tortoise clan is the largest with more than half of the population; next largest is the Lion clan of animal keeping and responsibility; then the much smaller Bee clan of architects and measurement; and the smallest of all is the Snake clan of healing and herbology. The fly does not see the relative numbers of the clans from high in the air; what he does see is a great deal of milling activity in front of the Snake clan temple of the moon, so stopping to rest only twice he can make a perfectly zig zag course over the roofs to where an active procession is finally proceeding in search of a warm puddle.

Finding a variety of people in long and short red skirts pushing carts of covered smells and with warm brown pools for eyes is very exciting to a young fly. To his misfortune the carts are protected by the same fanning motions as the bakery, wicked slapping fanning motions meant to demolish his body rather than simply send him away. Furthermore circling everyone's eyes is a layer of repulsive green malachite powder. While he is resting in disappointment on a broad woman's shoulder, the woman who a second ago was marching along talking with hands floating in the air before her is now whirling and suddenly smacking the fly with a hard finger across his face.

Spinning over and over through the air the disoriented fly realizes that much of the vision is dimming on the right side where one of his bright new multi-sided eyes is injured. Lurching now in an ugly unformed zig zag the fly lunges for the sheltering hair of a rectangular shaped girl who is imitating older women in a procession while pushing a cart with two small children and not watching out for what gets into her hair. Finding a shiny black coil of protection under the red bandanna the fly crouches in the shadow of a silver headpiece keeping quiet and resting, dizzy from all the adventures of entering a new body.

Meanwhile the procession is passing a distracted woman in a white dress with yellow trim who is anxiously calling "Margedda, Margedda!" and after a while the procession is passing out of the courtyard with the oak tree and onto a street that leads past the stable.

Mice Born Over and Over Again

Inside the stable a village of born over again mice lies mainly sleeping in their nests, little and big ones mixed together with their furry bodies touching. In the newest nest a little pile of furless pink infants lies mixed together in a puddle.

A mama mouse whose alert eyes peer from the straw has nests and gathered stashes everywhere in the stable. She has found by staying near the floor that by staying in one place all kinds of usable objects fall from the bodies of passing animals and humans. What she likes to gather in her stashes are feathers, bits of bone and leather; things dropped by the humans such as string and shiny pins and beads, even a heavy metal ring that took so much long neck stretching to carry.

All these usable objects she put in several places of storage along with large chunks of vegetable greens growing on stalks around the stable door and most of all the continual grains that so often fall from the mouths of perpetually chewing donkeys who live in the stable. Her grown sons from the first litter live in little bachelor nests or sleep in the daytime with their sisters. Her daughter mice have nests of their own or sometimes come to sleep with her and her newest born infants.

For herself the mama mouse is exceptional at digging, at hollowing, at hiding and at finding. She is very good at squealing. She is somewhat good at climbing and very good at looking after her children, at cleaning and at storing. She is extremely good at shredding. She is not at all so good at weaving, at pounding, at pouncing or at growling. In her village inside the stable she likes to make a lot of paths, she likes to have a lot of nests to sleep in and a lot of storage. She does not care so much for open spaces except on mating nights when she loves to run wild and dancing in the open where she can be certain to be chased and where she can make certain that the mate chasing has enough running enthusiasm to be advantageous to mice.

The mama mouse was a careful self-contained individual who enjoyed washing her face while sitting in the early morning sunshine and running up the walls to find interesting high perches. She loved to eat the greens that grew outside the door of the stable. She was never so foolish about what to bring home for storage as her brother mouse who ambitiously attempted one night to drag away a donkey by its hock, and who was mashed under the hay for the enormity of his vision. The mama mouse lived for a period of two years and three months, and bore an average of eight babies every two months following her own two-month childhood, totalling ninety-six new mice of whom fifty-four were females, eleven of those living to have babies and each of them producing a number of daughters though only one lived as long as their original mother did.

By the end of her life the mama mouse had been already responsible for contributing 2,916 of her own kind to the world, some two hundred fifty or more pounds of mice, most of whom had made a wealth of living for the various barn owls, shrews, voles and moles, hawks, frogs, snakes, ants, wasps, beetles, cats and weasels who pass through stables and other mousely places. Many of those she fed depend so thoroughly on her provision that her habits have completely formed their body shapes, eyesights, hearings, sleeping patterns, body movements, stances, attention spans, habitats, digestions, nervous systems, states of mind, and relative positions in the world. In return they gave her their undivided attention and plenty of reason for living.

Of this her second litter, thirteen babies had been born. One was immediately dead which she pushed out efficiently along with the turds, uneaten scraps and other trash. The rest of the new babies pleased her immensely not so much yet as individuals as a moving warm conglomerate with pretty pink faces sucking milk from her breasts and twittering with cries that she left only after the second day and then only for the water she could extract from a melon rind dropped by a passing human.

The new babies were five days old when Margedda's fingers found them, folded all around themselves to form a ball with a labyrinthian middle in a similarly round house of straw and shredded apron left hanging over a rail by a stable hand from the Lion Clan, to judge by its blue color. The blue fibers mixed attractively with the straw bundle surrounding the twelve who lay in a softly padded hollow with their big sister sleeping curled around them. The sister mouse who was half grown and covered with bright straw-colored fur did not squeal but ran out of the house when Margedda's monstrous hand lifted the outside layer of shredded hay with her big fingers reaching in to gather three of the stretching clean warm babies.

"It's only me, the human owl," she whispered, carefully replacing the nest with its curled outer sheath and topping hay. As she reached her fingers holding one pink naked infant toward the little triangle of owl beak showing through bedraggled fluffy facial feathers she remembered that Blueberry Jon had said he thought the mother owl might chew up the baby's food before feeding her. Margedda's own face recoiled in horror at this possibility, and she was greatly relieved when the little beak opened and the little mouth closed over her offering. "That's a good baby," she murmured, offering a second helping. When the owl did not accept the third naked mouse she wondered if she had been too hasty in taking three at one time.

"Margedda, Margedda," suddenly she could hear her mother calling her along the street outside the stable. She could tell it was her mother not only because it was her name being called and who besides her mother ever called her name? In addition, she could tell because her mother Gedda had a way of pronouncing words that differed from everyone else in the city, differed from Blueberry Jon's words and even differed from her daughter Margedda's words.

She jerked to her feet with the birdcage bobbing against her arm. Gedda would not appreciate her long disappearance and the search she had to make to find her daughter. She would not appreciate, Margedda felt certain, her crouching in a stable in her festival dress hunting for mice. Most of all, she would not appreciate the precious pink mouse infant clutched in her palm like a piece of fig candy, nor were there any pockets or secret places in the ceremonial dress.

"I'm keeping this for you until later," Margedda whispered fiercely to the startled ball of owl clinging to the side of the slatted cage, and then she popped the warm little body into her mouth where it lay quietly sleeping between her tongue and cheek.

Small Purchase
Natalie Kusz

I have bought a one-eyed fish. Drifting around the tank near my
desk, his skin ripples silver like well-pressed silk, and he moves
under the light and hovers with his one bronze eye turned toward
me, waiting to be dropped shrimp pellets or cubes of dried worms.
His body is smooth and flat, like a silver dollar but twice the size, and
his fins are mottled gold. He is a relative to the piranha, a meat eater
with a bold round mouth, but even when the smaller fish challenge
him, swishing their tails at his eye, he leaves them alone and swims
off. He has not eaten one of them.

I call him Max, because my sister said I should. She did not remind
me, when I brought him home, that I had wanted no pets, nothing
with a life span shorter than my own, nothing that would die or be
butchered as soon as I had given it a name. She just looked up, with
her face very serious, as if she knew well how one could become attached to a fish, and she said to me, Max. Yes, that should be his name.

I had told us both, when I bought the aquarium, that fish were low-
maintenance animals, without personalities and incapable of
friendliness, and if one of them died you just flushed it away and got
another. And besides, I said, I needed a fish tank. I had begun to feel
stale, inert. I needed the sounds of moving water in my house, and
I needed, too, a live thing beside me, something interesting to stare
at when I stopped typing for a moment to think.

Last summer, when I was tired and the writing was going badly, I
got superstitious about the sea and thought that the lurch and pull
of waves would freshen my ears and bring on clean thoughts. So I
packed some books and a portable typewriter, drove to Homer on
the coast, and rented a cabin near the beach. Something about the
place, or its fishy air, or my aloneness in the middle of it, worked
somehow, and I breathed bigger there in my chest and wrote more

clearly on the page. I had forgotten about tides and about the kelp and dried crabs that came in with them, and every morning I shivered into a sweater, put combs in my hair, and walked out to wade and to fill my pockets with what I found. I liked it best when the wind was blowing and the sky was grey, and the sounds of sea gulls and my own breathing were carried out with the water.

Kelp pods washed up around my feet, and I stomped on them with tennis shoes to find what was inside. I collected driftwood, and urchins, and tiny pink clamshells dropped by gulls, thin enough to see through and smaller than a thumbnail. When the tide had gone far out, I climbed the bluff back to my cabin and sat writing in front of the window, eating cheese on bread and drinking orange spritzers or tea. The walls and windows there had space in between, and they let in shreds of wind and the arguing of birds and the metal smell of seaweed drying out on the beach. When the tide started back in, I took pen and notebook and sat on a great barnacled rock, letting water creep up and surround me, then jumping to shore just in time. An hour later, the rock would be covered, three feet or more under the grey, and I would only know where it lay because of the froth and swirl of whirlpools just above it.

When I came home I threw my bags on the bed and unfastened them, and a thousand aromas opened up then into my face, drifting out from the folds of my clothes, the seams of my shoes, the pages of my notebook. I had carried them back with me, the smells of wet sand and fish fins, of eagle feathers floating in surf, of candle wax burned at midnight and filled with the empty bodies of moths. I had grieved on the drive home for that place I was leaving, and for the cold wind of that beach, and I had decided that somehow water should move in my house, should rush and bubble in my ears, should bring in the sound of the sea and of the wind and the dark currents that move it.

So I bought an aquarium, and fish to go in it, and a water pump strong enough to tumble the surface as it worked. I bought plants for the tank and waved their smell into the room, and when I thought I was finished I made one more trip to a pet store, just to see what they had.

The shop was a small one, in an old wooden building with low ceilings, and the fish room in back was dark and smelled submarine — humid and slippery and full of live things. All light in the place came from the fish tanks themselves, and the plants inside them absorbed the glow and turned it green, casting it outward to move in shadowed patterns on my skin. When I closed my eyes, the sound was of rivers, running out to the coast to be carried away mixed with salt. And the fish inside waved their fins and wandered between the rocks, opening and closing their mouths.

I glanced but didn't look hard at the larger fish, because I had found already that they were always very expensive. I browsed instead through tetras and guppies, baby gouramis and cichlids, trying to be satisfied with the small ones, because after all it was just the water and its motion that I really wanted. So when I saw the wide silver fish and a sign that said "$10," I assumed it was a mistake but decided to ask about it while I ordered some neons dipped out. With my neck bent forward, I watched as fifty neons swam fast away from the net that would always catch them anyway. "Was that big fish back there really only ten," I said.

The clerk said, "You mean the metynnis with one eye. He's such a mellow guy."

I swung my head to look at her. One eye?

The woman stared at my face for a moment and opened her mouth. Her cheeks grew pinker, but when she answered me, her voice stayed even. She said, "Yes, his former owners thought he was a piranha and put him in the tank with some. They ate out one eye before anyone could get him up."

"They go for the eyes so their lunch will quit looking at them," I said. I told the woman I would take the metynnis. I thought we were a match, I said.

And I was right. As absurd as I felt about my affinity with a one-eyed fish, I found myself watching him for the ways he was like me, and I did find many. Max had already learned, by the time I got him, to hold his body in the water so that whatever he was interested in lay always on the same side of him as his eye. In the same way that I situate myself in movie theaters so that my best friend sits on my right side, Max turns his eye toward the wall of his tank, watching for my arm to move toward the food box. When I drop a worm cube down to him, he shifts his eye up to look at it and then swims at it from the side so he never loses it from vision. If the smaller fish fight, or behave defiantly around him, he turns his dead eye against them and flicks himself away to a further corner of the tank.

I don't know if it is normal to befriend a fish. I think probably not. I do know that as I sit by Max's tank and write, I stop sometimes and look up, and I think then that he looks terribly dashing, swimming around with his bad eye outward, unafraid that something might attack him from his blind side. I buy him special shrimp pellets, and I feed them to him one at a time, careful always to drop them past his good eye. My friends like to feed him, too, and I teach them how, warning them to drop his food where he can see it. Now one of my friends wants to introduce me to his neighbor's one-eyed dog, and another wishes she still had her one-eyed zebra finch so she could give it to me.

That's just what I need, I think — a houseful of blind-sided pets. We could sit around together and play Wink-um, wondering was that a wink or just a lid shut down over a dry eyeball. We could fight about who got to sit on whose good side, or we could make jokes about how it takes two of us to look both ways before crossing the street. I laugh, but still I intend to meet the one-eyed dog, to see if he reminds me of Max — or of me. I wonder if he holds himself differently from other dogs, if when he hears a voice he turns his whole body to look.

And I wonder about myself, about what has changed in the world. At first, I wanted fish only for the water they lived in, for the movement it would bring to my house, the dust it would sweep from my brain. I thought of fish as "safe" pets, too boring to demand much attention, soulless by nature and indistinguishable from their peers. But I know that when the smaller fish chase after Max, or push him away from the food, I find myself fiercely angry. I take a vicious pleasure in dropping down shrimp pellets too big and too hard for the small ones to eat, and I find pleasure, too, in the way Max gobbles the food, working it to bits in his mouth. When he is finished, he turns a dead eye to the others and swims away, seeking things more interesting to look at.

May's Lion
Ursula K. Le Guin

Jim remembers it as a bobcat, and he was May's nephew, and ought to know. It probably was a bobcat. I don't think May would have changed her story, though you can't trust a good story-teller not to make the story suit herself, or get the facts to fit the story better. Anyhow she told it to us more than once, because my mother and I would ask for it; and the way I remember it, it was a mountain lion. And the way I remember May telling it is sitting on the edge of the irrigation tank we used to swim in, cement rough as a lava flow and hot in the sun, the long cracks tarred over. She was an old lady then with a long Irish upper lip, kind and wary and balky. She liked to come sit and talk with my mother while I swam; she didn't have all that many people to talk to. She always had chickens, in the chickenhouse very near the back door of the farmhouse, so the whole place smelled pretty strong of chickens, and as long as she could she kept a cow or two down in the old barn by the creek. The first of May's cows I remember was Pearl, a big, handsome Holstein who gave fourteen or twenty-four or forty gallons or quarts of milk at a milking, whichever is right for a prize milker. Pearl was beautiful in my eyes when I was four or five years old; I loved and admired her. I remember how excited I was, how I reached upward to them, when Pearl or the workhorse Prince, for whom my love amounted to worship, would put an immense and sensitive muzzle through the three-strand fence to whisk a cornhusk from my fearful hand; and then the munching; and the sweet breath and the big nose would be at the barbed wire again: the offering is acceptable. . . . After Pearl there was Rosie, a purebred Jersey. May got her either cheap or free because she was a runt calf, so tiny that May brought her home on her lap in the back of the car, like a fawn. And Rosie always looked like she had some deer in her. She was a lovely, clever little cow and even more willful than old May. She often chose not to come in to be milked. We would hear May calling and then see her trudging across our lower pasture with the bucket, going to find Rosie wherever Rosie had decided to be milked today on the wild hills she had to roam in, a hundred acres of our and Old Jim's land. Then May had a fox terrier named Pinky, who yipped and nipped and turned me against fox terriers for life, but he was long gone when the mountain lion came; and the black cats who lived in the barn kept discreetly out of the story. As a matter of fact now I think of it the chickens weren't in it either. It might have been quite different if they had been. May had quit keeping chickens after old Mrs. Walter died. It was just her all alone there, and Rosie and the cats down in the barn, and nobody else within sight or sound of the old farm. We were in our house up the hill only in the summer, and Jim lived in town, those years. What time of year it was I don't know, but I imagine the grass still green or just turning gold. And May was in the house, in the kitchen, where she lived entirely unless she was asleep or outdoors, when she heard this noise.

Now you need May herself, sitting skinny on the edge of the irrigation tank, seventy or eighty or ninety years old, nobody knew how old May was and she had made sure they couldn't find out, opening her pleated lips and letting out this noise — a huge, awful yowl, starting soft with a nasal hum and rising slowly into a snarling gargle that sank away into a sobbing purr. . . . It got better every time she told the story.

"It was some meow," she said.

So she went to the kitchen door, opened it, and looked out. Then she shut the kitchen door and went to the kitchen window to look out, because there was a mountain lion under the fig tree.

Puma, cougar, catamount; *Felis concolor*; the shy, secret, shadowy lion of the New World, four or five feet long plus a yard of black-tipped tail, weighs about what a woman weighs, lives where the deer live from Canada to Chile, but always shyer, always fewer; the color of dry leaves, dry grass.

There were plenty of deer in the Valley in the forties, but no mountain lion had been seen for decades anywhere near where people lived. Maybe way back up in the canyons; but Jim, who hunted, and knew every deer-trail in the hills, had never seen a lion. Nobody had, except May, now, alone in her kitchen.

"I thought maybe it was sick," she told us. "It wasn't acting right. I don't think a lion would walk right into the yard like that if it was feeling well. If I'd still had the chickens it'd be a different story maybe! But it just walked around some, and then it lay down there," and she points between the fig tree and the decrepit garage. "And then after a while it kind of meowed again, and got up and come into the shade right there." The fig tree, planted when the house was built, about the time May was born, makes a great, green, sweet-smelling shade. "It just laid there looking around. It wasn't well," says May.

She had lived with and looked after animals all her life; she had also earned her living for years as a nurse.

"Well, I didn't know exactly what to do for it. So I put out some water for it. It didn't even get up when I come out the door. I put the water down there, not so close to it that we'd scare each other, see, and it kept watching me, but it didn't move. After I went back in it did get up and tried to drink some water. Then it made that kind of meowo-wow. I do believe it come here because it was looking for help. Or just for company, maybe."

The afternoon went on, May in the kitchen, the lion under the fig tree.

But down in the barnyard by the creek was Rosie the cow. Fortunately the gate was shut, so she could not come wandering up to the house and meet the lion; but she would be needing to be milked, come six or seven o'clock, and that got to worrying May. She also worried how long a sick mountain lion might hang around, keeping her shut in the house. May didn't like being shut in.

"I went out a time or two, and went shoo!"

Eyes shining amidst fine wrinkles, she flaps her thin arms at the lion. "Shoo! Go on home now!"

But the silent wild creature watches her with yellow eyes and does not stir.

"So when I was talking to Miss Macy on the telephone, she said it might have rabies, and I ought to call the sheriff. I was uneasy then. So finally I did that, and they come out, those county police, you know. Two carloads."

Her voice is dry and quiet.

"I guess there was nothing else they knew how to do. So they shot it."

She looks off across the field Old Jim, her brother, used to plow

with Prince the horse and irrigate with the water from this tank. Now
wild oats and blackberry grow there. In another thirty years it will
be a rich man's vineyard, a tax write-off.

"He was seven feet long, all stretched out, before they took him off.
And so thin! They all said, 'Well, Aunt May, I guess you were scared
there! I guess you were some scared!' But I wasn't. I didn't want him
shot. But I didn't know what to do for him. And I did need to get
Rosie."

I have told this true story which May gave to us as truly as I could,
and now I want to tell it as fiction, yet without taking it from her:
rather to give it back to her, if I can do so. It is a tiny part of the
history of the Valley, and I want to make it part of the Valley outside
history. Now the field that the poor man plowed and the rich man
harvested lies on the edge of a little town, houses and workshops of
timber and fieldstone standing among almond, oak, and eucalyptus
trees; and now May is an old woman with a name that means the
month of May: Rains End. An old woman with a long, wrinkle-
pleated upper lip, she is living alone for the summer in her summer
place, a meadow a mile or so up in the hills above the little town, Sinshan. She took her cow Rose with her, and since Rose tends to
wander she keeps her on a long tether down by the tiny creek, and
moves her into fresh grass now and then. The summerhouse is what
they call a nine-pole house, a mere frame of poles stuck in the
ground — one of them is a live digger-pine sapling — with stick and
matting walls, and mat roof and floors. It doesn't rain in the dry
season, and the roof is just for shade. But the house and its little front
yard where Rains End has her camp stove and clay oven and matting
loom are well shaded by a fig tree that was planted there a hundred
years or so ago by her grandmother.

Rains End herself has no grandchildren; she never bore a child,
and her one or two marriages were brief and very long ago. She has
a nephew and two grandnieces, and feels herself an aunt to all
children, even when they are afraid of her and rude to her because
she has got so ugly with old age, smelling as musty as a chickenhouse.
She considers it natural for children to shrink away from somebody
part way dead, and knows that when they're a little older and have
got used to her they'll ask her for stories. She was for sixty years a

member of the Doctors Lodge, and though she doesn't do curing any more people still ask her to help with nursing sick children, and the children come to long for the kind, authoritative touch of her hands when she bathes them to bring a fever down, or changes a dressing, or combs out bed-tangled hair with witch hazel and great patience.

So Rains End was just waking up from an early afternoon nap in the heat of the day, under the matting roof, when she heard a noise, a huge, awful yowl that started soft with a nasal hum and rose slowly into a snarling gargle that sank away into a sobbing purr. . . . And she got up and looked out from the open side of the house of sticks and matting, and saw a mountain lion under the fig tree. She looked at him from her house; he looked at her from his.

And this part of the story is much the same: the old woman; the lion; and, down by the creek, the cow.

It was hot. Crickets sang shrill in the yellow grass on all the hills and canyons, in all the chaparral. Rains End filled a bowl with water from an unglazed jug and came slowly out of the house. Halfway between the house and the lion she set the bowl down on the dirt. She turned and went back to the house.

The lion got up after a while and came and sniffed at the water. He lay down again with a soft, querulous groan, almost like a sick child, and looked at Rains End with the yellow eyes that saw her in a different way than she had ever been seen before.

She sat on the matting in the shade of the open part of her house and did some mending. When she looked up at the lion she sang under her breath, tunelessly; she wanted to remember the Puma Dance Song but could only remember bits of it, so she made a song for the occasion:

> You are there, lion.
> You are there, lion. . . .

As the afternoon wore on she began to worry about going down to milk Rose. Unmilked, the cow would start tugging at her tether and making a commotion. That was likely to upset the lion. He lay so close to the house now that if she came out that too might upset him, and she did not want to frighten him or to become frightened of him. He had evidently come for some reason, and it behoved her to find out what the reason was. Probably he was sick; his coming so close to a human person was strange, and people who behave strangely are usually sick or in some kind of pain. Sometimes, though, they are spiritually moved to act strangely. The lion might be a messenger, or might have some message of his own for her or her townspeople. She was more used to seeing birds as messengers; the four-footed people go about their own business. But the lion, dweller in the Seventh House, comes from the place dreams come from. Maybe she did not understand. Maybe someone else would understand. She could go over and tell Valiant and her family, whose summerhouse was in Gahheya meadow, farther up the creek; or she could go over to Buck's, on Baldy Knoll. But there were four or five adolescents there, and one of them might come and shoot the lion, to boast that he'd saved old Rains End from getting clawed to bits and eaten.

Moooooo! said Rose, down by the creek, reproachfully.

The sun was still above the southwest ridge, but the branches of pines were across it and the heavy heat was out of it, and shadows were welling up in the low fields of wild oats and blackberry.

Moooooo! said Rose again, louder.

The lion lifted up his square, heavy head, the color of dry wild oats, and gazed down across the pastures. Rains End knew from that weary movement that he was very ill. He had come for company in dying, that was all.

"I'll come back, lion," Rains End sang tunelessly. "Lie still. Be quiet. I'll come back soon." Moving softly and easily, as she would move in a room with a sick child, she got her milking pail and stool, slung the stool on her back with a woven strap so as to leave a hand free, and came out of the house. The lion watched her at first very tense, the yellow eyes firing up for a moment, but then put his head down again with that little grudging, groaning sound. "I'll come back, lion," Rains End said. She went down to the creekside and milked a nervous and indignant cow. Rose could smell lion, and demanded in several ways, all eloquent, just what Rains End intended to *do*? Rains End ignored her questions and sang milking songs to her: "Su bonny, su bonny, be still my grand cow. . ." Once she had to slap her hard on the hip. "Quit that, you old fool! Get over! I am *not* going to untie you and have you walking into trouble! I won't let him come down this way."

She did not say how she planned to stop him.

She retethered Rose where she could stand down in the creek if she liked. When she came back up the rise with the pail of milk in hand, the lion had not moved. The sun was down, the air above the ridges turning clear gold. The yellow eyes watched her, no light in them. She came to pour milk into the lion's bowl. As she did so, he all at once half rose up. Rains End started, and spilled some of the milk she was pouring. "Shoo! Stop that!" she whispered fiercely, waving her skinny arm at the lion. "Lie down now! I'm afraid of you when you get up, can't you see that, stupid? Lie down now, lion. There you are. Here I am. It's all right. You know what you're doing." Talking softly as she went, she returned to her house of stick and matting. There she sat down as before, in the open porch, on the grass mats.

The mountain lion made the grumbling sound, ending with a long sigh, and let his head sink back down on his paws.

Rains End got some cornbread and a tomato from the pantry box while there was still daylight left to see by, and ate slowly and neatly. She did not offer the lion food. He had not touched the milk, and she thought he would eat no more in the House of Earth.

From time to time as the quiet evening darkened and stars gathered thicker overhead she sang to the lion. She sang the five songs of *Going Westward to the Sunrise*, which are sung to human beings dying. She did not know if it was proper and appropriate to sing these songs to a dying mountain lion, but she did not know his songs.

Twice he also sang: once a quavering moan, like a house cat challenging another tom to battle, and once a long, sighing purr.

Before the Scorpion had swung clear of Sinshan Mountain, Rains End had pulled her heavy shawl around herself in case the fog came in, and had gone sound asleep in the porch of her house.

She woke with the grey light before sunrise. The lion was a motionless shadow, a little farther from the trunk of the fig tree than he had been the night before. As the light grew, she saw that he had stretched himself out full length. She knew he had finished his dying, and sang the fifth song, the last song, in a whisper, for him:

> The doors of the Four Houses
> are open.
> Surely they are open.

Near sunrise she went to milk Rose, and to wash in the creek. When she came back up to the house she went closer to the lion, though not so close as to crowd him, and stood for a long time looking at him stretched out in the long, tawny, delicate light. "As thin as I am!" she said to Valiant, when she went up to Gahheya later in the morning to tell the story and to ask help carrying the body of the lion off where the buzzards and coyotes could clean it.

It's still your story, Aunt May; it was your lion. He came to you. He brought his death to you, a gift; but the men with the guns won't take gifts, they think they own death already. And so they took from you the honor he did you, and you felt that loss. I wanted to restore it. But you don't need it. You followed the lion where he went, years ago now.

The Buck at Noontime
Patricia Monaghan

Magic is something
you don't recognize
when it happens,

something that
ordinary.

Yes.

That is what you said,
afterwards.

Remember?
At dusk, at dawn,
across the nettles and willows,
under the sighing pines,

we would see
roe deer, fallow deer,
staring at us from the tall
dying grass — sometimes

a single doe, sometimes
two or three, once
a herd of seven

63

but never
at midday
at the crossroad
a single buck

holding us with fixed gaze
until you said

If I move will he run?

You danced in front of him.
I watched him watching you.
You called and sang.
He never moved.

In the long space
between us, the long time
between us, something passed.

What passed is the stuff
of legend. I could tell
it that way. I could say:

two young children, lost in
the forest and turning down
its savage paths, were saved
by a guardian angel; or,

twins escaped a dungeon
beneath a tower and ran
into the forest to find
a magic dancing circle; or,

a man and woman went
to the forest for initiation
into the languages of winds
and birdsong; these are stories,

like those told by anyone
who sees something,
something ordinary
— a buck
at the crossroads
at noontime —
and knows magic
and has no words for it

all the stories
say the same thing,
all the stories tell us

how magic speaks:

in a voice so familiar,
so commonplace, that we
create prayers and myths
which capture and belie its
sacred ordinariness.

Meditation on a Cat
Mary TallMountain

Preferably at that time toward twilight when visible outlines enter a blurred surrealist aspect, and motion settles in languid pulsation, and the day draws a tired breath; when the city's freeways crouch for one last lunge of homegoing, and the swords of the marketplace are silenced of their restless clangor — then should one say lazily to a waiting cat, "Do you want. . ." Before the question is fully put he has risen and like grey mist has drifted into one's lap where, basking under one's fatuous approbation, he commences a sequence of the utmost languor consisting of small preparations: the complete bestowal of his furry and sinuous body upon one's own; the tiny adjustments necessary to the draping and arrangement of himself accompanied by minute changes in lashes, brows, and other facial appurtenances; the exquisite frowning intensity as he prepares for this ceremony, lays his paws out, their furred fingers indrawn preparatory to commencement of the rhythmic clenching with which his atavism, pursuing ancient memory, kneads — what? Jungle bark on a lofty perch? The mane of his mate? The ineffably smooth gesture of his head bent back to bare his throat so delicately furred and the little underlip, pinkly moist, rarely seen (the gesture so trustful as to muffle one's heartbeat!), the tender and peremptory burying of his leonine head into one's opened palm, the nuzzling in — all these factors create the humility of him displayed in his totally abandoned self before one's luxuriously sleepy gaze.

Then there is the whole question of the temperature and texture of his fur. Along his length one's stroking palm meets different sensations: here in his ruff an airy coolness as if he has just come in from a summer dawn; over his lean skull and between his ears a silky grey carpet of skin-warmed satin, graduating more densely down to his haunches, each bearing a feathery weightless fluff which after being flattened by one's hand springs up so that he appears to have recently settled to earth and folded a pair of wings (are these the answer to his mysterious vaulting flight?); the crinkled furs of his underbelly, neck, and throat, faintly moist, each of differing texture but with common secrecy and the hidden quality unique to his particular catness.

One gazes fascinated into jewels in the lamplight, nearly pupil-less, so that one sees the ineluctable beauty of the magical eyes opened to one's view, boundless behind their crystal windows, perfect spheres of celadon green flecked and freckled with the warmest sienna, these eyes narrowing to elongated and Orientally slanted curves, while behind the lids slide the tiny veils of brown that appear only when the total ambience has produced a state of highest euphoria.

In a sudden flicker of time, the eyes flash open, the ears move slowly to point forward, inward, focusing — where? Upon one's thinly ticking wristwatch! This attentive pose, so close as to render him cross-eyed, is seldom struck, for his dignity is impeccable. One is highly elated, having discovered in him another evidence of a quaint drollery one was always convinced he possessed.

But one has forgotten — has he forgotten, himself? — that marvelous equipment that speaks so silently, so wondrously alone, his matchless tail! Is it possible he has forgotten it, tip lightly twitching, cloaked in the fine trembling filaments of shining fur, dangling, floating with separate life upon the air, that inimitable plume which with his other appurtenances, to say nothing of his always command-ing presence, mark him, no matter what his recorded lineage, in-dubitably of regal descent? No. On further reflection we are con-vinced that there is nothing in his being of which he is not at any mo-ment totally aware, not only in its general appearance and color, grace, movement, or quality, but in its effect upon people or other animals, at any angle, against any background in innumerable emo-tional situations and states where he may be encountered. In short, we must say he knows that in his whole kingly person he is, as a wise friend once said about another of his like, ontologically perfect.

II.

The most difficult task the birds demand is that we learn to be equal to them, to feel our way into an intelligence that is different from our own.

Attack at Dawn
Cris Mazza

Yes I'm afraid of him.

But he grew up in my bedroom, under a light bulb. On his first night, however, the synthetic, substitute heat wasn't enough for Clarence. He woke me, two in the morning, calling frantically, his tiny beak thrust toward the ceiling. He was only a black fluffball with white, like spilled powder, on his head. I picked him up and held him against my neck, his shrill beak in my ear.

I took him to bed. Clarence slept on my stomach with the blanket pulled over his head. I woke first.

Always, since then, like today, I've risen before dawn to find him waiting.

He outgrew my bed. Black-and-white tail feathers sprouted. And around his neck, a fringe of thin silky hackles — part of the show. On his body, the edges of his feathers blended with no ridges, making him solid and smooth. He learned to carry and move his head to help display his large vinyl-red wattles and comb. His call no longer frantic, but hearty and demanding.

And his spurs: They emerged, tusk-like, from the backs of his ankles, two inches long, and sharp, curving up and in. Since then, every year in early summer the tips splinter off, honing them from base to tip.

My leg throbs. He continues to stalk me. I'd thought — when he left my room — I knew him.

Morning on any ordinary day — his first call is what pulls my body from sleep. Outside, I'll be aware of the watery scent of dew and the smell of wet rotting mulch leaves under the avocado trees, the earthy compost pile, new fertilizer worked into a vegetable garden, a husky odor of ripening tomatoes or the green scent of bell peppers. I'll feel the cool damp air splash on my face and spiderweb lines brushing my arms and legs. I'll hear any mouse who rustles the weeds, a cat stalking, a bird shaking the heavy night air from its feathers. But I'll always have to remind myself to think; sometimes even the reminder is sluggish. At least, usually, by the time I enter the coop, I'll be alert enough.

Clarence and a few of the hens are usually stirring around in pre-sunrise. The three avocado trees on the east side of the coop will keep the dawn murky, and the natural light is soft. A leftover coil of chicken wire stands on end by the screen door of the coop, and upright in the coil I keep a five-foot wooden dowel. Feed pail in one hand, dowel in the other, I'll enter the henyard. Clarence always raises his hackles and comes towards me, scratching the dirt, arching his neck and turning left, right, left, right, like his mythical serpentine ancestors rising, swaying, from a marsh.

"No, you don't," I usually say, keeping one blunt end of the dowel against his chest. Any smile I ever felt, I never showed him. We circle, always facing each other, until I reach the feed trough. The mash looks like honey as I pour it from the lip of the pail, and Clarence eats, bending to bolt two or three mouthfuls at a time before standing to glare again. He'll flap his wings, slapping his sides like whips, one orange eye always on me. And frost creeps up my backbone as I watch him.

Watching him now. . . I'm numb. No. . . there's the pain in my shin. As though we're enemies. Is it really him?

Clarence usually stays near the feed trough, head high, posing over the hens there — they look up at him while they eat, as their necks poke in and out. With unexplainable trust, the hens feed with their backs to Clarence, tails up in front of him. And with the same unquestioning acceptance, they are always ready for him. Upon some instinctive signal I've neither observed nor understood, the hen will calmly lower her body and flatten her back, making it possible for Clarence to mount her — pinching the back of her neck in his beak, one huge foot on each of her wings, crushing her chest against the ground as he presses the underside of his tail to the underside of hers. When it's over she'll resume eating, perhaps shaking a little to put her feathers back in order.

But with me, sometimes he jousts — as I back out of the coop, keeping the dowel like a lance in front of me. Always only a single skirmish, and only occasionally will one of us manage to reach past the other's defenses. So if a stout hit from his spurs knocks me to one knee, how can I be angry? I'll limp around outside the wire. And if I meet his charge with a well-timed kick, and he falls back, shoulders against the fence, I'll retreat outside then also.

Difficult to recall this tenderly now with the throb in my leg and blood on my hands.

As I banded a hen outside the coop not long ago, there was a small commotion: long hen-necks stretched and pointed toward a corner of the yard. Still holding the hen under one arm, I went around the outside of the coop to see what it was, stopped and stared, pulse thick in my ears. A king snake was oozing through the wire with his pellet-eyes on a new family of chicks. Clarence moved between the hatch-lings and the snake. The hen in my arms became a flurry of hysterical feathers — that was something I understood.

I took the dowel and slipped inside. The chicks scattered from me like leaves blowing over the ground. Taking advantage of the confusion, I pinned the snake by the head and took it outside. Clarence ran across the floor of the coop to the door, wings up and level. Like a hawk diving with talons extended.

"See, Clarence," I said, poking the snake's face at the wire. Clarence returned the snake's round-eyed stare.

I threw the snake far down into the canyon behind the house.

He's watching me. Clarence, when did your shiny black eyes become staring orange?

When summer is ripe, the fig tree on the west side of the coop is always heavy. The hens consume gallons of nearly rotten fruit: sticky-sweet pulp hanging in soft black bags. Along with the fruit, the tree is full of large buzzing green beetles, sitting in groups of five or six on a single fig, sucking the insides out of it.

Last night before sunset, I stayed by the tree for several hours picking figs and bugs for the eager chickens who lined the wire. But Clarence couldn't keep a beetle in his possession long enough to swallow it. Instinct compelled him to show off his food and call the hens over when he ate. So they obeyed and snatched the bugs from his beak. I tried holding his beetle up higher than a hen's neck could reach, where he could look up and pluck it from my fingers. They all stood at attention, stretching their necks up, pointing their beaks at the bug. But before Clarence decided to take it, a hen would jump, snap, land and swallow, and Clarence gnashed at the wire near my hands.

The figs were easier for him because I pushed twenty at a time through the wire mesh. Sometimes they were too big to fit through, and the wires split them, leaving fig-sugar there where the hens could've lapped it up, if they had tongues. But Clarence seemed indignant as I piled the squishy fruit on the ground around his feet. The skins broke and the rose-colored seeds glistened in the last rays of the sun. Clarence gave me a look before sucking the figs into his gullet, then looked again.

At seven-thirty it was almost dark, the feast was over and they filed through the small door of their shed to the sheltered perches where they sleep dusk to dawn. I could hear their muffled squawks and restless moving around as the hens jostled for a favored position near Clarence. A last crippled bug lay on its back, waving its five remaining legs. I thought maybe in the morning Clarence would find it first.

I'm afraid to look. Stand-off? Or am I cornered? It can't be you!

I was back at the coop this morning before light touched the avocado trees draped over the eastern top wire, but Clarence and a few others were already out. I could see the Reds moving against the ground, like dark-backed trout at the bottom of a pool. Clarence was a grey rock statue with one clear orange eye looking out of the darkness. An unripe avocado fell off the tree and nestled in the mulch leaves. The fig tree was silent, gathering strength.

I took the dowel and let myself into the coop. The hens milled around my feet, refusing to move for me to walk. I tapped their sides with the dowel and cleared a path to the feed trough. As I bent to spill the grain, I whispered low to Clarence, "There was a bug here this morning; did you find it?"

He muttered in his throat. I kept the dowel gently pressed against his breastbone while I poured the grain. A fine dust rose and settled.

I was drowsy and watched them eating. Squatting, the dowel forgotten, tucked between my knees and chest. A cricket finished his night-song. The sky was light but the earth under the trees was still dark. Dawn, as always, unhurried, not even a breeze to rustle the leaves. I don't remember shutting my eyes. Just for a second!

I trusted you — Why? I knew better!

Spurs up, Clarence slammed into my shins, at the same time snapped his beak over my wrist. I fell on my butt, but I got the dowel in front of me and pushed him backwards, hard. He toppled onto one wing.

Only minutes ago.

Now on my feet again, but I haven't retreated.

This isn't going to happen, Clarence, not with me. You know this isn't the way we do things. Stop it. Please stop.

Neck stretched, head near the ground, bobbing, jerking up then down. Hackles standing in a pointed circle around his neck, a black-and-white sunflower with an angry face. War feathers. The voice barely audible, a growl, a grim moan. Rocking back and forth, shifting his weight, the spurs freshly honed, long and curved, legs stiff, now side-stepping, circling, glaring, approaching, breath puffing, hissing. *What do you want? What're you doing! Stay away from me. Get back!* Wings held out, feathers separate and spread and rigid like a fringe of spears, tripling his size, getting nearer, coming closer, the violent-red comb the only color. . . anywhere.

You're not even you anymore!

I swing the dowel like an ax and feel the thud as it meets the side of his head, on his red earlobe.

Clarence's neck jerks sideways, down over his wing as though he's trying to tuck his head under. He falls to one side, one wing flapping, his crooked body thrashing in circles in the henyard dust.

I fall after him, again feeling my bruised legs. He flops, dragging his feet toes-down behind him. The rhythm slows. Slows. He stops beating. I take him and hold him against my neck. *I've killed you. I wish I never saw that snake, wish I waited for you to have a chance at it.*

He does not struggle in my embrace. Against my ear I hear his rough breathing. I rub his comb between my finers. My blood smeared across one of my wrists, his drips down my other arm. I hold him between my knees, pat him all over and make blood finger-prints on his granite feathers.

Clarence trembles.

Leaning away from him, I stand him up and hold him there. Both eyes open now, he blinks at me. Orange. His tail is up, stiff. He doesn't move.

I reach out a red-spattered hand — a beak-shaped gash on my wrist — touch his neck, his head, his comb and hot wattles, his hard narrow back, his high chest. No resistance. I pull him close to me again, but he moves away with one unsteady step.

His head is up, his tail is up. We stare at each other. My legs ache, I feel my pulse there, but I stand and step backwards. Clarence watches me.

He looks, and I look back.

Again I step backwards, and again. Each step a thousand pounds on my legs. I retrieve the pail and the dowel and retreat, still backwards, out the door.

We look at each other. Through wire.

Clarence remains, as before, a grey statue. The sun still waits behind the eastern hills — they are outlined in flame.

I don't put the dowel into the coil of wire beside the door — it's still in my hand as I leave. No sound from Clarence. Next to the cellar door I place the dowel across two stones and step in the middle. It cracks into a V. The cellar is dry and dark and musty. Dusty bottles of wine on their sides in a crate. Crock jars of olives curing. A newly painted chair on the workbench. Brushes in turpentine. Rat traps hanging in rows. Rubber aprons and metal tubs, an ax, burlap sacks, a top-loading freezer. I can hear the hens quibble as they eat. Are they looking at him? In the cluster of tools inside the cellar door, I find an old corn broom, worn away on one side, too soft now even for dusting a blanket. Fit only for a scarecrow.

Sparrows are stealing in and out of the large mesh wire. Doves in the avocado trees stir then are silent again, but a mockingbird calls. A hen pauses in front of Clarence, lowering her head a little, waiting, but he glides past her, head up, like a seahorse. I put the broom into the empty coil of wire, bristles up.

Still Another Road Kill Still Another Initiation

Joan Dobbie

having to do with the deer
that flew up over the front
of our car
that lay heaving by the roadside
& fluid slowly flowing
out of its mouth
how i thought
there is nothing that we can do
how we tried to call *someone*
to shoot it
how no one came

how ted tried to kill it
while i didn't look
me — who should have had healing power
me — practiced yogini
    who should have seen
how i backed off thinking
there's nothing i can do anyway
& its eyes that were deer eyes
somehow peaceful

why were we so god-awfully sure
that being alive & dying
meant being in pain & needing
to be dead?

why could we not simply be quiet?
allow it the dignity of its dying?
why not pray?

why ted had to pound on it
for mercy's sake
in desperation for the life
that refused to leave
why i had to walk away
& pick pussy willows
off a nearby bush
thinking of my mother
& how she misses us
& janet trying to pull ted away
saying it's not your fault it's not your fault
until ted backed off
to pace the gravel roadside
back & forth
    & back & forth
while andy, eight years old, sat still
in the glass-ridden car
& would not look out

when the deer finally was dead
i went over & stared down at it
it was flat like a rug
i felt like vomiting then
i felt we had failed everything then
i recognized deer spirit only then
when it was too late
& understood only then
how perhaps with faith
we could have spoken to it

The Elephant-Hearted Woman
An Interview with Pat Derby

Theresa Corrigan

Twelve years ago, during one of my bookstore-hopping jaunts, I was in a little store in La Jolla when a book leapt up and shouted, "Buy me, buy me." I took it home and spent the next day falling in love — with Chauncey Cougar, LuSeal Seal, Neena Elephant, Rijo Tiger, Sweet William BlackBear, and most especially with Pat Derby, the woman who cared for these animal friends and brought them so alive for me in The Lady and Her Tiger.

Then a few years ago, a woman came into the bookstore that I now own and while talking of animal books, she inquired, "Have you ever heard of The Lady and Her Tiger?" *I said, "Are you kidding? It's one of my favorite books." "Well, do you know Pat has a shelter not thirty miles from here? Would you like her phone number?"*

The next Saturday, I brought my own animals to Pat's shelter: the butterflies that were dancing a jig in my stomach. I felt that I was about to take a test that would determine my future. I knew from reading her book that Pat judged people by their ability to interact with her animals, and if I failed with the animals, my chance of being allowed to know them would be terminated before it started.

I arrived at the PAWS (Performing Animal Welfare Society) shelter in Galt at precisely the time Pat had suggested. I had seen the pictures of Pat in her book, but the person who met me at the door did not fit my mental image. I expected someone large enough to handle big animals; Pat is petite. I expected someone young, forgetting that the pictures were at least twelve years old. I expected some odd combination of Hollywood glitter and animal trainer crustiness; I saw sweatpants, tiny sneakers and hennaed hair pulled back in stubby pigtails. I expected reserve and wariness; I received warmth, bubbly conversation and enthusiasm. But none of that quelled my anxiety because I knew that my ultimate challenge awaited outside — my first encounter with the animals.

I took my cues from Pat; I kept my ears and eyes open and my hands out of the cages, controlling my immense desire to "pet" the animals. I also paid attention when Pat said that most people want to volunteer to do what they assume is the "fun stuff" with the animals, not the shit jobs like fundraising and paperwork that make the animals' lives at PAWS possible.

Well, I must have passed Pat's test, because I've been doing volunteer work at PAWS for two years. My first job was fundraising.

While many of the animals at PAWS were once performers, today they are all retired. Pat is not. Along with Ed Stewart, the codirector of PAWS (and one of the nicest men I've ever met), Pat spends about fifteen hours a day feeding, cleaning enclosures, attending meetings to fight for animal rights, and most importantly, fundraising. In fact, finding the time to do this interview was quite a feat.

Theresa: How did you get started in the animal saving business?

Pat: I was working as an actress. I worked on a show that used animals and I just kind of backed into it. I just did what everybody does when you're around people who have animals: I started going out to the place where they kept the animals and volunteered. They never had enough money or enough food, so I used to bring food out and take care of the babies.

I never did train — not in the sense that people understand "training." Training generally is accepted as a relationship where a person imposes some sort of behavior on an animal, whether it's through a food reward or fear. There's a certain amount of discipline required in training, and I was never a disciplinarian. I always thought that animals were more interesting (including my dogs and cats) if they were allowed to be what they were.

I worked for Ralph Helfer at Africa, USA, as his baby animal nurse. I took care of animals that nobody else could get near, like the gorillas and baby elephants. They had a pair of baboons, and the trainers were so aggressive with them that they would charge at people. I used treats, and the baboons responded to me. Animals shouldn't be pushed to the point of no return; all you really have to do is sit with them. So I ended up having to work them because nobody else could.

I was able to do it because I never made them do tricks. You know, bears walking on their hind legs and stuff like that. Sweet William had been a circus bear, so that was already ingrained in him. But I hated having him do it. Neena [Elephant] was the same way; she had a whole act that she knew. Ted [Pat's husband at the time and an animal trainer] and I would argue all the time over that. He would say that they already knew the tricks. But I hated even seeing them do tricks.

I always liked doing things where the animal was responding to me because he wanted to respond, not because I was making him. And my greatest successes were with the leopards. The leopards would do anything for me just because I was there. If you put them somewhere else and I called them, they came. Chrissy [Cougar] would walk straight to me through fire or anything. Rijo would do it. Or like when we worked Seymour and Gwenny, we just let them be free and do what bears do. But trainers always wanted bears to stand up and salute.

After fifteen years of it I really got to hate it. It was something I did because it seemed like there wasn't any other way. Remember I started when I was young, before I really had my head set, and everything I know about today I learned about because I saw all the wrong things done. I could attribute everything I know about animals to Ralph Helfer in the most converse way in the world: because everything that that man did was so blatantly wrong. I just watched so many animals die and thought, "God, this is stupid." Later, when I worked with Ed, he would say, "What the hell are we doing this for? This is crazy. I don't even like it." I agreed, so that was it.

What I'm doing now is the result of years and years of moving in a direction. When I worked animals in movies, I always lectured to Humane Societies. I was always a closet animal rights advocate. I gravitated in that direction. And when we had the lodge [Howling Wolf Lodge, their previous shelter in Leggett, California], I developed that attitude more because we weren't working animals commercially, except for Lincoln Mercury. When we had a final schism with Lincoln Mercury, it was over principles. I just realized that animal rights activism was what I really wanted to do. I've never been really big on fame and fortune. Unfortunately, it's kind of dumb; if you're going to have an elephant and a grizzly bear, you should really think about money — a lot.

TC: You started your book by saying, "It has to begin with elephants. I was born in love with all elephants." What is it about elephants that you love?

PD: All my life has been colored by elephants. I really relate to them. Maybe in another life, I was an elephant. I don't know. I love their intelligence. All my life I've always sought elephants and as I've gotten older, I couldn't live without having an elephant living with me. I realized that when I lost Neena.

TC: So you got "71." How did you get her?

PD: In Zimbabwe, elephants are culled annually. To maintain a level population, over four thousand elephants a year are slaughtered. When a herd is sighted, men in helicopters shoot the matriarch first, which confuses the rest of the herd. As they group around their leader trying to help her, they are massacred. The babies in the herd are left standing, confused and terrified. Animal dealers are allowed to purchase the babies, although babies under forty-two inches high are traditionally killed, because they are too difficult to care for at that age. Most baby elephants suckle until they are six years old, and they are never very far from their mothers and the herd. Elephants are very social animals. The smallest elephants seldom survive the stress of the cull.

In 1984, Arthur Jones, the developer of Nautilus Sports equipment, rescued a group of young African elephants, orphaned in a cull. These elephants are now living at his ranch in Florida. Three years ago we took Mara, another elephant orphan, from the San Jose zoo to join the herd in Florida. It is one of the few places in the world where elephants can live as they were meant to [at least within the constraints of captivity]. It was on that trip that we first met "71" [71 was the number assigned to her after the cull]. She was the smallest of the herd and always had a terrible time keeping up with them. We saw her again the next year when we came back to see Mara. Unlike Mara, who is strong and healthy and has become a leader in the herd, 71 can survive only with constant human care.

Because the elephant is so intelligent, it's amazing to me how adaptable they are. They can replace other elephants pretty readily with people and they seem to do it by themselves. I've seen so many baby elephants do what she does; all those baby elephants in Florida do. It's like they say, "I can't have a mother, I'm not nursing, so I'll just suck on somebody's hand, and I'll do very nicely with this." Which is what's so sad about elephants, because it really doesn't take a lot; they don't demand a lot. And the people who train them are really awful. It would take very little to keep elephants happy.

With 71 we try and do what we can. She doesn't need us sitting on top of her, but she likes to know that we're here. We try to spend a lot of time with her, and usually when we leave her, we put hay or alfalfa down for her to graze on. In the wild they wander off from their herd to graze. When we first got her we slept with her, because she had been taken from the herd and she really was frustrated at that point. But she's got a certain kind of independence now. I mean they know, their infrasonic hearing is so well developed that she can hear me talking right now. So it's like she's in the herd because she knows where I am. But if we were totally off the property and there were nobody else here, she'd be very disturbed.

Elephants today are in serious trouble and the way they are kept in captivity is deplorable. It is a sad comment on our own society that the two animals with brains comparable to humans' — elephants and whales — are captured and used in demeaning performances to amuse us in the name of education. Killer whales jumping through flaming hoops and elephants standing on their heads are indicative of our inability to conceive of intelligence among other species.

During the past two years, we have observed elephants chained, hooked, prodded and beaten because they are elephants and elephants must be dominated (according to trainers' lore). It is not a pleasant sight and, because of the culls in Africa, many more elephants are coming into this country to be used as temporary attractions and dumped as they become larger and less manageable. There are no simple solutions to the problem. By taking 71, we are hoping to focus attention on the plight of all elephants and to develop a program to explore alternatives to the present practices of training and keeping elephants in captivity. 71 will be one of the only elephants in captivity who will never be chained or "disciplined."

I don't like relationships that are based on power, with people or with animals. I like a different kind of relationship. I think mutual respect is really important. I respect what 71 can do to me if she panicked. Her sheer size, if she fell on me, could kill me. But I'm not afraid of her. And I think that most animal training, especially with elephants and bigger animals that are dangerous, is based on the fact that the person who is working with them fears them, so they overcompensate for that fear with domination. I get really upset if Ed and I are kidding around and he holds me and I know he's physically stronger than I am and he won't let me go — I really hate that kind of dominance.

TC: The respect you talk about has two sides. You say you respect animals. How do they respect you?

PD: Well, there's a difference. If you ever watch animals, they're not aggressive in the sense that we are. An animal will never pursue an altercation except for a really valid reason. Oh, the male domestic cat will protect his turf. A female will defend her young. There are certain rules they have that will trigger an aggressive act. But if you don't trigger that, they just don't do it. So that's the kind of respect they have for you. I've never seen an animal that was normal (some are neurotic because of people) who just was aggressive for no valid reason.

So when I say I respect them, I mean I respect them enough to understand them. Like Harriet [Baboon], for example, the way we've told you to behave around her [don't stare at her, don't hold food where she can see it and not give it to her, and don't bare your teeth to her]. That's your respect for her because her behavior is ingrained. And if you do that, then Harriet respects you by behaving with you as she would with her own troop and she chuckles and grooms. . . that's the kind of mutual respect that goes down. Animals seem to say, "If you don't intrude in my space, I won't intrude in yours." That's the way animals generally respect each other.

Most people who love animals don't understand that you have to function within what that animal knows and understands. And they don't think about what they might be doing to trigger a certain kind of behavior in the animal. So that's why we don't usually allow people to approach the cages or go near the animals, but when we do, we really split hairs about just how far they go. You can't get careless, like you would with a cat or dog, because once you get a habit developed in an animal like 71 then you play hell breaking it. For example, 71 hasn't yet learned that she can use her trunk as a weapon and we don't want her to. We don't allow anyone to pound on her, even in play, because her instinct would be to swat back with her trunk, like she would with other elephants. We have to be very careful not to trigger her instinctive use of her trunk. One stupid act on our part can take forever to correct. We don't just want to keep her from hurting someone with her trunk; we want to keep her from learning she *can* hurt someone with her trunk. If she starts sparring with us, we just walk away from her so she doesn't get excited.

The best thing you can do for animals is be a calming influence on them. One of the worst problems with baby elephants, and Ed and I saw it immediately with Mara, happens in petting zoos where everybody pets and feeds the elephant. Once the elephant gets used to people feeding it, it gets frustrated if it doesn't get the food and it just becomes a nervous, little neurotic thing.

71 doesn't have any of that; we don't allow strangers to feed her. She eats at specific times; there's never anybody coming over with a treat or goody. Our behavior with her is carefully plotted and planned. It's the same thing with the sucking on hands. It could get out of control easily if we let her do that with everyone. She could start to grab people and pull their hands. Whenever she starts to grab somebody's hand, we stick our own hands in her mouth and ask the person to back away. She doesn't know her own strength and we don't want her grabbing people.

Everybody I've ever known who had a lion or tiger or a leopard for a pet didn't know what they were doing. When the cubs are little, the people think it's so funny to play hide and seek, to hide and let the baby stalk them. Then baby gets to be three hundred pounds and forgodsakes they're going to get killed. They don't realize it's a habit that they develop in these cats and it's impossible to break when they get older. But it's the same thing as raising kids. You know, you raise a kid and what you're trying to do is give him all the right values so that when he grows up, they're ingrained. You do the same thing with the animal. What you're trying to do is be a calming influence in his life, not to let him get excited, not to let him be neurotic, just to be the peaceful element that's going to keep him in his own social patterns. That's why training is bad, especially "affection" training. . . affection training is based on hand rearing baby animals on a bottle, giving them a lot of affection. Then when the training time comes you start with the discipline. So it's like a yo-yo. One minute you're loving them, the next minute you're cuffing them, and then you're loving them, and then you're hitting them, and then they're being forced to stay and then they can come. And it's tremendous turmoil and confusion for the animal. The psychological confusion and pain for the animal is the worst aspect of training.

TC: You talk about not wanting the animals to be frustrated, which is apparently them wanting something they can't have. Do you think there will always be frustration by virtue of the fact that these are wild animals who can no longer be wild?

PD: Yes, I do. There's always in them an unfulfilled area. The ones that are second or third generation captive-born have less of a need, but it's still there. You try to do the best you can. But there's always a point that you can't go beyond. I mean, you can't give the elephant Africa and a herd — unless you take her there. So you try to do the best you can and you replace all their needs with other things. An animal like Chrissy [Christopher Cougar] is the least frustrated. He is pretty well adapted to his life because he's totally imprinted. You can see the difference in him; he enjoys captive existence. He loves to play with his pine cones, and he is very set in his ways. There's very little frustration there. But with the grizzly bears. . .we're constantly trying to give them natural habitat, because changes in the weather really affect the grizzlies and we try to accommodate that. In the spring we let them out in the run more and we let the grass grow tall and we do all that stuff because there's something inside a grizzly bear that always needs a forest. So it's not the solution, but it's the best that you can do.

TC: What kinds of things do you think *you've* learned from the animals?

PD: [She sits quietly for a minute; then a soft smile creeps up the sides of her face.] Patience. How to die. That's sounds funny, but I really have. How to accept things. Patience is probably the biggest lesson. I never had any. And how to control my temper. I always had an awful temper.

When you're around animals a lot, you discover that they have a tremendous patience in everything they do. In the wild, they can wait for days for a kill. Baby elephants take forever to learn to use their trunks. Everything they do is kind of: "Well, I have to learn this, and no matter how hard it is or how long it takes, I have to learn how to do this." Their whole existence is based on that patience. I never had any patience about anything. If I wanted something I wanted it yesterday. But I've learned; it's kind of like the Buddhist philosophy. You keep growing and you keep moving. I've learned over a period of time with animals that the goals that you have that you want immediately, it may take you ten years to get. And then suddenly, ten years later you say, "Oh my god, ten years ago, this is what I really wanted and now I have it. Isn't it funny."

It's what you learn when you have defeat. I'm sure if I hadn't had animals, I would have lost my mind because I've certainly had a checkered life. When my father died, I didn't accept that well at all. But from the minute I got my first animal, I began to understand more about life. And now I think I'm capable of living through anything. There's absolutely nothing that could devastate me. As long as I'm alive, if the sun goes down tonight and I sleep through the night and wake up tomorrow, no matter how awful things are, I'll be able to start doing something about it. And that's the animal's attitude, which is what's so very sad about animals in captivity — it takes a lot to make them give up. They have this enormous patience with everything. And it's a tremendous philosophy. They also accept things. It's like "OK, this has happened to me and now I still have to survive, so I'll just get on with it." And they don't feel sorry for themselves. All of that I've learned about from animals — and I think those are the greatest lessons.

TC: But some animals do go crazy?

PD: Yeah, but there's always a reason. There's no real neurosis in animals. Animals that have been in the wild should never be in captivity. Those are the ones who go crazy and that, to me, is the worst thing for an animal. I would infinitely rather see an animal that's been wild destroyed than left to live miserably.

TC: Now that you are out of the animal training business and are working solely as an animal activist, what do you think of the work done by the animal liberation front, the militant people who liberate animals?

PD: Animal liberation people have made tremendous strides. I draw the line at violence; I would never advocate hurting people, but going into labs and pulling animals out — yes, I'm all for it. They had a commando raid on a California university just yesterday and they took their own minicam crew in and pulled all these cats. They filmed them in there — horrible, just awful. When they brought the cats out, they turned the film over to the media. Not the cats — they won't tell anybody where they are. Before we had tapes of the labs people never even discussed animals in labs. I'll give you a really good example. Roger Caras was really on the other side — "we need animals in research." Now Roger's thinking has done a complete change because you can't refute the stuff that those people have pulled out of the labs like the Gennarelli tapes [of head trauma experiments on baboons]. You see it. It's in black and white; you can't say, "Oh, Pat, that doesn't really happen." It does really happen.

Most research is useless. In the past some of it may have been necessary, but today, with computers and everything else they have, it's unnecessary. But using animals is cheap and there's a tremendous profit for people in research. And the only way we're going to stop product testing is to boycott every goddamn thing that tests their product on an animal. I think people are starting to realize that.

I'm a fourth-generation vegetarian. I think my great-great-grandfather probably got into it for health reasons. But it developed in our family because my mother and my father were really nonviolent. They didn't believe in killing anything — not bugs, nothing. When I was a little girl the worst crime I could commit would be to step on a bug. And my father spent a lot of time with me, explaining to me, and it stuck with me all my life, that the universe is composed of all these different worlds and that above us is a bigger world and below us is a smaller world, and they're all important. The little ant that crawls along the ground lives in a whole world and has a whole society, and I don't have any right to destroy any part of that. I grew up understanding there was a reason for every form of life, and the reason wasn't for me to just snuff it out because I "needed" to. So that's the reason for my vegetarianism. I also don't think that healthwise we need meat. I think I'm living proof. I'm an extremely healthy person. I have excellent teeth and I've been to the dentist three times in my life.

On the other hand, I know that my animals who are carnivores have to eat meat. And I think people who try to make vegetarians out of leopards and lions are crazy, because there is, in that aspect of nature, a predator and prey relationship based on controlling the species. I don't think you can go against what they normally eat. But if it came down to me having to slaughter something to feed my animals, I'm afraid they'd have to learn to eat tomatoes. Because I couldn't do it.

TC: How do you resolve that contradiction? You don't eat meat, you don't support the slaughter of meat and yet your household consumes a lot of meat.

PD: If somebody said to me, "OK, today we're going to stop all the slaughter of meat, totally stop it," then I'd start looking at some synthetics to feed my animals and hope to hell that science would come up with some. I firmly believe that if everybody stopped eating meat and we stopped producing meat, someone would develop a scientific alternative for carnivorous animals. But I think we're a long way from that.

Certain aspects of the manufacture of meat are more odious than others, like the slaughter of baby animals like calves for veal. I think that if animals are to be slaughtered, they should have some sort of quality of life and then be slaughtered. And I've always said that what I would like to do is to take old animals and let them live peacefully until they died. And when they died, feed them to my animals. That's an alternative we could use right now. I used to get old horses that would be brought to Africa, USA to be slaughtered. I would run in and grab them and take them to my place. I'd keep them and float their teeth and get their hooves trimmed and bring them back and they'd live another year or two. Then when they died, I'd slaughter them for my animals. Once they're dead, they're dead.

TC: Would that include people too?

PD: I don't know why not. I mean meat is meat. When you look at nature as it really is, things die and they decay and then they become something else. I really believe in a form of reincarnation. I just don't believe that the spirit ever dies. I think it goes from one thing that rusts and rots to another. With me I could care less. I'm an organ donor. If somebody can use my kidneys and anything else, hell, let them take the parts and if they want to feed the. . . the steaks to the animals, I would be perfectly happy, because my body's just a physical thing. . . it's going to rot and decay and it doesn't matter.

TC: That raises another question. What provisions have you made for the animals when you and Ed die? Some people I've encountered want their animals destroyed when they die. Their feelings are that it's better for the animals to die than to risk being abandoned or abused.

PD: That's why Ed and I formed PAWS. I hate non-profit organizations, just the paperwork is a pain in the ass. You have to call a board of directors meeting every time you have to make a decision that you know you're going to make anyway. And it's scary because there's always the possibility of somebody undermining it and trying to take it over; you never really have that total control. And I don't like that. But if Ed and I got on a plane tomorrow and were killed, not only would the animals continue but everything that we're doing would continue because we're training people to take over our work.

I just think that killing animals when humans die is terribly selfish because a lot of people can and do care about animals. Nobody is exclusive to that. You just have to sit down and show people how to care for exotic animals because everybody hasn't spent twenty-five years doing all the wrong things to learn how to do it right.

We stop the interview for one of 71's five daily feedings. I look forward always to time with the animals. As we head out the back door, we first encounter Harriet Baboon, born at the Lodi Zoo thirteen years ago and shipped to the Oakland baby zoo. Because she was terrified of people, she screamed all the time. An employee from Oakland contacted Pat because she was afraid they were going to "surplus" Harriet out to a research lab. Love and concern from Pat and Ed have calmed Harriet's anxieties. Her favorite pastime is picking imaginary fleas from Ed's arms. As social animals, baboons need grooming exchanges from their troop mates — Ed and Pat are Harriet's troop. I knew I had become an auxiliary member when Harriet began picking at freckles on my arms.

When anyone at PAWS gets fed, Harriet gets fed; she insists. Today we slice her some oranges. She stuffs the orange quarter against her teeth to make the same kind of wide-mouthed smile I did as a kid.

Next is Tuffy Bobcat, who was born in an animal breeder's compound for the exotic pet trade. Only two and a half weeks old when he arrived at PAWS, Tuffy had to be bottle-fed every two hours. Pat says he thinks she and Ed are his parents. Tuffy turns his buff, fluff tail to Pat for a quick scratch before we proceed.

Christopher Cougar, very old and arthritic, is next, showing an unusual spark of energy as he pounces on his pine cone, a gift from a recent human visitor. He is a retired actor from the Lincoln-Mercury car commercials, as are Flo and Spike Cougar and Rick O'Shay Bobcat.

We stop to pet the dogs. There's no visiting the exotics without a brief stop with Rusty, a demanding pup recently recovered from being abandoned without food or water when his humans decided to leave town without him. Oh yes, Pat shelters more commonplace animals as well — three dogs and forty-three cats, to be exact. Rusty lives in a grassy enclosure with Puppy, a blonde mutt foundling from the highway, and Jonquil, an old bloodhound.

As we approach Elsa Lioness, I feel my usual surge of excitement. It took me over a year to begin to earn her trust. When we first met, she would flatten her ears and lunge at me, obviously displeased. At the first sign of displeasure, I would walk away. Captive animals have no control over their interactions with humans; leaving them alone when they request it is one way of respecting their wishes and allowing them some control. Today when I greet Elsa, she runs up, falls over belly-up and sucks her foot, like a two-hundred-pound kitten. Elsa spent most of her cubhood chained to a tree in a suburban Sacramento backyard. Animal control agents asked Pat and Ed to keep her until the "owner" could set up better conditions for her; the owner was never heard from again.

Mica Wolf is pacing next door. She belonged to a woman who raised wolves as pets. Mica escaped and was captured by animal control agents. Pat says, "She's a garbage wolf. She's so interbred that she's no pure strain of subspecies. People who have wolf packs want pure strains, so we can't find a home for her." Although Mica has calmed down considerably since her arrival at PAWS, her pacing clearly evidences the distress of a wolf without a pack.

Seymour and Gwendolyn Grizzly are next on our tour. Seymour, who worked on the "Grizzly Adams" series, was born in the Minneapolis Zoo in 1968. As often happens with captive animals, his mother was unwilling to care for him, so he was raised by humans. After four months he had so imprinted on humans, he couldn't be reintroduced into the bear enclosure. Fortunately, Pat heard about him, and he's been living with her ever since. Gwendolyn was born of the same parents in the same zoo as Seymour and ended up in the same predicament. Once again Pat and Ed to the rescue. Today, Gwenny is asleep, snout to rump, like a huge hedgehog rolled in a ball. Seymour is out in the run wreaking havoc on an old tire.

Lucretia and Lucifer Leopard reside in the newly constructed twin towers. They are a pair of Chinese leopards purchased from an endangered species breeding compound in Florida by film producers for a TV movie, "The Runaways." Pat worked with them on the film and took them when the film was completed. They have been kept separated, but with Lucretia's recent spay, as soon as the connecting run is built, they will have the choice to cohabit again.

The newest resident at PAWS is Spook Coyote, so named for her extreme fear of people. A local Sacramento resident had found her, taken her home and kept her chained for nine years in a 55-gallon metal drum. Now she has a large run with grass, a log to burrow under and a house in which to hide.

Across from 71 is J.C. Lion, one of an unwanted litter born in Lion Country Safari in Southern California. He's old, cantankerous and seems to take great pleasure in looking docile until one gets too close and then letting out a roar that will curl your toes. He especially likes to do this with cocky old men.

Bearing apples, carrots and grain, we finally reach an eager 71. She's now five years old, and permanently stunted by her earlier deprivations, though still weighing in at over twelve hundred pounds. She dances a sidestep as we approach, extending her trunk for her favorites — the apples. In between bites, she reaches for Pat's hand to suck. We spend about fifteen minutes with her before returning to the laundry and the interview.

TC: The focus of our anthology is the relationships between women and animals — all different kinds of relationships, political, psychic, spiritual, emotional. So I wanted to ask you whether you think that animals recognize gender differences in humans?

PD: They definitely do. The most simplistic example is the male African lion. I have raised probably sixty-five male African lion cubs. And when every one reached sexual maturity, his whole attitude towards me changed. J.C. is a wonderful example. Ed and I raised him together and up until he was three years old, J.C. was my cat. I was mommy; he was my baby. When he got to be three, that was it. He was Ed's cat. I was the female and I was to be totally subservient. He will tolerate anything from Ed because Ed is male and he tolerates none of that from me. There are times when I can see even he gets confused about why he's doing it. If a human female is having her period, lions are just crazy.

Harriet absolutely knows that I'm female and Ed's male. Everything that she does with me is the kind of behavior that baboons do to competitive females. What she does with Ed is typical baboon behavior with a male who's the leader of the troop, which he is. She defers to whatever Ed requires. She never challenges Ed, never. And she gets jealous over Ed.

The ones that don't appear to notice as much are the bears, because bears in their own activity are together for a brief period of time, they mate and that's it. [She laughs] I think they hardly note sexual differences in other bears.

Not all societies are male dominated. Wolf packs are matriarchal which people have just now begun to realize. The dominant female is more dominant than the dominant male.

It was real interesting to me when we had Orphans of the Wild. We had a huge ranch, with lots of wolf packs. Nahani was an extremely dominant male. He and Ophelia and their cubs were a pack.

Once Nahani reached sexual maturity and was with Ophelia, Ted could never deal with him and yet I always could. As a matter of fact, when we had to move them, I was able to walk in, put a leash on Nahani, and get him to leave Ophelia and the cubs while we transferred them. I was also able to take Ophelia away from her cubs and to pick up the cubs. Nobody else could do it. To every one of those wolves I was the dominant female, even though Ted had raised every one of them with me. I realized that whoever the mother wolf is in the pack, her authority exceeds the dominant male's, because the cubs that she's raised never lose their respect for her authority. At a certain age the male wolf cub will challenge the dominant male, but they'll never challenge the female. As far as they were concerned I had birthed them all and was their divine matriarch.

Elephants are also matriarchal. 71 responds differently with Ed and me. I mean she loves us both, but her response is different. She treats me like her mother; she gravitates to me when she wants protection. Ed's her pal and buddy; she plays with him.

TC: Obviously they're responding to something, but they don't get down and look between our legs to find out what we are. Do you think it's sound, maybe the different sounds of our voices — ?

PD: I'll tell you what happens with animals. It's the basis of all that we don't understand about animals. Animals have a tremendous capability — it's not even ESP. An animal just knows everything; they know — this is a corny phrase — all the secrets of the universe. Every animal, every cat, every dog, is born with this innate understanding of everything. They just know what goes on. They're tremendously in tune with nature. They pick up vibrations and they have a sensitivity that transcends anything that we have. They just understand. They understand everything that I am and they understand everything that you are. The minute somebody walks through the door, every goddamn cat in this house could do you a computer reading on that person. A person walks through the door: male, beep beep, doesn't like cats, beep beep. And the exotic animals have it too, to an even greater degree. If you are ever here on a day when people in three or fours go through, you should just sit and observe the animals' responses to people. It's right on target every bloody time and it's not a big deal to them. The minute somebody comes through, they pick up all the vibrations and all the energy and it goes through their little computer brains.

TC: Do you think cross-species communication is possible?

PD: Oh, definitely. These domestic cats communicate with Elsa. When Clyde [a domestic cat] invades 71's turf, they definitely communicate about it. Clyde understands what 71 is saying, and she understands Clyde. There's no doubt about it. But humans. . .we're just not in tune with anything but each other. And we're really not in tune with each other.

TC: What do you think about studies to teach chimps and gorillas to sign?

PD: I hate them! It's really just teaching a primate to do a trick. And if it's really an intelligent primate, he learns real quickly what to do to get you to give him the treat. You're not really communicating; it's like a conditioned reflex. The person who's taught the animal sign language is the one who's telling us what they're saying. But they're interpreting what they hope the animal is saying. I have a lot more respect for Dian Fossey, who went into the area where the gorillas are and spent her life trying to relate to the gorilla on the gorilla's terms. And I think that Dian Fossey probably understood gorillas a lot more than primatologists who study captive gorillas.

But that's not even what I object to most. I agree that gorillas are extremely intelligent. All of the qualities that humans have that gorillas don't possess have been given to the animals in these studies. They begin to act like spoiled, bratty kids. I object a lot to that. I think that if we're going to communicate with whales and communicate with dolphins and communicate with gorillas, why do it from our point of view? Because maybe we're not superior to them. My theory is that people only demean animals; we bring them down to our level and put them on a PT Barnum level. What Dian Fossey did with gorillas is everything that's noble about animals, and people. That's what I aspire to do. Forcing a gorilla or chimp into a kind of lifestyle that isn't theirs spoils them. It's just like parents wanting their kid to be a doctor; they're going to mold her into just what they see her being whether that's what she is or not. This is manipulation, and trained animals are manipulated animals.

TC: In some ways, it's even worse than a parent who wants his or her son or daughter to be a doctor. It's more like studying a different group of people. . .like studying what Soviet people are like by bringing them over here, separating them into individual labs, and studying them —

PD: The only way to understand a Russian is to go to Russia, to live in Russia, to learn to speak the language, and live in their culture. And then *maybe*, you'll learn. But to bring a Russian to America, teach him English, and teach him to respond to what we respond to, you're not getting what's Russian. You'll never understand what gorillas are like by teaching them sign language and keeping them in cages.

TC: So how then do you learn to communicate with the animals? Do you learn baboon, for example?

PD: You know the great line that Elia Kazan said to Geraldine Page when she was in a play? He said, "For god's sake, Geraldine, don't just do something, stand there." People think they always have to be doing, and it's so hard to explain that the easiest way to understand animals and to communicate with them is not to do anything; it's just to be with them. It's a process of osmosis. You just absorb it. Everything I learned about elephants, I learned from elephants, not from any experts. Before 71 arrived, the vet said, "Do this, do this, do this and do this, otherwise she'll die." The minute she got here, I thought, "Thank god, she's mine" because I just know in my gut that's not what I'm supposed to be doing. I knew they were feeding her the wrong food and the wrong amounts. She should have been on a bottle, but it was too late for that. I had a gut response from what I've absorbed from being around them. The experts learn out of textbooks; I learned from just being with elephants. I mean if you're not stupid, if you can just sit and be quiet and shut up and stop thinking about what you want them to do, you'll learn everything there is to know. That's really what behaviorists do. I think the ultimate behaviorists are people like Jane Goodall and Dian Fossey, who have the ability to go quietly into a habitat and sit there for hours and just absorb. That's really all it is. And that's what I've done.

The way you communicate with animals is to stop trying to do anything, or to know anything. They communicate differently. Everything with them is vibration. You just have to get really in tune with what they're sending out — their sounds and everything. We're born with a tremendous empathy with animals. Most small children have a great empathetic response to animals. When we learn to talk, we begin to deviate from our natural ability to communicate with animals. We learn deviousness and dishonesty through speech. A human can say one thing and mean another. Animals don't do that. Animals say what they mean. When little kids learn to lie, they lose their ability to relate to animals. Some of the people who communicate best with animals have a difficult time with humans because they are more likely to say exactly what they are thinking and feeling. I'm that way, and people frequently misunderstand.

TC: So perhaps part of the key to communicating with animals is to learn to be more honest in our communication with other humans. So how do the animals at PAWS fit with your Russian example? These are Russians who are now in the United States. And so you're trying to communicate with them. They're already out of their home country, so are you. . .?

PD: Building little Russia, that's what I'm trying to do. To give every one of them their own country. We spend time with Harriet and let her groom. We do all her sounds. We give her the tree that goes up so high because we know that she doesn't go any higher. And Tuffy has his stump that he can grub in and we determine the heights of his platforms based on what he can jump to. So with everyone we try and create their country.

There's a certain amount of just plain sensitivity you need to communicate with animals. I think you have to come from the kind of background that I did which is nonviolent and supportive of all life. If you have that and you spend a great deal of time with an anteater and you observe that it does not respond to cold cement and then you put it on grass and you see the response, you have to, if you're not totally stupid, know that the anteater was meant to be grubbing on grass. You have to develop an empathetic response to everyone and everything.

TC: Many people assume that all you need is to love animals.

PD: There's loving animals and there's *loving* animals. If having an animal is an extension of your own ego, that's not love; that's selfishness and the animal suffers from that. It's like the parent who says, "I love my kid; therefore, I want him to go to college. I want him to be a doctor. I want him to marry the perfect woman. I want him to have children. I want him to do everything I want him to do. Because I love him so much." And they get the kid who doesn't like girls; he likes boys. He doesn't want to have children. Doesn't want to go to school. He wants to play drums in a rock band. And the parent goes crazy. The ultimate parent is the one who sublimates their own feelings for their child. . .what my kid wants to do, I want to help. It's the same thing with loving animals. The person with a French poodle who says, "Oh, I love animals," and feeds it chocolate and kills it. That's not loving animals; that's loving yourself and the animal is an extension of yourself.

The person who really cares about animals, and I've said this a lot in my seminars, may be the one who is never going to own one. I mean I have a lot more respect for the person who says, "I really care about animals, but I would never own one because I'm not capable of giving it what it needs." It's like me. I used to think I didn't like kids, but now I think I like kids a lot, because I have enough sensitivity to children to know that I wouldn't want to own a child.

TC: Do you consider yourself owning these animals?

PD: Not at all. I think they own me. I mean I'm not kidding. Look at my domestic cats. [Her outstretched hand motions around the room — a cat is perched on every comfortable surface from floor to eye level.] I mean if I owned them, they wouldn't be clawing up the furniture and peeing all over everything. And I wouldn't be up at four o'clock in the morning before somebody important comes here, trying to get rid of the stink. I don't interfere with what they do in their lives. I really think, in a sense, I'm just sort of the servant — I do whatever is necessary for them to be comfortable. And that's a choice that I've made. Right now, look, Valerie is lying on the clean clothes. I'm not going to stop her and she knows I'm not going to. So that's the difference between owning something and not.

I believe, and this is really what we work on with PAWS, that it takes a lot of sensitivity to animals to have them and to spend time with them. I really believe that if rich people want to have animals, I would love to see them do it. I mean if Michael Jackson wants to own animals, I think he should, but I think that Michael Jackson, not hired hands, should learn how to do it. I think that's where the buck stops. People with money who can acquire animals should have to prove themselves capable of caring for them properly.

I don't think, at this point in time, for whatever reasons, that animals should be brought in from the wild. I think there are enough animals in captivity and god help us if the zoos don't stop breeding. They breed Siberian tigers to get one perfect male or one perfect female and if the female has a litter of seven, they take one and there are six left. We have so many animals that are born in captivity that need special people to care for them. I don't think there's any reason to import. I really believe that if they're going to die in the wild, let them die in the wild. If Africa is going to become a concrete jungle and they're going to kill all the elephants and kill all the gorillas, at least let the last gorilla die in Africa.

I was opposed to taking the condors out of the wild. I don't care what the rationale is. I think that last condor, if we're screwing up his habitat, should be allowed to fly till he drops. I really feel strongly about that. But the ones who are born in captivity, the little giraffe who's right now sitting in Sacramento zoo on the surplus list, I think he's entitled to a quality of life and if there's a rich guy who's going to give that giraffe forty acres of land to move on, I would love to see that. But only if the rich guy has enough sensitivity and enough intelligence to give the giraffe what he needs and requires.

That's what our work is all about.

Landcrab II

Margaret Atwood

The sea sucks at its own
edges, in and out with the moon.
Tattered brown fronds
(shredded nylon stockings,
feathers, the remnants of hands)
wash against my skin.

As for the crab, she's climbed
a tree and sticks herself
to the bark with her adroit
spikes; she jerks
her stalked eyes at me, seeing

a meat shadow,
food or a predator.
I smell the pulp
of her body, faint odor
of rotting salt,
as she smells mine,
working those martian palps:

seawater in leather.
I'm a category, a noun
in a language not human,
infra-red in moonlight,
a tidal wave in the air.

Old fingernail, old mother,
I'm up to scant harm
tonight; though you don't care,

you're no-one's metaphor,
you have your own paths
and rituals, frayed snails
and soaked nuts, waterlogged sacks
to pick over, soggy chips and crusts.

The beach is all yours, wordless
and ripe once I'm off it,
wading towards the moored boats
and blue lights of the dock.

Afternoon with the Cat Lady:
An Interview with
Jean Bilyeu
Stephanie T. Hoppe

I park by the railroad tracks and cross Mason Street to the corrugated metal warehouse on the corner. One of our members owns it, and donates the use of it free of charge. Coming around to the entrance on Clara Street I can see our sign through the overgrown shrubs in the setback: "Domestic Animal Protection Society," and on a smaller board below: "No Animal Facilities." Animals are left all the same, dogs leashed to the doorknob, frightened and often hurt or starving, puppies and kittens in paper bags and boxes.

I go into the small front office, which is airless in summer, frigid in cold weather, but pleasant enough on this sunny November Northern California afternoon. Behind the worn gray metal desk, donated like all the other furnishings, sits a woman of what convention calls years — she is almost seventy — but with also the ageless aura of bright energy of those who have found their proper work: Jean Bilyeu, cat lady, principal founder of DAPS and many-time Board of Directors member, tireless rescue worker.

Before I can open my mouth Jean starts talking, worried about money. This time, she says, DAPS is really hitting the bottom, emergency veterinary expenses are over five hundred dollars a month and cutting into the funding for our spay/neuter program. DAPS is fully certified under state law as a Society for the Prevention of Cruelty to Animals and eligible to receive five hundred dollars a month from the County, but the powers that be in this county think animal welfare a luxury we can't afford. Beyond selling healthy dogs to the University of California for research, the Mendocino County pound makes little effort to place unwanted animals, and puts to death some five hundred dogs and cats every month.

The oversized Garfield telephone on the desk interrupts. A veterinarian from Willets, a small town to the north of us, is irate — I can hear her from where I sit across the room — about our decision to limit the use of our subsidy certificates to the local Low-Cost Spay Clinic and those vets who meet the clinic's prices. Jean begins to explain yet again that we are in the business not of subsidizing veterinarians but of spaying and neutering the maximum number of animals — and our supporting the clinic best serves that goal.

The conversation looks to go on a while. I wander into the warehouse space in back, tables and aisles piled with rummage, where half a dozen persons are quietly searching the piles of castoffs. Periodic sales of donated rummage form an important source of income for us. We have a reputation for high quality and low prices: our policy is to move things through.

When I return to the office Jean is dealing with a woman come seeking help for her mother, a problem of a dog that needs an operation that the mother, an elderly widow living in a trailer park on social security, can't afford. The little dog is the center of her life. She even wants it buried with her, the daughter worries. I bleakly consider the likely outlook for an aging dog on losing both person and home. This little dog, though getting on, apparently has some years left — if the operation can be done.

Garfield trills. A woman in Hopland, a small community ten miles south of us, reports that she's picked up a cat that was hit by a car. The woman is willing to keep and care for the cat, but she has no money to pay for veterinary expenses. Jean takes down particulars and promises to call back.

The woman who is here in the office starts to explain her own finances, why she can't help her mother with the little dog. Jean grows curt. She has an angel. She will see what she can do. She'll call. But even telephoning is complicated; a time is set that the woman will go to a neighbor's and wait for Jean's call.

Closing time: the rummage room is shut up and the volunteer in charge reports eighty-seven dollars in sales and a fifty-dollar donation. I remark that Jean has just spent more than that. Jean plugs Garfield into the answering machine. I describe the anthology I am planning with a friend, on the relationships of women and animals; how we want to record Jean's work, day-to-day like housekeeping, years on her own as well as with DAPS, trying to pick up after the messes that are made of animals' lives in our communities. We arrange to meet at Jean's home, a small house with a jungly yard in an older neighborhood, which she shares with, at last count, forty-two cats.

There, a few days later, the two of us settle at the kitchen table under the inspection of the indoor cats. Jean talks to them and to me, working through their stories toward a point that serves to start her own.

W e moved to Mendocino County, on the coast, in 1951. I was talking to one of our neighbors, and I asked him if there was a humane society in Mendocino County. He said, never heard of one, why? And I said, oh I like to get involved with things like that. Well, he said, you ought to go to Fort Bragg and see their pound. I said, what do you mean? He said, enough said! Just go see it.

I was sorry of that! It was just a small shed, wasn't any bigger than that end of my kitchen. Built on the ground, on the dirt. There was no floor on it or anything. No windows. And it was in a gully, not very far from the ocean, where it was always damp. One side of it, maybe about three feet, there was some chicken wire strung across where they — if they did come in with a cat, they threw it in there. And the dogs, they just opened the door and threw them in.

That was the awfulest mess you ever saw. The dogcatcher was the worst sonofabitch. When he'd pick up a cat, he'd bang its brains out on the side of the truck. I've seen him do it. Well, I got him fired. After he arrested me and I had to go to court, I ended up getting the bastard fired.

But when I saw what they called their animal shelter, I thought, my godalmighty this is a barbaric county. And I started talking to people and — it's the honest to god truth! — people in this county do not care about cats and dogs. They don't care. It's too damn bad. They just do not care. Worse than any place I've ever lived.

We moved over here [Ukiah] in 1965. I started in again. Raising hell with the pound.

I had a rotten neighbor. She was trapping people's cats and taking them to the pound, and she got one of mine. Lorraine was working at the pound at the time, and she was a bitch. When I couldn't find little Otter, why I called the pound and I described her. "Yeah, we got her down here." Boy, I was mad! I was madder'n hell. I said, OK I'll be down to get her as soon as I can find somebody to take me out there. "Well, if you ain't here by ten she's going up the chimney with the rest of them." I said, now listen, Lorraine, it's going to take me a little while to find somebody to drive me out there but, I said, I'm going to tell you something right now. My cat better be there when I get there or you're not going to have any place left to work.

So a friend who lived out in Talmage came and got me. She said, now Jean, you're not even going to get out of the car. I'll handle this, she said. You're too mad. So we get out there, and Jan takes the carrier and gets out of the car and goes up, and they wouldn't let her have the cat. She gave them a little guff and they still wouldn't let her have the cat. So she came to the car. She said — she was mad! — those sonsofbitches won't let me have the cat, they got to give it to you. It was Riley and Lorraine. I hate both of them. I went up there and I had the carrier and I said, go get my cat. And Riley went and got her and she was hanging down from his hand and she was absolutely coated with urine and shit, just coated. And she stunk so bad it would gag you.

He stood there holding her like that and I said, put her in that carrier, you big fat sonofabitch. "Not until you pay your money." I got my money out and I slammed it down there, and I was cussing them, and Jan was hitting me and saying, Jean! Pretty soon I got mad at Jan. I said, you hit me one more time and I'm going to knock you on your ass, and about that time Lorraine said to Jan, well, if you people had any brains you'd put collars on your cats so they'd have identification. Jan lost her cool. She reached through and she got ahold of Lorraine. She said, I'll jerk you out here and stomp a mudhole in your ass. I informed Riley that I was going after Ted Erickson [of Animal Control]. Which I was. So what do those sonsofbitches do but they call Ted. And every place I call, "Oh, I'm sorry, Mrs. Bilyeu, you just missed him."

I kept that poor cat in the condition she was in for two hours because I was going to make Ted Erickson hold her and look at her. We could not find that little sucker any place so we finally gave the cat a bath. We took a lot of pictures of her first. Of course the pictures didn't smell.

Then I went before the Board of Supervisors again. I took the pictures and showed them the condition my cat was in. I said, I just wish that the pictures smelled like she smelled, and I said, she was sick, it cost me over a hundred-dollar vet bill to get her back to health.

Now the cages that they had for cats at that time were round-bottomed with no drainage. Those cats would lay in those cages for days and pee and crap in there and lay in it. Well, I did get the damn cages taken out of there. They got rid of those.

The Animal Protection Institute (API) had advised me to set up a crew of people, they said at least twelve, to go in pairs, once a week, make a surprise investigation of the pound. Not the same two people and not the same day, not the same time. Al Beltrami [County Administrator] agreed to it. Ted Erickson wouldn't. Beltrami said, you have to; she's got the Animal Protection Institute behind her and you've got to do it. I said, there's one other thing — and I was talking to Ted — I said, I get damn sick and tired of hearing you and the people who work for you say, "These animals are going up the chimney." And Al Beltrami said, what do you mean? I told him and he turned to Ted and he said, is that what you use, the phrase you use? And Ted said, yeah, and Beltrami said, I don't want to ever hear it again. Well, I've never heard it since.

I'll be honest, had I known how hard it was going to be and some of the things that were going to happen, I don't believe I'd have guts enough to do it. Because it's — it's such an emotional thing. You get too involved in the animals. Particularly the ones you can't help. That's the bad part.

I had the DAPS office here in the house for a year and a half, and that was terrible. Terrible. I'd close the office at two and I would be so emotionally drained that I'd go in the bedroom and lay down across the bed and — and cry. You know, to get rid of it. Dad, my husband, he was very supportive, he was so good. He knew better than to really sympathize with me because I don't take sympathy. Once in a while he'd say, you got to remember, mama, if you're going to roll over a big rock you got to be prepared for what crawls out from under.

But you're not. You really aren't. Every time you think, by god, I've heard it all now, you haven't. You have not. Just like the guys out there in Talmage that took that longhaired cat and poured gasoline all over it and set it on fire. People say, oh don't tell me about it, I don't want to hear, it makes me sick. That's what's the matter with people. They won't listen. Until they do listen and do get sick nobody's going to do anything. People say, oh I don't want to read it. God damn you, read it! There's too many people ducking the issue in this county. Just yesterday I told Kathleen two instances, of the dog that was hung in the tree and hung there until it choked to death. And the kittens that the man held with their mouths pried open while the kids poured the liquid tar down to see how much they could get in them before they died. And she said, oh that makes me sick. You're goddamn right it makes you sick. So do something about it!

It's terrible what people do. And you think, you're living next door to these people. You're breathing the same air they're breathing. They call us human beings! About five years ago I withdrew from the human race and I joined the animal kingdom and I've been a hell of a lot happier. The animals, I can trust them, I know what they're going to do. I've got their love. People — the hell with that.

But I'll tell you another thing. This is the most rewarding work I've ever done. Hungry people — yeah, I sympathize with them. I think for a town this size to have as many hungry and homeless people doesn't reflect very good on us. But on the other hand there's Plowshares, there's the churches, there's all those organizations and groups for the people. The animals have only got us. That's why DAPS is so damned important! You can't consider the pound for the animals — that's a hellhole. People can holler and yell and fight back. Animals can't. They're right at our mercy. And by god we can't let them down. We just have to take care of them.

[Sighs.] I did take care of the little dog the other day. So that turned out all right. But the kitty didn't and I can't get that poor cat out of my mind. I know you can't save them all. Just like Elizabeth [DAPS Board member] says, we got to cut back on emergency. We've been spending so much, four, five, six hundred dollars a month. Like this girl, she calls, OK, she's hard up, maybe she's telling the truth, maybe she ain't. But you have to look at the animal that's suffering, not whether that person is telling you the truth or not. I wish that we didn't have to turn anybody away. It always hurts me when we turn somebody away because I always think of the animal, that we're turning our back on an animal, and I hate that. I feel like, well, I'm not doing my job.

I love all animals. Cats of course are my weak spot. The gal asked me yesterday how many I had. Frankly I'm not sure. When I feed a cat twice a day every day, then I figure it's my responsibility. And it's around forty-two. There's one I call the Midnight Rider. He always comes in around midnight and he eats. Some of them that eat twice a day here I'm pretty sure have homes. But they spend the biggest share of their time here.

Every once in a while somebody will say, wouldn't you give one away, to the right person? I say, there is no right person. I'm the only right person. [Laughs.] Now there's Lois and Kathie and Ann. Them I could give one of my cats. It would hurt me. But I could give one and know it would be OK. That's the only three that I would feel comfortable, because I know them very well personally and I know exactly what they'd do with them. And yes, I'm the first to admit that I've got by far too many. But what're you going to do when you don't trust anybody?

I've had quite a few experiences. I stay out of it now. I will never myself adopt out another animal. The worst DAPS adoption I ever did was these people lived up here in west Ukiah, a young couple. They had this black and white dog, it was about nine, ten months old. They were both working, and they decided he needed more companionship and so they registered him with us.

Some people came down from Willets to adopt a dog. We had pictures of all the dogs, and I showed them Buck's picture. "That's just what we want." While we were talking, Buck's owners come in. So I introduced them to one another, we all sat and talked. I explained the adoption procedure, everything it entailed. Everything was fine. The four of them leave and go up to the house. They're up there quite a long while. Finally the people from Willets come back and they've got Buck. They come in and they pay their fee, they get their papers, everything, happily. Go home.

It was about two months. I was sitting at the desk and I saw this pickup pull up across the street. It had this old dog sitting in the back. That was the most miserable pitiful-looking old dog you ever saw. This couple came in, and it was the young couple that had had Buck. They come in, and she was crying, and I said, can I help you? He said, we just wanted to show you Buck.

That was Buck. He was nothing but bones. He had scars all over him. And the way they got him back, the people drove down and threw him over the fence in their yard.

They had to put the dog to sleep. The dog was less than a year old. I called Animal Control. I gave the name, address and phone number of the people who did it. "Oh. You didn't see them do it. We ain't going to do anything." I called the district attorney. "If Animal Control won't do anything, we can't do anything." I will see Buck to my dying day. He was a young healthy full-of-life dog. And three months later he was an old dog that had to be put to sleep.

And your so-called well-known people! We had a cat in the adoption program, a beautiful longhaired female cat, and this doctor, he's a gynecologist in Willets, he adopted her. He was a total pain in the ass. He came down here, looked her over, oh, guessed he just had to have this cat.

So he took her. Had her for close to a year. We had the office over where it is now, and I was getting ready to go to work and dad said, there's a guy walking in the driveway. I went to the door. I didn't recognize him. He said, I've got a cat I want to put on referral with you. I said, well, you'll have to wait until I go over to the office. I think I was opening then at ten. I said, you can come by then.

So. After I got over to the office I got to thinking about it, and I thought, god, that guy looked familiar, and I kept thinking and I finally realized it was the doctor from Willets. Well, I got real busy and I forgot about it, but he never came in.

Along about one o'clock I had a slack period and I thought, hey, that guy didn't come in. But I didn't think any more about it until my husband come after me at two. He said, well, how was your day? And I said, oh, busy as usual. He said, well, it ain't going to get any better when you get home. I said, why? Well, he said, when I got back home after bringing you to work, there was a box on the porch. He said it had been all taped up but the corner of it was torn out and it was a cat. I said, what does it look like? and he told me, and I said, that dirty sonofabitch. So before I ever left the office I called that doctor and I told him, I said, now I'm going to give you twenty-five minutes, and I said, that's liberal, to get down here and make amends for this or I'm going to send the sheriff after you for abandoning an animal. "Oh, you wouldn't do that!" I said, oh, yes I will. I said, I will enjoy doing it. I said, twenty-five minutes. I was furious.

We came home. And here was the cat, scared to death. I brought her in the house and dad said, what are you going to do? I said, I'm not sure, but one thing I am going to do, I'm going to call the police right now, because I think this sucker, because he's a doctor, is going to need to try to throw his weight around a little bit. I said, I'm not going to stand for it. So I called the police. I told them, I think I'm going to have a little problem and I'd like to have somebody stand by. So a cop and one of the trainees, a young kid, came out here.

The doctor had got here, and he was trying to tell me how rotten this cat was, and she was lying in the middle of the table. I said, you've had that cat for a year and all of a sudden she's rotten. The cop came in and said, what do you need? and I said, I just want you to stand here a little while because I — I was furious! Dad was sitting in on the davenport and I'd hear him every once in a while, give 'em hell, ma, give 'em hell. I started in on this doctor and I chewed his ass out good. "Well, what do you want me to do?" I said, well, there's a referral fee. I said, you're going to pay everything, this cat has to go back and have a complete examination and everything else and by god you're going to pay for it. And I said, you will never get another animal through DAPS. I said, you are what is called a rotten person for an animal.

The cops begin to side with the doctor a little bit. "Don't you think you're being a little hard?" I said, not near as hard as I'm going to get. The doctor said, well, how about a little check? Will that make you feel better? I said no, but it'll help. Well, he said, how about twenty-five dollars? I said, well, you cheap sonofabitch. And the cop said, all right, Mrs. Bilyeu. I said, you just stand there, that's all I want you here for. And the doctor said, well, how about fifty dollars? I said, come on, you cheap sonofabitch. So he gave me a check for a hundred dollars. And I said, OK, I've got your check, now get your ass out and I don't ever want to hear of you again. I rushed right downtown and cashed that check real fast because I was afraid the sonofabitch might stop payment on it.

We always laughed about our hundred dollar cat! And then who adopted the cat but Dave Crew, our vet.

It was March 17, St. Patrick's Day, 1982. We had an appointment with Dave at four o'clock to examine that cat. My husband had an appointment with the doctor that day. The doctor told him, you're in better shape than you've been for years. He said, I don't want to see you for six months. Good. We came home. He lay down, took a nap and I was laying there reading, and it was about, oh, quarter after three, three-thirty. He said, let's put our clothes on and take that cat out to Dave's, see if he'll take us a little early and then let's make a big pot of potato soup for St. Patrick's supper.

I said OK. We got dressed, put the cat in the carrier and got in the car and drove around the corner and my husband died.

We just got around the corner in front of Creative Workshop and he stopped right in the middle of the traffic and the horns started going and I looked over at him and I said, you damned fool, you can't stop in the middle of the traffic. He said, I'm dizzy. I said, OK, let's edge the car over to the curb. Well, he said, I can't see either. So I put my hand over his and we pulled it over. I said, well, I'll go run in and get some help, and he looked over at me and grinned and he said, I'll be all right, and he died.

Ah.

You know, it was wonderful for him. I will always be grateful and thankful that he went the way he did.

I'll never get over it, him going the way he did, but how awful it would have been for him to lay in the hospital or something like that, week in and week out. He'd done enough of that as it was.

You know, I can say it now, he looked over at me and smiled and he said, I'll be all right. I — I can say now I know why he was smiling. Because he was leaving me in such a hell of a mess. And he was getting out of it. Kathie, my adopted niece, once in a while, gets aggravated at me. I say, Kathie, if I don't retain this sense of humor I'll never make it. She says, but your sense of humor is so twisted! I say, yeah, I know it is, and that's what keeps me going.

But bless his heart — he was so supportive. And he was very, very proud of DAPS too. Very, very proud. It was such a struggle. Godalmighty, we'd have meetings and sometimes I'd be the only Board member there. Sometimes it'd be just Dave Crew and I. And my husband. And the only reason my husband went to a lot of the meetings was because he had to take me. And Margaret Bold, she wasn't even a member, but she'd show up. For the first couple of meetings, two or three meetings we had, there'd be twenty-five, thirty people. People hate meetings, including me, I don't like the damn things either. It would have been awful easy for any of us to have dropped it the first year, year and a half, two years, because it was such a hard struggle. Nobody believed in us.

Now we've got a reputation, a terrifically good reputation. We don't have what you'd call a big membership, but it's around two hundred, bigger than what I ever expected. For this size county [human population about 70,000] we should have a bigger membership.

A lot of people think DAPS is a cockamamie outfit that don't amount to anything. You know, they used to call us the old biddies with the brooms trying to get the shitflies out of the barn. I said, you can make fun of us old ladies all you want to, but who did it? It was us old ladies that did it, by god. It wasn't them smartass men. And it wasn't any vets either!

One very bad thing with DAPS is the veterinarians don't like us. What they'd like to see is us crawl back into the woodwork, you know, and stay there. We're doing something that they should be doing and they know it. About the third year, the Mendocino County Veterinarians Association wrote us a very, very flowery letter of support — very flowery! — and a pledge of five hundred dollars, which we never got a penny of. And we never got an ounce of support. The only support we've gotten is from the Mendocino Animal Hospital. And from Dave Crew. If it hadn't been for Dave Crew being willing to take the chance with me, DAPS may never have gotten off the ground. His being a part of DAPS at the outset gave us the credibility we needed to get people to take notice of us.

About Dave Crew. [Laughs.] Right after the law was passed allowing senior citizens to have pets in low-cost housing, we decided to give that a shot. I approached that place Autumn Leaves. Absolutely not, I was told. "I don't care what the law is." I was talking to Dave about trying Walnut Village, and he suggested we go there together instead of phoning. We made an appointment and away we went. Now David can charm the birds out of the trees, the cats away from catnip, and the dogs from a juicy bone, but not the managers of Walnut Village. Dave put his charm in overdrive and still they were just two cold fish. He finally gave up and we walked out. They had a big brand new motor coach sitting at the curb. Dave walked over and kicked one of the tires and said, let's go back to the clinic, get two or three big dogs and bring them back here to piss on the wheels.

The rest of the vets have given us crap. It makes me feel good to jab 'em a little bit. I like that. Gee, when we started our spay/neuter program they gave us so much crap that it was pitiful. It's tampering, according to the vets. It's tampering with veterinarians' prices. This was their reasoning for not wanting a low-cost spay and neuter clinic, that it lowers the quality of veterinary practice, which is a goddamn lie, and you know it as well as I do, and so do they.

I've had people say to me, are you trying to wipe out the cat and dog population? Jesus Christ, do you realize what an utter impossibility that is? There are people who do not believe for religious reasons in spaying and neutering. And men — oh, god, men take it personal. I get a big kick out of men when you start to talk about neutering dogs and they get so indignant. I feel like saying, I'm not talking about you, I'm talking about your dog.

Since we started we've spent $32,831 alone on spaying. That spayed around two thousand animals. When you figure that money all came from people like you and me — people taking out memberships and who cared enough to make a donation. There is no public funding in that whatever. I think that is one hell of a good record.

I do believe — I have to believe — that we will have a completely free spay/neuter program. If we had a completely free spay/neuter program, within three years you wouldn't believe the difference you'd see! It'd be fantastic. It makes me sick that it is so simple, it's so easy to see — why do other people have such blind spots? I get so damn mad at people. I don't expect everybody to feel like I do. But when you stop and think that your tax money's what is keeping that hellhole pound down there going. By their own admission they don't give a damn about adoption. "Kill 'em or sell 'em," that's their motto. And we're busting our butts to save as many as we can and spay as many as we can to keep this from happening. I dunno, sometimes I think, oh god, why the hell don't I stay home and mind my own damn business.

I would say the majority of my adult life was more or less spent being involved with animals, seeing what I could do with them. There's nothing that's a bigger challenge to me than to have a frightened animal and get its confidence.

One time — I was about, oh, twenty-two, twenty-three — I lived out in the country. My back porch was up off the ground about two feet and I went to go out the back door one morning and I heard this dog growl. So I went out away from the porch and lay down on the ground and looked under. All I could see was its eyes and I thought, oh dear. I went into the house and I got some food and I came out and lay down and I kept coaxing and coaxing.

I coaxed the dog out to where I could see it. It was a gorgeous Australian shepherd and he'd been shot. His leg had rotted and there was maggots in it and, oh god, it was a mess. I thought, well, I'm either going to get the hell bit out of me or I'm going to do something.

So I went into the house and I got a pan of water and some cloths and some peroxide and I came out. The dog had crawled clear out from under the porch then and was eating. I sat down on the ground and I kept talking to it and finally its tail thumped a little bit and I said, well, old fella, I'm going to touch your leg and I hope to god you don't bite me.

I put my hand on his leg up above the wound and he kind of shivered and shook but he didn't growl and I said, I'm going to help you. I took a rag and got it real wet and squeezed some water on him and he flinched but he didn't growl. I got his leg all cleaned up and I bandaged it. I sat out there for a long time. I worked with him all day. I'd pet him, you know, and talk to him and that. I got his leg all well and when I went to town I told everybody about it — I knew he was somebody's work dog.

I must have had that dog, oh, seven or eight months, and we were in the house and the dog stood up — he was laying on the floor — he stood up and his hair all bristled up and he started growling. I called him Duke. I said, what's up, Duke? He went to the front door and, boy, he was mad. I opened the door and there was a pickup and this man and woman in the pickup. That dog went out on the porch and, my god, I tell you, he was furious. This guy said, yup, that's him, that's my dog. He started to get out and I said, if I was you I'd stay put in that pickup. And his wife told him, you stay there. He said, well, I want my dog. I said, well, you're not going to get it because, I said, this dog will eat you. I said, if he's your dog then you done something. It made him mad and he left.

A couple of days later my brother came. He knew the guy, and he told me, that *is* his dog, Jean. I said, Bud, that dog will kill that man. He said, I know it, he's the one that shot him. He said, they were working the cattle and the dog got tired and went to get a drink and he shot him. I said, well, I'll tell you one thing, he can get the sheriff, he can get anybody, I will not give the dog up to him.

So he had a brother, this guy did. I knew his brother and he was a real nice guy. He came up a few weeks later and he wanted to know if he could have the dog, and I said, what're you going to do, take him and give him back to your brother? He said no. He said, I would kill him before I'd let my brother have him back. But, he said, he's such a good work dog. So I let him have him. That was such a rewarding experience, to get that dog's confidence when he was really hurting as bad as he was.

A black kitten is playing with my pen. She bats it over the edge of the table and stares after in obvious astonishment that it dropped to the floor. A fair-sized black area rug that had materialized on the living room floor is up and after the pen in a flash, the kitten staring after with enormous eyes.

That's Willy Fred. That's cat, that's not hair. That is a big cat. And there's China — I went to go out the back door one day. I just saw on the step there was something there so I stepped over it and turned around. I thought the cat was dead. It was all covered with tar and oil and I thought it was dead. I squatted down and touched her head and she opened one eye a little bit and I picked her up and walked out to the garage and I said, my god, dad, look. And he said, oh my god, that's the ugliest cat I ever saw in my life. I said, don't you ever say that again. She doesn't need to hear that! Well, he said, wrap her in a towel and I'll take her down and have her put to sleep. I said, no you won't, I'm going to work with her. I brought her in here and I really didn't think I could save her. It obviously hadn't been too long that she'd had kittens. And she was so starved. I got as much of the tar and oil cleaned off of her as I could and she was too weak to even eat. I had to feed her with a spoon.

I worked with her all night and every once in a while dad would say, you want me to help you? And he'd hold her for a while. By next morning I had practically all the tar and oil off of her and she still was too weak to eat. Dad — he'd look at her and he'd shake his head and I'd say, don't you dare say it! So he named her Miss America. When she got on her feet she stayed in the yard with dad. She went everyplace with him. And he'd sing to her: there she goes, Miss America. She's still here. When China came, it made Miss America mad, so she moved across the ditch, but she comes home every day to see me.

China — people lived next door had her and she was nothing but bones and she had big burns on her back and the vet said he was pretty sure it was cigar burns. We started feeding her special food, and I cleaned her coat up. The people had been given an eviction notice and dad said, oh god, I hope they don't take her with them when they go.

Well, they didn't. She was strictly my husband's cat and you know, I thought sure as hell I was going to lose her when he passed away. She wouldn't eat. She'd go in the bedroom, she'd hunt for him and then she'd cry. She loved our mailman, too. He'd stop every day and hold her and love her. And he'd come down on weekends when he wasn't working. I think between him — well, it was him that helped me get her through it. I didn't go into the bedroom to sleep for quite a little while after dad passed away. I finally thought, well, maybe if I go in the bedroom to sleep, maybe that'll help her. So I'd tell her, come on, China, let's go to bed, and she'd go in, she'd go around to dad's side of the bed, she'd get up, no dad, she'd get down and leave. I'd go to bed and I'd call her and she'd come back again, look again. "Well, he still isn't here." I had a terrible time with her and she still is a man's cat as far as that goes. She's lost a little weight but she's the cutest thing. Hey cutie! Hey skinny little cat! Mama's little skinny cat! She's got short legs, she looks so funny!

Jean shoos China toward me. She looks like a racoon with Siamese-cat markings. I hold out my hand and she jumps onto my lap between the two cats already sleeping there. Jean regards all of us with approval.

I tell you, Stephanie, my life with cats — I wouldn't trade it for anything. Absolutely nothing would I trade it for. It's an experience. It's wonderful, because every day something different happens and they do the cutest things and the orneriest things and the silliest things.

We had one cat that — my husband liked to watch Roller Derby — and he'd turn the Roller Derby on and she'd sit there. Our TV was a black-and-white and it was a console that sat up off the floor, and she'd get right up there and those skaters'd be going around and she'd grab 'em. And she'd look in her paws and it was gone. So she'd look under the TV to see if she dropped it. She'd sit there by the hour catching those skaters. We had more fun watching her than we did the damn Roller Derby.

And they're so damned smart! They're so much smarter than people that we don't have a chance. Like I say, the cats don't live with me, I live with them. I do what they require that I do. But I enjoy it. So much. It's — it's such a good life. I mean you get so much out of it. You get more out of it than what you put in. You know, when you've got the love of an animal, I don't care what kind of animal it is, but if you got their trust and their love that's more than you really can ever expect to get from life. And I've sure got it. I've really got it!

Now when I was going to grade school and junior high my ambition was to be a veterinarian. But when I found out how I couldn't stand an animal suffering I knew I could never be a vet because you see too much. I knew I'd never make it. So then — I was in the ninth grade — I said I will have an animal orphanage some day. That was my goal and it was right up until the third year of DAPS when my husband saw how I was fighting a losing battle. I was getting people to donate to the building fund — I ate, drank, slept, everything was animal orphanage. And dad sat down and set me straight. He drew up an ideal small animal shelter, ten dogs, possibly twenty, twenty-five cats. Out of that ten dogs there're probably maybe four that are adoptable. You're going to have six left. What the hell are you going to do with them? Out of the cats, maybe five or six are adoptable. All right, those animals are going to live out their life in that shelter or you're going to have to kill them.

Well, I saw that I was fighting a losing battle. So then I forgot that and concentrated on the spaying and neutering. Which goes to the root of the problem. Don't try to cure it after it's full blown. Nip it in the bud. You know — these women, I get so mad at women, mothers, they'll come in the office. "We want a female cat." Mostly it's cats, some dogs. I would see what we had and then I would talk to them about spaying. "Oh, no, no, no, I want my children to see the miracle of birth." I can't stand that. It chokes me. So I tell people, you take your children down to the pound and show them the agony of death, which is caused by the miracle of birth, and go to the library and get films and pictures and show them the miracle of birth. Don't use an animal!

The short winter afternoon has worn away and night is closing in. Through the unshaded window I see the outside cats gathering. Before I leave Jean takes me to meet two old ladies who live apart in her bedroom behind a screen door, Dynamite, 17, and Effie Mae, 15. While she tells me their stories, the two sleek shorthaired black cats slowly blink their eyes.

We turn to go, and I pat this cat or that while Jean tells her or his story. She lets me out the front door, and as I walk away up the drive I hear her talking to the cats, straightening out which is to be indoors or out for the night.

Storm/Cat/Me

Nan Sherman

C at and I think it's the weather.
We feel wild and unruly.
Storm warnings rustle the air;
the wind quickens, then stealthily
rallies cloud-forces for the sneak attack.

Nervously Cat and I
scurry from room to room,
window to window,
peering into each other's eyes,
fragmented, alarmed as the
clouds hesitate over us, rumble,
shatter our ears with their
fiery, streaking explosions.

And then . . . the rain,
torrential, heavy,
relieves itself on the hills,
spanks the palm tree fronds,
slams relentlessly
against the window panes.

Cat is looking for a fight,
claws outstretched; so am I.
We glare at each other.
The storm has exposed cat/human wiring,
we are electrically charged.

Thunder cracks the sky wide open, claps
shake through the rooms,
chasing wailing Cat and me,
seeking to escape this applause
from clouds etched against the moon,
whirling through the black, wet night.

At last the wind sighs away
as the storm moves on
leaving sliding human objects
on flooded, shifting ground.
The magician's fire trick disappears
behind a benign scarf of clouds.

Cat and I lie breathless, drained,
curled around each other in front of the fire,
fur drying, bones melting into velvety cushions,
warmed, mesmerized by the flame dance.
The storm reverberates, vanquished,
in the distance. Snoring gently,
we are content.

Queen Jane, Absolutely
Karen Kidd

The woman was all air and water when she came up the canyon — all pasty and ladylike — and sure of nothing walked into the big tipi unprepared and unpreparable for what would occur there. Here Goat Spirit began in her, and brought her nearer to the earth.

Crosslegged in the deep Colorado night, she sat like all the peyote eaters, facing the fire that waved its arms like a wild conductor. All except the woman were singing — indecipherable songs that threatened to wash her away. She was rising like a wisp of smoke, up toward the smokehole like a balloon. Afraid she would float right out — afraid she would vanish in the black night air while the singers, lost in song, never noticed a thing.

Old John Hawk saw her clawing the ground as if to hold herself down. He hopped over on his only leg, and kneeling, pressed one finger to her forehead and whispered, "Just look at the fire." As one song ended another one spilled out of it. People were puking into the dust, fresh peyote going around. "Watch the fire, Longbone." His eyes were floating diamonds, his grin flooded her. Then he vanished, dragging himself through the shadows as if brokenwinged.

Momentarily, the woman zeroed in on the fire, and it held her tight as mystery, then passed her down, as if into a nest deep within her being. Unswayed by air and water then, she became present to the shapes and music — the person stretched out before the half-moon altar for whom the singing had been called. Then she took up the thread of a song.

Pulling her along, the song soon burst into the occurrence she could not have prepared for — she felt herself suddenly singing her own long face into the long dark face of a goat, and singing into being the soft nubs of horns that suddenly pushed up through her scalp and slanted over the top of her head. Reaching up, she felt her face, furred and newly angled, and horns like twin blades, piercing the shadows. She sat like that, singing and touching until dawn threw patches of light on the tipi walls and the fire withdrew.

"Leave her alone, she's turning into a goat," someone wisecracked astutely, after someone else commented on how Longbone seemed to be stroking curves of air that peyote night. She laughed, but knew those horns were there, and felt them rubbing the sky during her solitary walks up the canyon. "It's my Capricorn, finally rising," she would think — the way she thought "It's my Pisces moon," when the river of her overflowed, or "It's my five planets in Libra," when she tended to drift. On her solitary walks, Goat Spirit followed — filling out her step, and the way she eyed the canyon's wall. Thus accompanied, she approached her twenty-seventh birthday, a month away.

On the afternoon of her birthday, Longbone and three longhaired companions returned to the canyon from a morning in town. They drove up in the yellow van — into a sea of neighbors' vehicles, parked helter-skelter. Neighboring dogs cavorted with the canyon's goofy setters. Around the big dome were gathered locals and hippies in assorted versions of dress-up — all whistling and clapping as Longbone rushed into their midst, feigning surprise. The air was lush with music and marijuana smoke.

Longbone threw up her hands and ran inside the big dome to change. She was requested to stand behind the chicken coop until she heard a voice yell "READY." She stood in a ratty black velvet dress, listening. She heard the blue bus pull up, then the yell. As she rushed down, the side door of the blue bus slid open and out popped Longbone's birthday present, arrogant and bucking, flying at Longbone while they all sang "Happy Birthday."

She was a black Nubian goat with an aquiline head, long petal-shaped ears and delicate redstreaked legs. Someone had put four strands of pearls high up on her neck. Pushing at Longbone and bringing her down, the shining goat licked neck and ears, nibbled at wrists and edges of sleeves. Streams of Longbone's hair caught in small goat teeth. Longbone laughed, gasped and cried as she kissed the long black lips and pressed her face against the goat's dark face — her dream horns against the silvery, solid ones. "What're ya gonna call 'er?" someone eventually inquired. And the goat said, right into Longbone's round eye, "Queen Jane."

Like the embodiment of something ancient coming up out of the river of herself, is how Longbone felt Queen Jane. The "something" that had begun that peyote night, with a song that came and went. "And did I begin with her?" she would wonder. "Did I pull at her with the foretaste of myself — bones, eyes and hair fluttering around her while she stood patiently in the sunlight of her corral?" She didn't guess that the sly goat had scattered bubbles of herself, which worked like a net, and at a precise instant, had gathered up the comrades of Longbone as they circled the goat pens, searching for exactly the right one.

And the net contained Longbone, the red rock canyon where she lived, and the canyon walls that Queen Jane was born to climb and Longbone was afraid to.

Deep into the canyon traveled humans, the black and silver cats, the silky redhaired dogs. Some went all the way to the caves in white sandstone, where mountain lions lay coiled like clay in the drying sun. Some went, but not Longbone. Not trusting her body to scale unyielding panels of rock or to carry her from ledge to ledge leaping through space, she only dreamed, gazing up at the white sandstone that frosted the red — waiting for the climbers to return bloody and exhilarated, from beyond fear. "Where did you go?" she would ask them. Nine times out of ten they had no reply, or would shrug, "I just blended in."

Queen Jane, on the other hand, took to the canyon as if born from it — her destiny simmering there. She was pregnant when she arrived that fall. Her legs seemed impossibly thin, her hooves impossibly tiny, to carry the widening wedge of her belly up the steep rock. But up she scrambled, shale streaming behind her, rolling one blurred eye at Longbone, trembling below. Sailing from ledge to ledge, dancing, gazing down in mock ruefulness, Queen Jane captivated Longbone and drew her upward.

Legs refused to unbend, and quivered. Hands like claws grabbed everything in sight. Like that, Longbone pulled herself along — a little farther each time they went out, Goat Spirit nudging her. By degrees, her tenacity overwhelmed her fear. Fingers spread out, feet put down roots. By degrees, she came closer to the white cliffs and tantalizing caves — the singing mouth of the canyon. One day, deep in fall, Longbone saw Queen Jane just above her on a ledge of white that ruffled the mouth of the cave. With one upward motion, she stood beside Jane at the seam of white and red — and saw the valley stretched wide beneath her, Mount Blanca like a whitelaced fairy godmother saluting her from the opposite side. And felt her body and being mellifluous with the being and body of earth and sky, Goat Spirit opening wide.

The winter clamped down, leveling everything out with its gaudy sheet. The canyon's cold shoulders were unclimbable, so humans, dogs and cats all came in and wrapped themselves around fire. Queen Jane knelt by the potbellied stove with triangles of orange light in her brushstroke eyes, Longbone's hand on her face.

In the middle of February, Queen Jane crawled unceremoniously under the big dome and gave birth to a couple of kids. The first, a dark and glossy replica of herself, she swiftly murdered with a kick when it tried to nurse. The second, white where Jane was black, with circles of black on her flanks and face, Longbone just as swiftly retrieved and took to her bed, bottlefeeding it Jane's syrupy milk.

The defiant Queen Jane made a run for it, rushing toward the canyon's icy stare. "I have not chosen the life of a milkgoat, confined to lower ground," she bellowed. Night after night, while Longbone lay with the kid, Jane stood facing the arroyo and breathed her milk into air. This went on for weeks — Longbone squeezing ever diminishing sprays of white from Jane's black tits, while Jane danced in and out of the bucket, one blurred eye rolling. The kid grew brave on evaporated milk, in cradles of brown human arms.

One morning the still wobbly kid stepped out into thin sunlight on legs like furwrapped sticks, and flung out her own net of bubbles. A few days later, an old green Cadillac came up the road — Walter Cisneros and his eleven-year-old daughter, Mati. "A lover of goats," Longbone observed to herself, as Mati jumped out with eyes aimed at the kid. And the kid marched up to the young girl, all show biz — her destiny flashing around them like a hallucination. In it, the kid rolled in the Cisneros' meadow, down in the valley, and the girl rolled beside her, soft nubs of dream horns shyly pushing through Mati's curtain of black black hair. Within hours, Mati, Walter and the tiny goat went back down the road in the front seat of the Cadillac. And by the time they got to where the lower land meets the highway, the kid had called herself Littlebird.

Then spring came. Sage and juniper tinted the air. Each dawn, dogs, cats, humans, and goat flew out the triangular doors of the big dome. Potatoes and onions hissed on the outdoor stove — prelude to the symphony of motors, blades, hammers and flowing water that coursed through the days. At dusk the bats sailed out from the caves and lowered themselves, singing night awake while the humans laughed and smoked below them.

In spring's tenderness, Queen Jane's capricious part released itself — dancing on the rooftops of vehicles and streaking in and out of doors with mouth streaming articles of clothing, household objects, wads of tobacco. Impatiently, Jane nagged Longbone at whatever task she was up to — nudging her toward the next dose of mystery.

When the temperature remained safely above freezing, John Hawk and the other men reappeared with sacks of dried peyote. As if in welcome, the rattlesnakes, emerging from dormancy, glided into the high grass of the upper meadow, then down to the woodpiles to coil. They lay dryly among the corpses of fallen pinyon that reddened on the lower land.

Longbone's dormant dream emerged also — her dream of rattlers, her dormant fear. Wearing long yellow eyes, it reared its head one night and hung there, taunting her as though she were still a tourist in the canyon. But that spring night she made light of the dream, believing herself to be enveloped in Queen Jane's veil of protection. As she imagined that it was Jane who pulled her up the canyon walls, Longbone imagined that Jane would inevitably steer her away from all that was dangerous — mine fields of rattlers. Soon Longbone would have to pick her way through the mine field of her own dangerous imaginings.

In summer they walked, Queen Jane, Longbone, and a darkskinned whitehaired woman named Ivory, who was the beginning of something. They walked slowly up the rutted road, past the big and little domes and the gardens, headed toward the greenfenced national forest boundary. On a rise about a mile up lay the skeleton of an old cabin — a cool place to sit. The women sat in almost wordless conversation, under a hole that let in sky and watery sunlight. Jane grazed and raised her head periodically, testing the soft heat between them. Then Ivory went back down the road alone, leaving the canyon for a while, with her five horses. Mouth hungry, Longbone watched her from in front of the ruined cabin.

Longbone was about to cross over to where Queen Jane stood, when Jane came suddenly flailing toward her, and Longbone followed along a fading path that wound through the grass there. Running on air, Longbone had her arms spread, her hair falling out of its leather string. She was about to let out a whoop, when Queen Jane suddenly rose before her and leapt sideways into the grey grass some distance from the path, startling Longbone. Then Longbone looked down — eight or so feet in front of her coiled the tapestried snake of her dreams.

The rattler had been dozing on the path, in a stretch of perfect warmth. Now she reared up, leveling her long eyes at Longbone, slowly hissing her rattles. Frozen, Longbone treaded terror, barely breathing. Queen Jane was an ebony carving of a goat. The snake held still.

In one part of herself, Longbone swam in nausea, thinking, "She's gonna get me and what will happen — will Jane get help somehow or just stand there, watching me glaze over and die?" Another part of her experienced as real the boomerang curve of the snake, springing open-mouthed — the instant of splitting pain as she planted her fangs in Longbone's vibrating flesh. Real, the poison's milky stream rushing toward her heart. The rattler remained poised.

The part of Longbone that had been coaxed by fire and rock, her horned and rooted part, remembered suddenly the horses of her childhood, before cities, when she ran breathless up to the hills with the pockets of her overalls full of apples — never enough. How the horses formed a line, then a ring around her where she stood, trembling and holding out apples, tiny in relation to the animals thrusting their muzzles against her shoulders, their heavy restless feet stamping around her. This part remembered also the feeling that drove her to the hills, which she summoned to stop her trembling — which came from the river of her and radiated out upon the horses — her love, greater than her fear. Pressing her terror back into its lair, this part of Longbone struggled to love the rattler as she had loved the horses — as she loved Queen Jane.

Then the rattler's eye fired out a message — "What choice is there, really?" And when she looked, Longbone saw that the snake was at least as wise and fearful as herself, with no particular desire to kill. The snake simply awaited a change in emotional tone. Seeing that, Longbone then instinctively loved her — love's clear stream unraveling and radiating out upon the rattler. Swiftly, the russet snake unwound and slid into the grass opposite where Queen Jane still stood. Longbone fell against Jane's chest, all her parts in awe.

The summer of the rattler was also the beginning of secrets, whispered in Jane's long ears by Longbone. A secret thing about herself, held like a lonesome jewel, began to throb. The beginning was Ivory, who returned to the canyon near the end of summer. Longbone and Ivory walked back up to the cabin, near where the rattler had been that quivering morning. There, where they had talked on a red-striped blanket, they whispered — going deep inside each other. Outside, Queen Jane wandered from shade to sunlight and nibbled at the fingers of trees.

High above them, limping on ridges, a ragged old mountain lion looked down with a wistful expression.

In shedding fall, almost a year from the moment that Queen Jane came up the canyon, the reedy strawcolored woman and the rounder sunburnished one traveled to the city on a kind of honeymoon-supply run-birthday trip. In their envelope of femaleness, they walked, taking in the city's wisdom and smell, and slept in a city bed, in a blue motel room — getting in deeper. Longbone was turning like the leaves of northern aspen — shimmering like coins. Turning queer, and liked the feel of it.

Alone for days, Queen Jane picked up speed and distance, moving along the national forest border to another canyon, silver-blue. She studied the shaggy longhorn goats shaking their heads on the high peaks and dreamed their wildness down into herself, for future reference. For safekeeping, she dreamed Longbone down into the nest of herself — she felt the pulling threads between them, as if Longbone might be sliding into some other life. Then she came back down the slick red rock to wait.

Spotting a leap of blackness that was Jane, the lion considered venturing down to the canyon floor — down where the fact of human presence was a sour vapor. "Am I foolish or brave?" he asked the wind, who shrugged and turned disappointingly away. Pondering, he paced the ridge. He was tantalized by the sight of Queen Jane, shining and oblivious, but he was held at bay by the swirl of human activity. Then the sun fell and evening gathered all the dome-dwellers indoors. There was nothing for the old lion to do but sleep on it.

In the blue motel room, in night's deepest part, Longbone let out a yell and woke up shaking from a city dream. "Something or someone attacked me." She shook her head rapidly back and forth, as if to loosen the dream and lay it on the bed. But the dream remained amorphous, releasing only a dim sensation of hands like paws raking Longbone's back and shoulders. "Time to get out of town maybe," Ivory whispered, and they decided to return to the canyon the next day.

The morning was full of hot air, a day for play unfolding in the canyon. Still bargaining with the wind, the mountain lion crept lower, scanning the creekbed, the rutted road, the picked-over gardens. Mouth opening and closing, he tiptoed down. He saw the dogs and humans pile into the blue bus and take off in the direction of McHenry's Pond. He eyed Queen Jane as she dozed on the dome's wide porch, with only flies for guardians.

They were flying back — Ivory with her bare feet on the dash of the yellow van, Longbone driving. Behind their seats were cartons of kerosene lamps and cases of foods not available in the stores near the canyon. On her feet Longbone wore the silver cowboy boots that were this year's birthday present, and from Ivory, strings of malachite, coral and turquoise hung from the rearview mirror. The blue motel dream was a thick curtain between Longbone and the cliffs rushing past. She saw the highway as an arrow aimed at her beloved canyon, her splendiferous family, Queen Jane. Tender as butterflies, the dream's paws swiped at Longbone's mind. Her eyes held the white line. They were flying back in apprenhensive silence.

In a puddle of shade, in morning's final moments, Queen Jane had a dream and, waking like a shot, stood listening for its message. Delicate terror skittered along her backbone. From out of the blue, someone or something had brushed her like an ominous wing, and ducking under she had felt herself tumbling in a spin of bruising pain.

Beside himself with temptation, the lion tiptoed lower.

With the wings of her dream churning the river of her, Jane careered around the big dome, bleating into silence. The humans and dogs, she knew, wouldn't return from the pond for hours. And Longbone? Would she return and fling herself like some big loose bird upon Jane's neck, chasing off all this apprehension?

"Hey," a human voice yelled out from the direction of the gardens. There, in front of the silverpainted little dome, stood John Hawk and two of his cronies, all of whom had arrived sometime during the night and crashed out up there.

Jolted, the mountain lion turned and bounded upward through

the boulder corridor that led back to sacred obscurity, back to his senses. Impressed with his own speed and fluidity, he perched and wondered at the risk he had considered — for a while believing himself desperate enough to chance a fool's death. With his eye of knowing, he saw the hungry-eyed neighboring ranchers with rifles who would surely hunt him down to protect "their livestock." The black goat, he realized, might well have been his last meal.

John Hawk pushed back his new straw hat. His black lawn of hair bristled as he hobbled toward Queen Jane — a can of tobacco in one hand, the other steering his crutch around anthills. Jane was circling with her head and snorting as she trotted toward him. "What's goin' on?" His tone was austere. The next moment, John Hawk felt within himself the wing, and the tumbling over of Queen Jane's dream. Then they both felt the clattering thud that was the yellow van landing upside down at the bottom of a pine-studded ravine.

Flying back, propelled by Longbone's dream, they had seen almost no one on the road. Seventy miles to go, Longbone shifted her eyes toward Ivory and touched her fingers to Ivory's cheekbone. Then, rounding a curve, they came suddenly and irrevocably upon a circle of vultures on the white line, gathered like the petals of a black flower around a center that was bright, open death — sleek bodies leaping in and out. As the van flew toward them, they rose angrily backwards in air. Across the white line lay the streaming corpse of a dog.

One furious vulture lifted, then turned at a slant and flung itself upon the van's windshield — face beet-red, ominous wings covering the glass. Longbone was trying to slow the van, swerving — and over the edge they went, tumbling down in a bruising, battering spin. Snapping branches, the van rolled in a haze of dust, then landed with a clattering thud.

Queen Jane flashed her eye of knowing and took off down the road.

Down the rutted road to the spot where the earth turns from red to pale grey-brown, and immense twin cedars straddle the line — down there, Jane ran. And turning in circles, she faced the canyon, the peaks beyond the canyon, whitelaced Mount Blanca in the distance below the canyon. From there she summoned Goat Spirit. And when Goat Spirit flew down from everywhere, Jane shuddered, and dispersed herself in a great leap — the river of Queen Jane sailing out like light to meet the river of Longbone. And Goat Spirit accompanied her along a trail of dusking sky.

The yellow van lay mingled with the lower branches of a low-slung pine, softly rocking. Still conscious, and seeing her life in diminishing circles, Ivory slid out the open side window on her back. She felt broken all over and compelled, as she crawled around the front of the van, by a dream of fire — the engine exploding, and fire swallowing them like a giant hot mouth. The door on the driver's side was mercifully openable — a shock to see Longbone upside down and utterly dislocated between seat and steering wheel. In slow motion, Ivory unwedged her and, pulling her out, saw that Longbone's face wore a mask of blood. In slow painful motion, Ivory dragged her to shade and pine needles — where Longbone lay like a pale flattened weed, and Ivory slumped beside her.

Disfigured, in a disarray of broken boxes and shattered glass, the van settled into the long arms of the pine, and didn't burn.

Ivory floated down beside Longbone like someone tangled in seaweed — the seaweed was Longbone's hair, matted with blood. Longbone's nose was broken — possibly her neck, Ivory thought. The eyes behind the blood mask were swelling shut. "Alive or dead?" — the words crisscrossed Ivory's mind until she fell into a pool of sleep, everything turning purple around her.

Between life and death, voiceless and sightless, Longbone fluttered, slippery in her body. "I'm here, struggling to live," one part of her ached to communicate, before the maw of pain bit down and she slid into motionless dark silence.

Another part, though voiceless, felt a song, familiar and indecipherable, weaving through her, and took up the thread. Though sightless, she saw a line of dancers on the highway's edge — each with a goat mask. Then the dancers became shadows with flashlights, stumbling down the ravine, and the song turned into the whine of an ambulance, rushing Longbone and Ivory through deepening night.

Longbone was still sliding down.

Here, Queen Jane entered, river to river, and shouted, "Climb with me." Jabbing at the dark motionless silence, she whispered, "Live with me." Goat Spirit poured full force, through Queen Jane, into Longbone — awakening that part that had been coaxed by fire and rock, her horned and rooted part. "Are you really here?" Longbone asked the swirling air. "Yes," whispered Queen Jane, "Absolutely." Then, though motionless, Longbone made the leap and came swiftly back to earth.

Interface
Gloria Anzaldúa

for Frances Doughty

She'd always been there
    occupying the same room.
It was only when I looked
    at the edges of things
my eyes going wide watering,
    objects blurring.
Where before there'd only been empty space
    I sensed layers and layers,
felt the air in the room thicken.
    Behind my eyelids a white flash
a thin noise.
    That's when I could see her.

    Once I accidently ran my arm
through her body
    felt heat on one side of my face.
    She wasn't solid.
The shock pushed me against the wall.
A torrent of days swept past me
    before I tried to "see" her again.
She had never wanted to be flesh she told me
    until she met me.
At first it was hard to stay
    on the border between
the physical world
    and hers.
It was only there at the interface
    that we could see each other.

See? We wanted to touch.
   I wished I could become
pulsing color, pure sound, bodiless as she.
   It was impossible, she said
   for humans to become noumenal.

What does it feel like, she asked
   to inhabit flesh,
wear blood like threads
   constantly running?
I would lie on the bed talking
   she would hover over me.
Did I say talk?
   We did not use words.
I pushed my thoughts toward her.
   Her "voice" was a breath of air
stirring my hair
   filling my head.
Once Lupe my roommate
   walked right through her
dangling the car keys.
   I felt Leyla shiver.
I named her Leyla,
   a pure sound.

I don't know when I noticed
   that she'd begun to glow,
to look more substantial
   than the blurred furniture.
It was then I felt a slight touch,
   her hand — a tendril of fog —
on the sheets where she'd lain
   a slight crease, a dampness,
a smell between candles and skin.
   You're changing, I told her.
   A yearning deluged me —
her yearning.

That's when I knew
she wanted to be flesh.
     She stayed insubstantial day after day
     so I tried to blur
my borders, to float, become pure sound.
     But my body seemed heavier,
more inert.

     I remember when she changed.
I could hear the far away slough of traffic
     on the Brooklyn-Queens Expressway,
the people downstairs were playing salsa.
     We lay enclosed   by margins, hems,
where only we existed.
     She was stroking   stroking my arms
my legs, marveling at their solidity,
     the warmth of my flesh, its smell.
Then I touched her.
     Fog, she felt like dense fog,
the color of smoke.
     She glowed, my hands paled then gleamed
as I moved them over her.
     Smoke-fog pressing against my eyelids
my mouth, ears, nostrils, navel.
     A cool tendril pressing between my legs
entering.
Her finger, I thought
but it went on and on.
     At the same time
an iciness touched my anus,
     and she was in
and in and in
     my mouth opening
I wasn't scared just astonished
     rain drummed against my spine
     turned to steam as it rushed through my veins
light flickered over me from toe to crown.
     Looking down my body I saw

    her forearm, elbow and hand
sticking out of my stomach
    saw her hand slide in.
I wanted no food no water nothing
    just her — pure light sound inside me.
My roommate thought I was
    having an affair.
I was "radiant," she said.
    Leyla had begun to swell
I started hurting a little.
    When I started cramping
she pushed out
    her fingers, forearm, shoulder.
Then she stood before me,
    fragile skin, sinews tender as baby birds
    and as transparent.
She who had never eaten
    began to hunger.
I held a cup of milk to her mouth,
    put her hand on my throat
made swallowing motions.
    I spooned mashed banana into her bird mouth,
hid the baby food under the bed.
    One day my roommate asked
who was staying in my room,
    she'd heard movements.
A friend recovering from a contagious
    skin disease, I said.
She ran out saying, I'm going to the Cape
    indefinitely. See you.
    We had the house to ourselves.
I taught her how to clean herself,
    to flush.
She would stand before the mirror
    watching her ears, long and diaphanous,
begin to get smaller, thicker.
    She spent a lot of time at the window.
Once I caught her imitating
the shuffle of the baglady.

No, like this, I told her.
Head up, shoulders back.
I brought in the TV.
This is how humans love, hate, I said.
Once we sat on the stoop
watching a neighbor sweep the sidewalk.
Hello, he yelled, hello, I yelled back,
eh-oh, she whispered.
Watch my lips, Ley-la.
Say it, Ley-la.
Good. I love you.
Ah uff oo, she said.
Soon Leyla could pass,
go for milk at the bodega, count change.
But no matter how passionately we made
love
it was never like before
she'd taken on skin and bone.

Do you ever want to go back, I asked her.
No, it's slower here and I like that.
I hate summers in NYC, I told her,
wish it was winter already.
The temperature dropped 10 degrees 20
and when a chill wind began to blow in Brooklyn
I told her to stop
messing with the cycles that affected others.
I watched what I said
and let Leyla run the place.
She had snow in the livingroom
and a tree in the bathtub.
Nights I lit the illegal fireplace.
Once when reaching toward a high shelf,
I wished I was taller.
When my head touched the ceiling
I had to yell at her to stop,
reverse.
How do you do it, I asked her.

You do it, too, she said,
my species just does it faster,
    instantly, merely by thinking it.

The first time she rode the subway
    I had to drag her out.
I suppose it was the noise,
    the colors flashing by, the odd people
that held her open-mouthed gaze.
    I had to do a gig in L.A.,
speak at a conference, was short on cash,
    but she wanted to come.
She walked past the flight attendants
    didn't even have to hide in the lavatory.
She laughed at my amazement, said
    humans only saw what they were told to see.
Last Christmas I took her home to Texas.
    Mom liked her.
Is she a lez, my brothers asked.
    I said, No, just an alien.
Leyla laughed.

Cinderella Dober-Mutt

Anne Cameron

*for my Sweetie. . . more than seven years and it's still more than
yesterday,less than tomorrow!*

I would never have met Cinderella if I hadn't fallen deeply in love
with her Person.

It was Spring Equinox,and I went to a piece of women's land to
deliver a rose bush and an apple tree;"if you love me,if you really,
really love me,plant a rose for me. If you're gonna love me for a
long,long time,plant an apple tree,and a rose for me".

I was standing talking and joking with some women,and suddenly all I could see were eyes as blue as the sky,eyes so blue you could
have dove in and swam. And a voice,low,throaty,as rich as cream,
richer than cream,richer than all the mythical treasure chests of all
time,laughing,introducing the Woman behind the blue,blue eyes.
Cornflower blue eyes. Forget-me-not blue eyes.

I learned about softball games when I was seven. I learned about
pitching when I was nine. I learned about sliding into third base
when I was eleven. And there were the blue blue eyes,inviting me to
dive into something that I knew was going to change my life. There's
this thing happens in a ball-player's stomach when she knows it's slide
or hit the bench,a lurching that is scary the first few times it happens,then energizing and increasingly welcome once you've learned
how to land without breaking your butt. You run,you feel the lurch,
you take the dare,you slide,and whether you make it or not,the spec-
tators join your team in a loud yell that makes the occasional bruise
well worth the discomfort.

I felt the lurch and thought about my life,where I was in it,what I had learned,what I hadn't yet learned,what I knew,what I hadn't bothered to find out,what I wanted,what I needed,what I intuited and I just let go and slid. They were cheering before my feet left the ground! And the loudest cheer was my own.

I didn't meet the yellow-brown eyes until I knew the blue eyes and the Woman who lived behind them. I didn't meet Cinderella until after her Person and I had danced together,laughed together, talked together and been through the usual tentative getting-to-know-each-other preliminaries.

And then,there she was,Cinderella Dober-Mutt,giving me the lookover,coming over,tail half-down,sniffing at my jeans,sniffing at my sneakers,ignoring the hand I held out,palm down,fingers loose. She gave me the most total going-over I ever had,then looked up and stared at me. Stared. Stared.

People say a dog stares as a mark of defiance. People say a dog stares,but cannot out-stare a person. People say a lot of stupid things, and that is one of the stupidest. Cinderella Dober-Mutt knew something was growing between her Person and me,something that would have an effect on her life. She wanted to size up this new person.

She stared. Then gave a distinctly audible sniff and walked off,tail still half-down,still not wagging. She did not lick my hand. She did not invite me to pat her head. She checked me out and went off to think about it.

A few months later,I was seeing a lot of Cinderella Dober-Mutt. She was black and tan,marked like any Doberman you ever saw,but she was smaller,shorter,wider,probably some lab in there,or maybe terrier,or maybe good old Canadian Basic. Just your typical bush-mutt,wise to the ways and vagaries of bears,wise to the sneakiness of racoons,wise to the ferocity of cougars,wise to the ways of people.

She had shown up full-grown,and full of milk. No sign of puppies,no collar,no tag,no identification,and obviously no idea of how to get "home". Nothing would chase her off,she waited in the rain, shivering,eyes pinned to the door,not begging,not pleading,just sitting in the yard,obviously ready to die if that was what was going to happen next. And when "shoo" didn't work,when "scat" didn't do it,when "take off,mutt" didn't move her,it was "I can't leave her out there any more,she deserves to live as much as anybody does".

She might have been two years old,or she might have been three years old,how do you tell with a Dober-Mutt? She ate,she drank,she lay down with a grateful sigh,and she took over as Resident.

She had other litters of pups,and not one of them was worth the powder to blow it to hell. She was a good mother,but her opinion of her own pups showed her intelligence. She knew they weren't worth "scat". But nobody would believe Cinderella Dober-Mutt's pups were never going to be half the dog their mother was! People not only wanted the pups,people paid money for the pups,and the money was saved until there was enough of it to take her to the vet and have the whole pup-business put to an end.

Cinderella Dober-Mutt knew she wasn't big and strong,she knew she wasn't rough and tough,she knew she wasn't old fucka da moun-tain. If another dog started a fight,Cindy had only one chance to de-fend herself;and she went straight into their faces. If that didn't work,she'd lose the fight. It always worked! One high thin enraged yip,totally unlike her usual deep bark,and she was all over the other dog's face. The same high thin enraged yip she used when Bear came around to snoop for the chance to take a chicken or rip up the garden and eat all the produce.

She never charged the bear's face,though. Nor the rest of the bear. Yip yip yip yip,just out of reach of the crushing,killing paws,yip yip yip until Bear roared a curse or two and left. If there is one thing a bear cannot stand it's a dog that won't go away and yip yip yip yips insults. In the bush you don't want a brave dog,in the bush you want a smart dog. The people up the logging road had a brave dog,a Rhodesian Ridgeback that even challenged and tackled the wolves which came down in the wintertime looking for housecats and fat, stupid pet dogs. The brave dog charged out when Cougar came around looking for lambs and all they found the next morning was the tail. The rest of Brave Dog had become dinner and Cougar had gone off,belly full.

Cinderella Dober-Mutt wasn't brave. She would yip yip yip until the bear went away, but if it was a pack of wolves she moved to the porch to do her yapping, and if it was Cougar, Cinderella Dober-Mutt had sense enough to whine and ask to be allowed into the house for the night. Not brave. Smart.

Smart enough to live long past the time most bush dogs have become memories, with a struggling rose bush to mark their final resting place. Smart enough for her muzzle to start to go white. Smart enough to know little kids want to tug your ears and examine your eyes so when they show up, fade into the ferns and brush where they can't find you. Smart enough to live long enough that she no longer bounced on her toes but moved flat-footed and increasingly slowly.

Cinderella Dober-Mutt lived so long she took most of the rules she had been taught and threw them away, developed her own rules, and when I showed up in the life of her Person, she set about teaching me the rules.

My Sweetie told me she had never been able to put Cinderella on a leash or a chain. "She won't move", my Sweetie laughed, "it insults her, it breaks her heart, and she just stands there, head down, body slumped, until I finally can't stand it any more and take off the leash. I built her a dog house, once, and she wouldn't go in it or even near it. She was totally insulted by it! And a leash just breaks her heart. The insult of it!".

Just to make sure that I knew she wasn't fooling, my Sweetie took my dog's leash, went over, clipped it to Cinderella's collar and said "C'mon, old girl".

Cinderella slumped. Her ears sagged. Her head lowered. She looked for all the world like a dog which has just been beaten with a tire iron. "See?".

But we were living in my house, and our neighborhood had been invaded by contractors two years previously, what had been "out of town" became a "neighborhood" and the Society For The Prevention Of Cruelty To Animals was being kind to them all by rounding up dogs,taking them to the pound,charging fifty dollars impound fee and three dollars per day board charge. Then,if you hadn't claimed your dog within three days the S.P.C.A. kindly destroyed them and incinerated their bodies.

Try to explain any of that to a bush dog. Try to explain any of that to Cinderella Dober-Mutt! Just across the street was a corner store where the school kids went to buy Coke,Ripple Chips or Cheezies. The trash bin was full of half-eaten sandwiches! And if an old dog plodded over and wagged her tail,the kids would swarm around her patting her head,giving her Ham'n'Cheese,giving her Salmon Salad,giving her Bologna,giving her cookies. Cookies! Pieces of cake! Chips! Cheezies!
"Cinderella Dober-Mutt,you get back here before the dog catcher gets you!".
"Cindy,you old tart,come back!".
"Cindy,you'll end your days in the electrocution cage. C'mon home!".

My Sweetie was working,and couldn't take the old girl with her,so suddenly it was Cinderella and me,trying to work out some kind of relationship. And MY dog was either in the house with me,or on a chain which ran along an overhead line,giving her lots of room to romp,but keeping her from going out where the S.P.C.A. could be terminally kind to her.

Cinderella's name began to change sometimes. "Sure,sure,Sarah Barnyard,now we'll do Act 2 of Camille,right?". "'Atta girl Katie Hepburn Dober-Mutt,into the tragic conclusion of the Russian Tragedy". "Sure,sure,Tallulah Bank-Mutt,give us the gears here". "Well,what can I say,Miss Academy Award Winner,who won't stay in the yard? Who's out there being Rambo-Dog with the S.P.C.A.?".

My Sweetie's big blue eyes filled with tears,but with the S.P.C.A. being so kind to all the dogs,especially old fat undeniably smelly dogs,what choices are there.

And then one day my brain clicked into gear. I went into town and got a brand new collar and a brand new blue nylon webbing leash. Took them home as if they were the Crown Jewels of Scotland,and made a big fuss. "Hey,CinderBinder,look at this! Come on,look at the new jewelry!",and before the dog could figure out what all the fuss and glee was,the collar was on,the leash was on,and she and I were heading up the road with my dog,also leashed,to the park.

Every day,right after lunch,into the routine. Big grins,loud yells, clapping of hands,and onto the leashes to go to the park!
"Oh God,I feel so rotten about her. It breaks my heart to see her so sad."
"She's not sad,she's pulling your string."
"Look at her! How can you say she isn't sad. Look at her eyes. Look at the way her head just hangs. Look at her look at me."

So I talked and my Sweetie listened and with much "see you later" and "have a good time",my Sweetie left as if she was going off to work. Got in her car. Drove away. Then I took Cinderella in the house for a few minutes and during that time,my Sweetie drove to within a block of the house,parked the car,and came home down the back alley. I put Cinderella back out on the chain,my Sweetie sneaked in the house from the back,and peeked out the window. There was old Cinderella Dober-Mutt,ears up,tail wagging,woofing softly at a couple of kids coming from the store with Egg Salad,coming from the store with Cheezies,coming from the store with grins and smiles and pats,and all the tragic drama was finished.

When the contraband was safely tucked in her belly I went out with the leashes in my hand. My Sweetie watched from behind the drapes.
"Hey,any dogs up for a trip to the park?".

Such glee,such dancing,such Gee you're a good pal licks and wuffs. On with the leashes and off we went up the road,Cinderella dancing and bouncing happily. She wuffed and snuffed,she wagged her tail in a circle,she flirted with me,she flirted with my dog,she

saw my Sweetie come from the alley to meet us. Down with the ears,down with the head,off with the glee and Sarah Barnyard's heart was breaking. Glimph glumph mumph,she barely hobbled and lurched. Look. See what happens when you aren't here. See what your friend does to me. Oh woe is me,oh woe is you,oh woe is all of us.
"You old whore", my Sweetie laughed. "You conniving old whore!".

Well,when the cat's out of the bag you might as well turn it all into a joke. We all went up to the park,and had a damn good time, leashes or no leashes,S.P.C.A. or no S.P.C.A.

As soon as we could we all left the city and moved back into the bush where dogs didn't need leashes or chain-runs. Unfortunately there were no more Tunafish sandwiches,no more Chips,Cheezies or Twinkies. Ah,but there are skww — urrls. Squirrels which sit in trees and insult the dogs,squirrels which throw pine cones and slander, squirrels which sometimes come to the ground and can be chased, and if there aren't skww-eee-urrls there are pack rats.

If you gave Cinderella Dober-Mutt a bath she would sulk for days. As soon as she could,she'd find something on which to roll.

The salmon were coming up the river to spawn and we went down to watch the miracle. Ah,you've already guessed what that dog did! When Pacific salmon spawn,they die,and some of them are eaten by bears,some by eagles,some by ravens or other birds,but some. . . rot. And there is nothing on this earth stinks worse than spawn-dead salmon.
"You filthy old horror! Yuck! Get away from me! You ride home in the back of the truck! Oh,how COULD you!".
"You don't fool me,you did it on purpose. G'wan,don't be so proud of your stinky self."

She got in the back of the truck with a "kiss my butt" look on her face and glared at us through the back window. Even with the windows closed we could smell her.

And then we got to rain-slick "Cindy's Hill". It wasn't called that before this incident,has been called that ever since. The pickup couldn't make it up the mud-slide incline. Not enough weight. Out we got,put rocks in the back,put wood in the back,finally. . . put ME in the back,all my weight on the wheel well. My Sweetie,who is a much better driver than I am,got behind the wheel,and took a run at the hill. At full speed,mud spewing behind us,me on the wheel well,we went up the hill and Cinderella Dober-Mutt came over to tell me she liked me.

Have you ever had a dog smeared with spawn-slime try to climb on your lap and kiss your face with a tongue that has been licking offal?

Have you ever had that happen at top speed up a slippery hill, with mud spewing and your Sweetie howling with laughter?

And then one night we came home from a movie and she didn't hear the car coming into the driveway,she just kept sleeping. I went over to check her,terrified I'd find her dead,but no,she wakened, looked at us sleepily,wagged her tail,and lay down to sleep some more.

Next day she moved so much more slowly. Her back end seemed weak,and it got weaker. Going down stairs was okay,going up got to be more and more of a chore. We took to lifting her rump for her, "Come on,old girl,you can do'er".

And she grinned. She looked exactly like anybody you've ever seen who has just smoked a half joint of home-grown Indica (although,of course,none of US has ever seen anybody do that illegal thing!). Grin grin,isn't life wonderful,moon june spoon croon peace love groovy. But she sometimes tumbled sideways or got up and flopped down again. Grin grin,look at the flowers,and isn't the cat the best friend we've ever had. Except she couldn't sit on her weakened back end any more,it was stand up or lie down. Grin grin,wag the tail,lemme lick your hand,you're my friend. Except sometimes in the morning there was a damp stain under her and she didn't even know she'd been leaking.

And the incontinence grew,grew until she realized she was leaking,and each time it happened she was totally humiliated.

And her belly just swelled and swelled. A film crew came up to do a Canadian Literature Series half hour on the resident writer,and the cameraman asked "Is that dog pregnant? Because if she is,I want a pup". So we told him No,she's not pregnant,she's dying. The man nearly wept,and Cinderella Dober-Mutt made her film debut. Nearly every shot includes her,grinning,grinning,grinning,wagging her tail,and spaced right out in the ozone.

I took her to the vet and he did X-rays. Showed them to me,and I said I couldn't see Anything.

"See all that white? It's fluid. That means it's either her heart or her liver. If it's her heart,it's congestive heart failure,if it's her liver it's what we call Garbage Gut.".

"Betcha it's Garbage Gut",I managed. "She's a bad old tart when it comes to garbage. Tunafish sandwiches. Twinkies. Chips. Cheezies. Chocolate Cake. She loves garbage.".

Of course there was nothing he could do. I brought her home and waited for my Sweetie to come home from work. We decided we'd just make her as comfortable as we could,as happy as we could, until it all got out of hand.

Inside a week it was quite totally out of hand,the incontinence was constant,she obviously didn't know where she was half the time, and the grin was beginning to look like a leer.

My daughters came up from the city because they knew how Momsie-Two felt about her old dog,and they knew how they felt about Momsie-Two. They helped dig the grave. It was not the all-time fun weekend.

One of the places Cinderella and I had always butted our hard heads was the question of where she would ride. In the truck,sitting on the seat,she insisted. In the back,like a dog,I insisted.

So my Sweetie got up in the morning,put on jeans,sneakers,and an old shirt,sat combing and brushing until Cinderella Dober-Mutt gleamed and glistened,then they headed off for their last walk together. I stayed home. Some things are just too personal,too private, too religious for a third party.

Usually,my Sweetie walks the dogs every morning for almost an hour,up the logging road and into the bush,running off their energy and fortifying herself for eight and half hours out there in the (you should excuse the term) real world. But the walks had been getting shorter,and shorter,and shorter as Cinderella weakened. That morning they didn't make it to the end of the driveway. My darling sat down,holding her friend of a dozen years,and wept openly. Cinderella grinned. She wagged her tail. She pressed herself against my Sweetie and licked her face. Finally,they made their slow way back to the house and my Sweetie brought out the brand new kerchief.

Cinderella Dober-Mutt always had a kerchief around her neck. It was so her Gang Of Rebels would recognize their leader. It was because we all wanted to live in the Wild West and be cowdykes. And she got a brand new kerchief for her last trip.

My Sweetie couldn't get the time off work,and we couldn't wait any longer,and so I was the one drove the Dober-Mutt to her last visit with the nice young man who easily admitted he had never known anything more wonderful than an old dog. She sat up front,on the seat,leaning against me because she couldn't really sit on her worn-out butt. Around her neck the brand new cotton kerchief,on her face that bright-eyed open-mouthed tongue-lolling grin.

The vet's eyes were wet and he made no attempt to hide how he felt. I stood beside her,patting her,tears pouring down my face,and he gave her a poke with a needle. She sighed,she lay her head on her tidy little dobermutty front paws. The tail wagging slowed. The vet reached for a second needle,then looked at me. "You ready for this?", he asked,his voice thick. "Yeah. As ready as a person can be,I guess".

He gave her the second needle and she just closed her eyes. I didn't even know she was gone until he told me.

She rode home on the front seat of the truck,too. Wrapped in her blanket,her poor tired body at rest,and she stayed in the truck until my Sweetie got home from work,and changed into her casual clothes. Then,weeping,we put the old farce in her place. And planted a deep red rambling rose bush. "If you love me,if you really,really love me,plant a rose for me". We hung her collar and the long out-of-date license from the trellis.

The hole in our lives seemed positively enormous. Reminders were everywhere. Snakes wriggled with no dog to harass them. Blackberries grew with no old brown and black muzzle to poke at them,no white strong teeth to pluck them off,no long red tongue to lick'em back,no old throat to swallow them.

It was awful.

And then some Townie dumped a litter of mutt puppies on the highway. And the smallest one couldn't keep up as the mother led her starvelings into the bush to try to catch rats,rabbits,birds,anything that might provide food and the slim,dim hope of life in the wild.

She was small,and black,like a labrador retriever,except for the whiskered wire-haired terrier face. And terrified. Left alone she would panic,then freak out pathetically. So because she was black, and because she sang the blues,I called her "Bessie Smith." But she didn't have the dignity,she didn't have the royal bearing to be called Bessie Smith,and it all got shortened to Smitty.

She was the glummest pup I ever met. Too traumatized to romp, or play,too aware of the permanence of insecurity to tumble and flirt,she would look at me with her yellow-brown eyes and I would feel overwhelmed with sadness.

She was sick when we got her,she was terrified,she was sad,she was half crazy. But she knew she was lucky. She knew we weren't the S.P.C.A.,there was no three-day limit,no electrocution chamber,no kindness for short terms only. And she began to respond to being left with a full bowl of food all the time,a full bowl of fresh water.

And one day,coming back from the morning walk with my Sweetie,Smitty smelled bear. yip yip yip,yip yip yip. Another day the bully german shepherd up the road charged her and Smitty knew she had one chance and one chance only,she went right up Freda's face,yip yip.

Every time we give her a bath she goes outside and finds something on which to roll. She bounces forward on tippy-toes,then rubs eye cheese on your clean clothes. She loves to sit beside you,leaning against you. Snakes have to be fast,squirrels better stay in their trees,and pack rats don't have a chance. Cats are either ours,and thus "sacred",or they're racing away,tails bushed. She leaps into the water to chase off the invading kelp,she heads for the ferns and brush if small children arrive,and oh my God is that a piece of cake,can I show you my Sarah Barnyard routine,let's go to the beach,can we go find blackberries,aren't I lucky to have my own People!

Sometimes,when the sun is high and the day is hot I look out the front window,and there she is,Smitty Whiskerface,curled up at the base of the rambling rose bush where Cinderella Dober-Mutt was placed,and I know it just is not possible,the christians taught me animals have no souls,reincarnation is nothing but pagan superstition,and death is final;but there she is,and the color scheme is different,the age is different,she's blockier,she's bulkier,she's just every bit as flirtatious and stubborn. Of course it's co-incidence,our lives are full of co-incidence,everything from education,to politics,to religion is stuffed with co-incidence,there are sixty thousand co-incidences every day of our lives,but we go to pick berries and a whiskeryface pokes out,the long red tongue appears,the blackberries are snoffled up,by the dozen,by the peck,by the bushel. And when Cougar passes by,she wants in the house,please,there are limits to what a girl's expected to do for a bowl of kibble a day!

No,she isn't Cinderella Dober-Mutt. There only ever was one Cinderella Dober-Mutt. But damn,when you see her moving sure-footed along a log,or bouncing over a rock pile,or staring at you, conveying her thanks for a life that doesn't include sleeping in the rain or slowly starving to death,you're reminded of the Leader Of The Pack Of Rebels.

And sometimes,when we're playing music and dancing together, Smitty gets right into it,old Bojangles Fleet-Foot herself,and we've got the old girl back for a while,not in the person of Smitty,but in our memories,in our hearts. And she is young again,with strong hind end and tiny neat feet,eyes bright,heart strong,liver functioning,all the pain,discomfort and fuzziness gone.

Native people say there is nothing deserves more respect than an old dog. And we have several roses,several apple trees. If you love me,if you really really love me,plant a rose for me,and if you're gonna love me for a long long time,plant an apple tree,and a rose for me. . . .

A Friend In Need
Dorothy Wood

A relative of mine had me put on conservatorship, meaning that my money (mostly an inheritance, which he wanted) was handed over to the Public Guardian's Office, to be doled out to me in small, monthly allowances, starting at $10 a month. I was placed in a board-and-care home, from which I could go wherever it suited me, as long as I was back in time for meals.

During the drab, purposeless years of my confinement I encountered a dog on one of my walks. He was a big, friendly fellow, and when I patted him, he leaned up against me, licking my fingers. It was the first contact I had experienced in six long years that bordered on affection. I began going by the place where he lived, but he was not often out. When he was, my heart leaped for joy. I called him to me to pat him and rub his ears. He reminded me a little of a dog I once owned. I had always owned dogs, but where I was now there was no place for a pet of any kind.

I prayed every night now for a dog of my own, though I knew I could not get possession of my own money, or find a place where a dog would be allowed.

The days turned into weeks without my new canine friend making another appearance. The house where he lived began to look deserted. The grass remained uncut and no car ever parked in the driveway. I still went by the house every day, but finally had to conclude that the family had moved away. This was no answer to prayer; but it came to me that I could take the bus to the nearest shopping mall. Once there, my steps led me unerringly to the pet shop where there were dogs of every description.

A wire pen out in front held a bright-eyed cockapoo who greeted me with wriggles of delight, trying to climb over the fence into my arms. I went to the mall every day to pet and talk to him. He licked my fingers and whined to be closer, even as I yearned to hold the loving little bundle in my empty arms. I named him "Wigs" and thought about him constantly. He was always there, at the corner of his pen, pressing against the wire, his paws reaching out to me. I tell you I did not just imagine he was looking for me.

One day two boys came by and started to pet him. He saw me coming and dodged their caresses to come to me as though drawn by a magnet. Oh, we were getting thick, Wigs and I. Our visits had to be brief since new people were always crowding in about us, so I would tear myself away to stroll the mall. After a while I would return for a good-by word and a joyous yipping from Wigs. Then, sadly, it was good-by until tomorrow.

But there was not always a tomorrow, as you may have guessed, and I already feared in my soul. One morning I approached with a toy I had fashioned out of an old sock. It had ears, head and tail, and I thought it would be something of mine they might let him keep, so he would not be so bereft when I had to leave him. How pleased the little fellow was going to be. Why hadn't I thought of this sooner?

But he was not in the corner of his pen. I quickened my pace, realizing in shock that two short-haired spotted dogs shared the pen. Where was my little Wigs? I went through the store, but he was not in any of the cages inside. He would not be there again. He had been sold. How I wanted that happy, frisky little Wigs for my own! They had no right to take him away!

I did not cry. I was too accustomed to reversals in my life. I stumbled back to the bus, throwing the toy I had made in the dust.

Where was my little Wigs tonight? I wondered as I climbed into my narrow cot. I did not sleep much that night, or during the dismal nights that followed. I did not go back to the shopping mall. I would only get attached to another dog, who was not mine, and would be taken away. Once again my days had become pointless. I walked by the house where the big dog had been, but there was no sign of life about the place. I did not know what to do with myself. The other board-and-care residents sat around staring at the walls. I had to have something to do.

About this time I was transferred to a retirement home where there were over a hundred residents. My allowance was increased, so that I felt I could afford a second-hand typewriter. I wrote several letters to the newspaper, and even wrote of my fate to some public officials who I thought might be able to free me from conservatorship. If I could get my money back into my own hands, and be allowed to move where I pleased, I would find a place where I could keep a dog.

Instead I made a trip to the hospital with a broken hip. Once up and on a walker, I was afraid my chances of ever getting a place and a dog of my own were slimmer than ever. I was soon off the walker, but unsteady on my feet so that when a small dog jumped up on me, I lost my balance and nearly fell to the ground. My balance remained poor for some time, and I told God that it was too late now. My dog-walking days were over. I would have to give up praying for a dog. I could no longer handle one.

Four years had elapsed since my move to the retirement home, and to my surprise I was granted my freedom from the conservatorship, and my finances were returned to me, together with an accounting, which did not account for everything, by any means. But I was free. I was seventy-three years old and free to look for a place of my own.

I answered a share-the-home ad in the paper, which mentioned a very reasonable rent to stay nights with an elderly woman who was afraid to stay alone. And wonder of wonders, she had a little dog — a cockapoo, who climbed up on the davenport beside me, and then into my lap.

"He's fourteen years old," his mistress was saying. "I guess I've spoiled him because he expects a walk morning and evening, and I can no longer take him out. You wouldn't have to go more than a block with him."

My balance was still poor. The little dog was lively enough to throw me, and I had already had it out with God. He had waited too long. I could not do it. The little dog was so endearing, I found myself petting him and yearning to try walking him a short distance. I finally said I would try it. His mistress fastened his leash and we were off.

He did not exert a strong pull on the leash and seemed content to sniff at things along the way. God had answered my prayers after all with a dog I could handle. Not my own — but he seemed almost my own as time went by and we walked farther and farther on our morning and evening excursions. My step was much surer than it had been, and little Taupe, as he was named, didn't appear to tire, even when we were gone for a solid hour on our rambles.

More and more I realized that this dog and this place had been picked for me. How lucky I was! If I got busy about something when it was about walk time, Taupe would come to me and bark demand-ingly. If I was still busy and paid no attention to him, he would ask to be let out in the fenced back yard. But when I opened the back door, he would turn and trot to the front door, barking his com-mands. We always left for walks by way of the front door, so he was making his meaning clear.

I enjoyed the walks as much as he did, and we never missed a morning and evening stroll together until he died in his sleep two years later.

The days seemed remarkably flat and pointless again without him, and I found I had little excuse to take walks anymore.

It was not long, however, before a neighbor brought an all-black poodle to me. "She almost got run over crossing the street," my neighbor said, dumping the little dog in my arms. "We can't keep her. We have two dogs of our own. But she's a little doll." I hugged her close. She was younger than the dog I would have had in mind, but she seemed content to snuggle in my arms, and I could not let her go back to the danger of our busy street.

I took her out, accustoming her to the leash. A short walk at first. Then, when she stopped fighting the leash, and understood my com-mands, we ventured farther. We named her Coaly, since she was as black as coal, and she learned her name and what was expected of her in a hurry.

She would jump up on a chair to get me to put on her leash, then away we would go — me with my very own dog, proud as punch. It had taken twelve long, lonely years to come to this, and every morn-ing was beautiful; every walk filled with adventure for us both.

But all good things come to an end, and I had to give my little Coaly away when I went to the hospital. As I take my sedate daily stroll from the retirement home where I live now, I like to recall the many good times we had together.

She will always be among my pleasantest memories.

Assurances
Becky Birtha

A blessing has come to this garden:
Four black and yellow spiders
spin their webs from vine to corner
petunia to geranium, and hang still
through the long hot days, waiting for food.
I make myself
simple meals from garden vegetables
eat with my chopsticks from the painted bowl.
I'm waiting too: word from you.
An answer. An ending. Your decision to
no longer share this life with me —
if a life can be shared!
The spiders' webs are complex,
intricate like handmade lace
symmetrical and open as windows.
Each is perfect and complete, each
is all it needs to be.
The spiders never speak
to one another, or visit, yet I know
each one is aware that the other three
share this same garden. And aware of me.
There's some way that
I'm connected, some sheer strand
that, by all logic, ought to break
when an obstacle slams into it,
or human hand, but holds.
The spider falls, plummets
carefully to safety and patiently
climbs to mend the web
to begin again.

III.

For life and death, the operative number is always one.

Rescue
Shirley Graves Cochrane

Whitman woke her as he always did, laying his huge head beside hers and sighing. His tail made a steady *thunk* on the floorboards, but otherwise he waited patiently while she reassembled her body and rose. Together they walked down the hall to the back door, where the goats waited in early light. Moonshadow and Touchstone, the last of James' herd. Today the man from Prufarms was coming for them.

After Whitman and the goats bounded away, she stood on the porch and tested the air. Winter's bite in it. Broom sage moved across the mountains like herds of animals, hard breathers climbing slopes. The light could pull at you like remembered grief.

As she stood feeling the dawn, her son came to her again. Like that picture of the wind in the story book he'd loved as a child. Sometimes as their faces touched, she could feel his mourning for her — almost an apology for his death. *Robbie.*

Even this long afterwards, she sometimes looked for him to come down the road with that rocking gait of his. She thought of his death as a mistake, coming so soon after James'. Divine miscalculation.

She went back inside to make her morning ablutions, as James' mother used to say. The house's best view was from the bathroom window. Above the breasts of mountains, clouds made larger mountains. Under the largest tree sat James' bench. It looked, he'd always said, as though it had been stolen from a London park during the reign of Victoria. The two of them would sit there on summer evenings, determined to have a piece of time to themselves. Besides Robbie, there had been her father and his mother, the two of them quarreling like a married couple. She and James seldom quarreled. With others around them, they did not even talk together much. But alone. . . no one would have believed the passion between them.

She'd been unable to forgive him his death. Starting back to teach too soon after the flu, he'd waved off her warnings, gone on. Two of his students came with the college physician to tell her. Angry, she'd been. Sometimes she could still feel that anger roiling inside her.

When she went outside, Whitman edged past the goats to leap upon her, almost dancing with her, greeting her as though he'd not seen her half an hour before. In wretched shape he was — his tail resembled the rutted road. Golden retriever mostly. The other part husky, James always said; *wolf,* she said. Those amber eyes. And pure wolf the way he placed his paws on your shoulders. James always talked courteously to him ("Yes, Whitman, I can see you need your breakfast"). She herself was often impatient, now saying, "Oh, for heaven's sake, Whitman, get *down.*" He went off up the road. Crossness always wounded his spirit.

The goats encircled her, gently butting, their milk bags extended. Touchstone was black with tan markings, stylish looking somehow. Moonshadow had a gentle striped face. Their eyes were green and wide set. She stroked each of them carefully, wanting them to remember her touch.

As she put out the goat feed, she heard Whitman barking. She walked up the hill, placing each foot carefully to miss crevices the rains had carved. Whitman had cornered a huge woodchuck. He danced about it, his shanks stained raspberry from the woodchuck's blood. The creature raised its head from time to time, showed teeth, then lay still. Dying? As she watched, Whitman grabbed its tail, shook it, threw it up, grabbed it again — a cruel game. "Whitman, come here!" she shouted. To her surprise he came at once. She grabbed his collar and hauled him up the road. He turned, looked back at the woodchuck but did not break away. There was nothing she could do about the creature — maybe kinder to let Whitman finish it off. "Aren't you ashamed, torturing a helpless creature that way?" she asked Whitman. On and on she went, meaning to stop but unable to; poor Whitman slinking before her. Scolding — the way she'd sometimes done with her son. She could see him, a stocky boy, at twelve almost as large as his father, walking ahead of her down the road, holding in his anger. Never turning on her.

All around her were summer's leftovers: daisies, black-eyed Susans, parasols of Queen Anne's lace. Yet every so often a quick icy little rain would come. She released Whitman to roam.

Close to the orchard now, she decided to get the apples. The fruit shone like jewels beneath the trees, so thick you could walk almost the entire orchard stepping only on apples. Their wine filled the air. As she gathered one apple in her apron, she would see a better one. The heaviest-bearing tree was circled with brambles, but its fruit was worth the thorny journey. Each apple seemed perfect. Then suddenly two bramble bushes caught her right leg, like a rabbit trap. Every time she tried to get free, the spikes drove deeper. Turning too quickly, she fell, her trapped leg helpless. She let out a cry, and Whitman bounded to her, romping, rolling on her, all but laughing. "Get off my leg, you fool," she cried. Whitman moved away, feelings hurt. "Help!" she screamed wildly, though who but the goats could hear? Finally she lay still, waiting for strength. "You are so useless," she flung at Whitman, and he turned, walked back to the road.

Ridiculous being trapped like this. She tried to remove the brambles, but her fingers would no longer mind her, keeping to their own gnarled rhythm. Then she heard Whitman barking. At an intruder? She lay helpless, as another icy rain began. She thought she heard a man's voice — like James, talking sense to a dog. And then she could see him on the road, wearing a green hooded windbreaker. He was slight and had James' strong, spare build. Whitman led him to her, once again bounding to her, rolling on her trapped leg.

"What is your dog's name?" the man asked, lifting his hood the way you would a hat.

She gave him the name.

"Whitman," he said firmly, "this is no time for sport."

Immediately Whitman withdrew, settled on his haunches.

"So." The man's eyes were a surprising green, a shade deeper than her son's. Startling with that black hair and dark eyebrows. A length of rope and various tools hung from his belt. He detached a pair of clippers and began cutting the bramble bush into short pieces, removing each one carefully without even snagging her stockings. It took him a long, careful time, but at last she was free.

"Now — can you get up?" He held out his hands, but she could not reach up to them. He had to go behind her and wing her up. At last she stood, looking at the landscape as though it had been years since she'd last seen it.

"No bones broken?" he asked.

She moved cautiously. Nothing but the familiar licks of fire between the shoulder blades. "None," she assured him. She attempted to walk but staggered.

"Should I carry you?" he asked.

"Oh no, no." She studied him hard. You could not be too careful these days. A man of thirty-five, she guessed. Younger than James had been when she first met him. His mouth was thin-lipped and wide, teeth even and white. Aquiline nose, a little large for his face but beautifully chiseled. Hands strong, well shaped. His face still held its summer tan, a bit of rosiness topping it. A man as striking as James.

"Here." He put a hand out to steady her. They seemed to fly — she could never hope to walk this fast alone. At the field where Whitman had captured the woodchuck, she asked him to stop. No woodchuck in sight. She felt exhilarated for the creature, escaped, if only to a private death.

They resumed their flying pace. The crazy thought came to her that this must be James' ghost, summoned by Whitman. But he did not seem like a ghost. Also, James would have known to steer her past the steep kitchen steps and around to the easier side ones.

"I'll fix tea," she said.

"Ah. . ." He looked around the kitchen. For something to do, she supposed. A man restless indoors.

"Would you like to make a fire in the stove?" She pointed toward the living room.

Soon she heard him outside chopping. How long since she'd had proper kindling! He chopped awhile, came back in, lit the fire, went out again to chop some more. She could feel the warmth creeping into the kitchen.

She made tea and coffee, ladled out some fresh goat's milk yogurt, heated coffee cake frozen since Christmas. She found linen napkins, silver teaspoons, lump sugar, other things she never used anymore. And the best cups.

"I don't have much company anymore," she told the man when she brought in the refreshments. "The road's got so bad. Only regular visitor is Alice, my daughter-in-law. My *former* daughter-in-law, I guess you'd have to say. My son's widow."

"The loss of a son is surely the worst thing that can happen to a woman," he said.

"I lost my son and husband within a single year."

He sucked in his breath. "Is your daughter-in-law a comfort to you?" he asked.

"Tries to be. Brings her baby out to see me. Baby by the second husband. She and Robbie talked about children. And now she has one and it looks exactly like its daddy. A little girl."

"I can see that a grandchild would be a comfort to you."

The want of grandchildren was like a third bereavement.

"Alice collected a good bit of money for his death. A man with a trailer that came loose. Ran into my son's milk truck." Some day she would go look at the place he'd crashed through the guardrail.

"Could I pour you some tea?" He came over and carefully filled her cup. It struck her again how much he resembled James. Especially his build — upper torso like a tree, not quite matching the slender lower half. And the strong features firelight set dreaming. He could be James' kinsman. A son even. After all, who knew what might have happened in his long bachelorhood, with all that passion in him and a scolding mother to escape? To all the questions about the days before their marriage, he would answer: "The questioning of the past is endless, is it not?"

Suddenly she found herself telling the stranger about her anger at James for dying. "As though he'd left me for another woman." A sound came out of her; it struggled to be a laugh, but ended up more cry.

"Anger in such situations is not unusual," the stranger said.

It was not so much his words as his tone that comforted her. She longed to confide more but forced herself instead to ask him questions. He came from Iowa, he told her — moved east just last month.

So then, he was not James' ghost or love child or even kinsman. "I guess you'd say my husband and I had an arranged marriage," she resumed their conversation.

He rushed in with assurances about arranged marriages. Oriental marriages, Jewish marriage brokers. "Amazingly happy," he gave such marriages his blessing.

"I guess you'd have to say James and I arranged the marriage," she told him.

He laughed deeply, taking this for joke and not exact description. James had been thirty-eight, she thirty-six. They'd sought security — financial for her, domestic for him. But on their wedding night. . . . She could still remember his gasp of surprise, their sure movement toward each other.

Her visitor rose, went over to the bookcase, where he fingered James' first editions, then the lesser books behind.

"You need someone to build more bookcases," he observed.

And prune the apple trees and make cider and fill in the ruts and patch the barn and catch the rat. . . .

"If you're looking for a place to stay," she said, "you're welcome here. You could have James' old study — it's got a private entrance off the porch. Fireplace, lavatory. . . . I'd give you room and board if you'd help keep the place up."

"Oh, no," he said quickly.

"You have a family?"

"No. An old bachelor." He laughed. At the *old*, she supposed.

Then why? she wondered but did not ask.

He allowed a few minutes to tick away, then he clapped his hands lightly, once in front, once behind, and said: "Well, I must be on my way."

She felt a desperate need to hold him. But he looked, for all his kindness, like a man who would escape even mild captivity. She led him outside.

"The goats. . ." He fingered the rope at his belt.

"Then you're the man from Prufarms?"

"Yes."

"But the truck. . ."

"I walked."

"All that way!" Didn't he know how long it took to walk roped goats down a winding road? He'd not last a week at Prufarms, where they believed in doing things zip, zip, zip, mostly with Mack trucks.

The rain had stopped and the sun was riding the blue sky. The goats appeared.

"This is Moonshadow. And Touchstone." She put her hand upon each sloping head.

The man spoke to them, the way you would to people.

"Will you tell Mr. Pruden to please call them by their rightful names?"

"Certainly. That is very important." He roped them courteously.

"Don't forget now, if things don't work out for you at Prufarms, you can come right here."

"Thank you, thank you."

Never in a million years would he take that offer, she knew, and felt again the swift anger toward men. One way or another, they always left you.

Whitman made a sound — not quite whine.

"Take Whitman with you," she said. "You'd be good to him. He just gets on my nerves."

"Oh, no. I couldn't do that. He's a good watch dog. You need his protection."

"I may be moving soon." That house in town Alice had found. Reasonable rent. Nice back porch. It would do. Alice just two blocks away with her baby. "Wouldn't you like a dog like Whitman?" she asked. "He's a beautiful dog when he's fixed up."

"I always wanted a dog." Some echo of boyhood sounded in his voice. He looked at Whitman, standing beside the goats. "But I must be sure he wants to go." He went to the gate, the goats moving with him. "Whitman," he said, when he stood just outside the gate, "you may come too."

Whitman gave a short bark but stayed in place.

"He needs your permission," the man said.

"Whitman, you may go," she said.

Whitman looked at her, walked toward the gate but turned just before he got there and went over to lie in the ditch. Whenever Alice came to take her to town, he'd lie down that way, roll his eyes, flop a paw at her when she came to say goodbye. Leave her with a load of guilt, while he, as soon as she was out of sight, would more than likely go bounding off, a goat again. But this time was different.

"Well, I can certainly see he doesn't want to leave," the man said. "It wouldn't be right to force him." A reprimand edged his voice.

"No, I suppose not." To her surprise she felt the rubbed-raw feeling that years ago had meant the coming of tears. Ice breaking up in a stubborn river.

"Well, thank you, thank you," he said.

"I should thank you."

"Goodbye." He took off down the road at a clip that was almost a run, the goats trotting beside him.

"I guess, Whitman, if we move to town you can find some dog friends to replace the goats." She spoke with courtesy, as though she expected him to make a sensible reply. They turned and walked back to the house.

Daji

Juanita M. Sanchez

for a day
for a night
i heard the cries

in a cottonwood
large and bare
my sister yells

look!
there he is
i see him

so small
thin from survival
his eyes as big

as any pond
i'd ever seen
orange and white his cloak

the colors of winter
he was the prince
of india

traveled all those miles
just to reclaim me
his brown-eyed jewel

his queen
who pays the rent
who feeds him

but he was a king
of the people
no dog was unwelcomed

as long as they
would play
with him

and the roof
now that   was the playground!
and me

with a fear of heights
and i thought we'd die
up there with too much laughter

it was winter
some ten, twelve years
i was in and out

one city to another
coming home
my king looked

too much like
when i first
met him

the disease progressed
so quickly
how could i notice?

he couldn't survive the winter
i wrapped him
in his favorite towel

a silly snoopy
beach towel
his kingly robe of security

i placed him
on the vet's table
i went outside

the tears wouldn't stop
inside
the vet waited

i had to be with him
i had to tell him   my prince of india
it was my decision

that i was sorry
that if only it was me
i would want to die

rather than face
too slow
a painful death

that i would be grateful
for dying with dignity
and i tried

Daji,
my friend,
you looked at me

for the last moment
with such trust
your eyes received

my body
my soul   my spirit

and i bathed
in the water of your eyes
i sank in the water of mine

i held you
in the car
on the way home

to the land of my grandfather
i dug the ground
i placed you in

i placed with you
your favorite towel
i placed with you my crystal

i gave you
a piece of pottery
from the chaco

the indian
the native peoples
of our beginnings

and i asked them
to accept you
in their travels

that they help
you now
that they know you

that they love you
that they remind you

of the brown beauty
who played with you
on the roof

Mrs. Schultz Walks Suzie

Rochelle Natt

Suzie squats.
Mrs. Schultz, owner,
looks away,
respecting Suzie's privacy.
Suzie leaves a steaming lump,
paws scratching, she seasons it with earth.
Mrs. Schultz asks, "Finished, baby?"
She doesn't look until Suzie yips twice.
Then Mrs. Schultz wipes Suzie's bottom,
tucks her under her arm
and walks on,
smiling at those who stop to say,
"What a pretty little dog!"
It takes Mrs. Schultz back thirty years
when she would walk,
arm around her daughter's shoulder,
and passers-by would call:
"How pretty!
You look like sisters."
Thinking of her daughter
who is hiding upstairs,
too heavy to tie her shoes,
the wadded-up letter
to no one
in her daughter's waste basket
scrawled in red crayon:
"I hate my mother."
Mrs. Schultz murmurs, "Suzie knows
I am the best Mommy."
Suzie looks away.
Mrs. Schultz coughs twice.

Harriet

zana

there is a lot of wind this time of year: it scatters mauve petals across the courtyard and roughs up waves on the pool. It sounds like ocean here in my cubicle. i wonder if you are outdoors or safe and warm out of the wind.

i have loved you since i saw you. i touched you and felt we understood each other, but that was just the deepest layer speaking. we both must unlearn so much of what we've known in order to reach that deepest layer again.

i am shy, not knowing how to approach you. at first i would greet you by bending quickly to stroke the fur between your ears. i hoped you would know that it hurts me to stand long, that i was hurrying to be in the hot pool, but wanted to say hello. but you drew down into your fur. i had not thought to notice what i was interrupting — were you thinking, daydreaming, enjoying your solitude?

you made a mistake with me, too, scrambling up on me so quickly the first time i sat low by you in the courtyard. can you understand how tender is my unprotected bare skin, how fearful i am that your long claws and nibbling teeth will make me bleed?

now i send you a greeting thought but do not stop when i have only a small part of myself to give. later there will be more; i will lie on a chaise near the bench you like to chew on, and perhaps you will come to me. then my hands will move through your fur, over and over and over, timelessly. i will have no thought of doing anything else. i will feel your bliss and contentment though you make no move or sound. my eyes will follow my hand through the patterns of your fur, down the delicate membranes of your long ears, into the ultimate softness around your nose and mouth. i am breathless at the intricacies of your body and spirit, so unlike mine.

when i swim, i do not know if you watch me. do you think of me when i am not near you? do you pick me out from other people walking past?

you followed me one day, nearly to my room, and i wanted so to lift you up, to put you in my bed with me, to hold you in the curve my body makes and kiss you and understand your secrets. but this i am far from ready to know how to do.

a strange thing has happened: i feel closeness with the man who cares for you. it is not often i drop my shield and let in vibrations from a man. i feel tender toward this man who is your familiar. your womon i see less often; when i do, we smile as if sharing a secret.

your life seems hard to me and i wonder how you cope. is it food-hunger that makes you jump into the potted plants and eat their bright flowers? or is it a hunger to set your feet on real earth, to eat food still live from the ground?

and i in my bungling am still one of the gentlest to enter your life. there are the children who grab you like a beach ball, yelling "ma, look, a bunny!" and the man who kept staring at you and saying "that's the dumbest looking rabbit i've ever seen."

i wonder if you can understand any words we say? perhaps our tone of voice is comprehensible to you, after all this time? you, after all, may have developed the skill of understanding a foreign tongue, since you are imprisoned in silence here, exiled from your own kind.

and you have developed trust; there was little choice. you cannot easily escape these large creatures who would pursue you. better to be compliant and hope for the best.

i was not here when your man's dog bit your leg and the man took you to have it amputated. i know you trusted this man as much as one can trust when in distress. as much as one can trust someone of a different species. but still. you could not ask him why, or how. i have seen photographs of rabbits strapped to tables for experiments. and i know that, like any creature, a rabbit can scream.

in a magazine, for easter, was an article on rabbits. there was one like you, very large and lop-eared, white with patches of varied browns. and there were other rabbits, too — many sizes, many shapes and colors, arranged on a spotless surface like a display of this year's new cars. the article said rabbits are "dim." dim but pretty. i could read nothing in these rabbits' glazed eyes.

what is the sadness of being so much in the power of others for an entire life?

i am sorry i called you "my baby," that i wanted to pick you up because you are small and soft, to cradle you and play toys with you.

now i have come to respect your age and pain; you are of unknown kinds of wisdom, an adult and not a baby except in the fact that there is some of the crone and some of the baby in each of us.

i am honored to spend time with you in this place, to have you lick my skin with your long, light tongue, to have you lie quiet against my foot, sending messages i will never know how to translate, but that some part of me understands.

Unexpected Refuge
Hope Sawyer Buyukmihci
(with Hans Fantel)

For the first few days in Turkey, I was entranced with the
kaleidoscope of new impressions: oranges, calendulas, pansies,
and roses along the streets; ragged children everywhere, their
wooden shoes worn to slivers; high-wheeled cabs drawn by skinny
horses, their brass-trimmed harness festooned with blue beads;
cobbled streets with tumbledown stone houses; men and donkeys
sharing the street on equal terms.

But, as a woman brought up in a western culture, I soon came to
despise Turkish customs and attitudes. The sight of women walking
a respectful distance behind their husbands enraged me, as did the
separate entrance for women on streetcars and buses. It seemed as
if I had been transported not just to another country but to another
era. My role as a "respectable" woman, I discovered, consisted mainly
in sitting at the window all day, awaiting my husband's return. And
since Cavit's work as a road engineer for the Turkish government
took him away for weeks, it was often a long wait.

In fact, my husband's family was extremely generous, and if I had
been able to encourage it, would probably have given me signs of
genuine affection. But basically they regarded me as a strange
creature to be gradually tamed and civilized.

One facet of my personality, in particular, seemed
incomprehensible to my Turkish in-laws — the way I felt about
animals. It distressed me to see the often cruel unconcern shown by
Turkish draymen to their horses and donkeys. Once, toward the end
of our stay, I expressed my feelings in a way that outraged the family.

As usual, I was sitting at the window when I saw a donkey being
driven up the hill. He was a scrawny little creature with huge and
gentle black eyes. His face bore a look of patient resignation and his
round furry flanks were like soft pillows. Piled high on his back was
his burden. Chairs, cabinets, strange-looking brass kitchen utensils

were arranged in a sort of tower on a platform over the donkey's spine. The awkward pile was clearly top-heavy, and its swaying from side to side made it difficult for the donkey to keep his footing.

Just as he rounded the curve in front of my window, the donkey slipped on a cobblestone. The violent swing of his burden pulled him off his tiny feet, and he came crashing down on his side. Rather than unburden the donkey of his load and help him to his feet, the driver began beating him with a strong, knurled stick and twisting his tail. The donkey struggled piteously. The driver lifted his club, swung it far back, and with a gesture of concentrated malevolence hit the little donkey right in the eye.

I don't know what came over me at that moment. Perhaps it was the memory of a story describing an English woman in India whipping a cruel bullock driver. But I grabbed a heavy cane from the umbrella stand and tried to rush out into the street to rescue the donkey. I don't know what would have happened if I had actually struck the driver. Fortunately, Cavit's uncle restrained me at the door.

I sat sullenly in the window for days and weeks. I soon ran out of reading matter, and the family — not wishing to encourage literacy in a woman — pretended not to understand my request for English books.

Thrown entirely on my own resources, I entertained myself with endless ruminations. Sometimes I fancied myself a caged animal. I kept pondering these parallels: My in-laws denied me my way of life. Not through malevolence, but through thoughtlessness. What stood between us was a kind of emotional ignorance, a lack of recognition for the needs of the other. Likewise, I felt, man fails to recognize the natural claims of animals.

It was during this period of searching for some anchor of meaning amidst the crosscurrents that threatened to swamp our marriage that the idea of the wildlife refuge took shape in my mind. At first, it was merely a vague notion of wanting to live in the country, surrounded by animals and close to the sustaining realities of nature.

If we couldn't afford a farm, at least we might have just a piece of land with streams and woods sufficient to give some shelter to forest animals, and, along the forest edge, enough open land for bluebirds to enjoy. Could I make Cavit see it?

I said nothing to him at the time, for he was bitterly struggling with himself. His loyalty was to country; his love was for me; and his wish was to live in America. He spoke little of this, but I felt his turmoil.

At times, as if to make up for his "disloyal" thought of leaving Turkey, he became more vociferously Turkish than ever. He would neglect me and speak harshly to me, as if indirectly to remind me what a Turk expects of his wife. At other times, the pendulum of his inner indecision swung in the other direction, and he and I felt a wonderful sense of loving solidarity.

What finally helped resolve these conflicts was the little donkey I tried to rescue when he was so cruelly beaten in front of our house. When Cavit returned after a long field trip, his uncle practically greeted him at the door with an account of my misdeed.

"For a donkey!" the uncle shouted. "She'd shame the family for a donkey!"

Cavit said nothing in my defense. Nor did he reproach me. He understood his uncle's feelings. And he understood mine.

He ate in silence and spent the evening reading quietly. Later, after we had gone to our room, he announced his decision to return to America.

My heart leapt at the thought of returning home. In my imagination I pictured us on a farm in the western mountains, perhaps near Mount Baker, where Cavit and I had spent such a happy time. I envisioned clear brooks sparkling in their rocky beds and looked forward to seeing bears ambling down into the orchards during the winter to munch on windfalls.

We reached New York at last on a bright day in the spring of 1954. Two little girls, Linda and Nermin, had meanwhile been added to our family. As we all stood on deck looking at the Statue of Liberty, I felt like an immigrant in my own country.

At the dock we tallied up our assets.

Expenses during the long trip had eaten into our last reserves but I hadn't realized how close we were to destitution.

"You count it," I said to Cavit, hoping he'd somehow come up with a bigger sum.

"Seventy-three dollars and thirty-five cents," said Cavit.

In the brief silence that followed, the dream of Mount Baker collapsed. Setting out across a continent with three children and less than a hundred dollars seemed foolhardy. We were stranded, and on the evening of our return to my homeland we found ourselves dependent on the hospitality of friends in Philadelphia. On the train from New York, we passed through the dismal industrial region of northern New Jersey. Junkyards alternated with ramshackle houses and smoke-belching factories.

"When do we get to America?" asked Nedim, who was old enough to sense that these surroundings were not what we had pictured as our destination. I didn't have the courage to tell him that this, too, was America.

"Soon," I said. "We'll get there soon."

A few days later — down to nearly our last dollar — we telephoned a friend whom we had known at Cornell and who shared our love of nature.

"I've got a trailer," he said. "It's parked in the woods in southern New Jersey. I go there to camp out on weekends. You can live in it till you find something better."

The low-lying land, laced with still waters, was far different from the snow-peaked mountains for which we had hoped, but I soon became attuned to the endless dialogue between the sky and the marshes as they reflected each other's moods at various times of the day.

Cavit found an opportunity to practice his specialty of metallurgical engineering at a laboratory within commuting distance, and by fall his salary enabled us to move out of our friend's trailer and make the down payment on a house with three acres of land.

As winter faded, I looked over the snowbanks for bluebirds — those childhood companions I had missed so much during my years in Turkey. I listened for the small sounds of their warbling amidst the gusts of the March wind. But none came.

I soon learned why. I chanced on an article in *Audubon Magazine* describing the plight of the bluebird, driven to near extinction in the short span of a few years by a combination of urban sprawl and the indiscriminate use of insecticides. I read more, and I came to feel that, if I succeeded in bringing bluebirds back to southern New Jersey, I would have done my small part in restoring the marvelous web of life which mankind has so disastrously torn. I built a number of bluebird houses and set them out on our land, hoping to provide the bluebirds with nesting facilities of which the growing cultivation of the countryside had deprived them. But the longed-for bluebirds didn't come, and commoner species, mostly starlings and sparrows, took over the houses I had built.

Another spring came and went. We had been back two years and still no bluebirds had visited us. My nostalgic longing for them grew. I began talking about them to my son. "Have you ever seen a bluebird?" I asked.

"Yes, lots of them," said Nedim. "Don't you remember how they nested over in the maple tree?"

"I don't mean 'blue jay,'" I said. "Bluebird. Do you know what a bluebird is?"

"Do they live around here?" asked Nedim.

"They should," I said. With a pang I realized that my children had missed one of nature's greatest delights. If I couldn't show them a living bird, at least I could tell them about it. So I dug out the pamphlets and brochures I had collected about bluebirds, and together we began reading. And then, unexpectedly, I came upon a hint as to why our own bluebird shelters had not attracted their intended tenants. I had previously overlooked a remark in one of the booklets that bluebird houses should not be placed close to human habitations.

On our three acres, it seemed, we just couldn't get the birdhouses far enough from the dooryard. This doesn't bother sparrows. But bluebirds like to be a bit farther away from people.

"What we need," I told Cavit, "is the right kind of land for putting up bluebird houses. We should have a creek or a pond with lots of rotten stumps."

I was thinking also of the rabbit family that used to hop leisurely around our lawn to nibble the dew-wet grass in the early morning. They had been murdered by hunters just outside our boundary. Nermin, my little girl, had been inconsolable that no more rabbits came, and during hunting season, she cried at the sound of gunfire. A grey squirrel who had regularly come to our oak and delighted the children with his graceful gambols had been picked out of a tree by a passing gunman. He evidently wasn't interested in the squirrel. He just wanted to kill him, and he left the small, shattered body for the children to find and mourn.

I desperately longed for a patch of land large enough to let me protect all the animals who lived there and in which our children could enjoy their companionship without having them murdered almost before their eyes.

"It has to be big enough," I said. "How does ten acres strike you?"

"It strikes me right between the eyes," Cavit said firmly. "I'm still paying the mortgage on our place and we've got to save for the kids' education."

That was all we said then, but we began to look at properties for sale. One inspection tour took us over an erratic sand trail to a forlorn clearing along a large, neglected lake. Though less than five miles from paved road, the place looked primordial. Dead trees protruded ominously over what seemed to be haunted waters. Near the bank, we came upon a small shack and a tumbledown barn. Half the barn roof had crashed down from the rafters, and smashed bottles and rusty beer cans surrounded the place like a beleaguering army. Yet despite the presence of all this trash and the predominant mood of decay, a kind of serene beauty inhabited the place. Great tall trees ringed the cabin and somehow gave the poor broken shack the aspect of a secret castle in the very depth of a great forest.

Cavit and I forced our way through the buttonbush, sweet peppers, and rank swamp grass that had grown up all around the pond. Branches of maple, oak, magnolia, and wild cherry reached down into the wild profusion of undergrowth.

Untangling ourselves from the maze of greenbrier, we scrambled over fallen trees and came to a small clearing opening the view toward the pond. Without a word Cavit and I stopped, as if to savor it. The halting of our footsteps restored a deep silence that reassured a song sparrow nearby. Suddenly he began to sing.

We went to talk to the owner, who at first treated us rather coolly. She was a rich, matronly woman with a rather stiff-backed manner, evidently in no hurry to sell anything at all. She asked us what we would do with the land. We told her our plans for an animal refuge. Her face registered disbelief and suspicion.

Crestfallen, I tried a new tack, counting on her feelings for animals. "I noticed the little elephant statues in your hallway," I said. "Are you fond of elephants?"

"Yes," she replied. "I'm a Republican."

We left it at that, but we felt encouraged when we discovered in roundabout ways that Mrs. Adams was making inquiries about us. Perhaps she thought that Cavit and I were a "front" for real estate speculators. This may have seemed a plausible explanation for our "crazy" talk about a wildlife refuge, and in my more mischievous moods I like to picture her surprise when she found out that we meant what we said.

A few weeks later she confronted us with an offer: "I wouldn't sell to a developer," she said. "But I like what you're trying to do. You'll have to take the whole parcel, though. Eighty-five acres."

The price she quoted was reasonable enough. But eighty-five acres was more than eight times what we had considered feasible. It meant a huge debt, even if we could raise the down payment.

Getting Mrs. Adams to sell had proved easier than getting Cavit to buy. True, he had been going with me to look at land and talk to realtors, but he had viewed these activities more as Sunday excursions than impending cash deals. As long as the land was unavailable, he felt safe. Now his bluff had been called, and he again retreated temporarily behind the newspaper.

His position, however, had already been undermined. Sooner or later, we both knew, we would jointly have to face the moral obligation I felt toward animals. We had already clashed on this point on several occasions. Each time, it turned out, Cavit came a little closer to my view — not as a matter of "giving in," but in the course of serious thought and honestly gained conviction.

The man who once dismissed the whole idea of an animal refuge with the curt remark, "Animals don't pay rent," was now weighing the possibility of devoting all his resources to such a project. We talked about it for days, he stressing the financial folly of such an investment, while I pointed out that the refuge represented both a way of life and a moral commitment.

At last he said sourly, "We'll have to use the kids' education money."

And with my delighted assent, that summer of 1961, he robbed our children, hocked our future, and bought the land.

A dirt road branching off toward the refuge from a paved highway a mile away was called Unexpected Road. I never found out what accounted for the unusual name, but its allegorical overtones appealed to me. It somehow pleased me to think that our home and haven was to be reached by Unexpected Road, and Cavit and I decided to name our land "Unexpected Wildlife Refuge."

It was too late in the season to rebuild the cabin before winter. But meanwhile the cabin served as base camp for exploration of the forest and swamp that now were ours. Skirting the pond, we made our way to the woods, where a dim path led along the shore and broadened out to a leaf-paved trail among the trees.

We pushed through tangles of greenbriers along the shore. "I hope we'll have beavers in our pond," I said. "Do you suppose there are any?"

Cavit was ahead of me, bending aside branches and reaching to foil the tough brier stems which grabbed at us.

"I'm at the dam," he called. Then, "Oh!. . ."

I came up to him, and we both stared at the dam. Dark water was falling over, and caught in the swift current was a dead beaver, his round furry body washed constantly by the rushing stream.

"There *were* some, anyway," Cavit said. "Hope that wasn't the last one."

We turned our eyes out to the somber pond, and looked across the expanse of lily rafts to the maze of dead trees beyond. Amidst their stark nakedness, far out, stood a huge pile of debris, heaped up in conical fashion.

"There's the beaver lodge," I whispered. "There *are* beavers here. Or at least there were." My eyes fell again on the dead beaver. "I just hope there's a pair of them left," I said.

As we walked back to the house, a crow appeared on top of a tall stub, and regarded us curiously.

"There's one crow, at least," I exclaimed. "A start on our wildlife."

"There may not be much more," said Cavit.

Indeed, we found few animals but plenty of shotgun shells. For many years, our woods had been a favored spot for hunters. I shuddered at the thought of the suffering that must have taken place. Our first step in turning a killing ground into a sanctuary was to post the land. We tacked up hundreds of *No Hunting* signs, not yet realizing that it would take far more than nails to make that message stick.

We spent every free moment at the refuge. To our immense joy, we gradually discovered that, despite past ravages, the land was not so depleted as it seemed at first, and our constant walking and watching was rewarded by many meetings with animals.

As summer and early fall went, most of the trees were swept bare, and all along the woodland paths lay leaves crisp and crinkled, for there had been no rain since they had fallen. Big flocks of robins lingered, feeding on chokeberries, persimmons, pears.

Water snakes still moved about, for the weather had not yet turned cold, but even the days were slightly chilly, and the snakes seemed sluggish, lying motionless on sunlit sections of the paths, and moving sleepily away when feet came near them or someone reached down and touched their tails.

That winter the persimmon trees were loaded with frozen fruit and became a feasting place for robins. The robins, three to six at a time, came early in the mornings, not making a sound when it was cold, but giving forth a few chirps on warm and rainy days.

Out on the iced-over pond, snow lay thick, and the skating was good where we cleared it off. Otters' tracks — a few steps and then a slide — crisscrossed the surface. Water lilies, their stems and roots visible beneath the ice near the shore, looked succulent and edible. We saw occasional tangles, gnawed on, evidently brought up when the ice had broken. From along the east shore, covered with deep snow, a woodcock flew up. I was surprised to see him on a bitter cold day. Once I saw a muskrat swimming under the ice. Then one day, when a warm spell softened the ice, I saw something that made my heart leap with happiness: sticks freshly gnawed by beavers!

Spring came early, and it came with a bound. In mid-February the red-winged blackbirds were back; and by March mourning doves had begun to call, herons were fishing in sheltered coves, and ducks were quacking in the pond. The ice was melting, and pussy willows had opened.

There was a wonderful smell in the air — damp swamp mixed with the perfume of swelling buds and future flowers. All around me new life groped upward, growing toward summer fulfillment. The time of long daylight enabled Cavit, after returning from his office, to join the children and me in our observations in various parts of the refuge. As we gained practice in being sufficiently still and unobtrusive so as not to frighten the animals, more and more different kinds disclosed themselves to view. Cavit, I, and the children usually went out singly to make our observations. Going in a group would have alarmed the animals. Every day at dinnertime, we would tell each other what we had seen.

It was still chilly, yet many nights we stayed out at the refuge, bedding down on the floor of the still-unfinished cabin. It was the time of year when we felt we had to get out there and be up early to hear, smell and feel the changing world. Bird song seems especially sweet in spring; for it is not yet the daylong chorus, but rather the occasional sounding of individual voices, like small, cheerful prophecies of the summer to come.

As soon as the ground softened, we started digging the footings for an addition to the cabin. We could hardly wait to get the cabin ready for permanent occupancy. For a family of five, the space might be a little tight, even with the addition. But with all the outdoor space around us, we felt sure we wouldn't be cramped.

Earlier we had all pitched in to clean up the place, hauling off endless loads of trash, containing an amazing proportion of empty beer cans, that the previous tenants had accumulated.

As Cavit dug the foundation of our future bedroom he uncovered baby turtles deep in the ground. Guided by instinct, they unerringly headed for the pond. Sorry to have disturbed them prematurely, we helped them down to the water. I watched one as he stood with feet partly submerged, looking about with perplexed curiosity. Having thus taken account of the world for the first time, he ambled into the water with an air of apparent self-possession and began to swim. His strokes were still feeble, but he evidently knew just what he was about. Then he encountered calamity. His shell caught against a straw on the water's surface, pulling him askew on his course.

The tiny turtle struggled valiantly to overcome the drag. His power was weak, but his persistence invincible. Ultimately, he overcame the straw and headed onward on his just-begun life journey. I sometimes think of the intrepid little turtle when I feel in need of inspiration and encouragement.

The biggest morale booster, though, came early in April, when I glimpsed the first bluebirds taking up residence at Unexpected. I stood in the cabin yard when I first spotted a small, sparrow-sized bird coming toward me from a long way off. As he drew nearer I recognized the rather fluttery, erratic flight typical of bluebirds. As he alighted on a nearby branch, I was able to verify his identity by the vivid blue back and brick-red breast with a fleck of white near the undertail. I also recognized him by his distinctive way of sitting on the branch, slightly bent over, giving a round-shouldered appearance.

"A *bluebird!*" I shouted, though there was nobody to hear me.

He took wing again, dipped into one of the birdhouses along the bank, and then flew away again. It was almost too much to hope that he would find a mate and come to stay. But the very next day, I saw a pair of bluebirds near another one of the houses I had put up. Evidently they were setting up housekeeping. I watched them for a long time, flying about the house, uttering their soft, warbling calls whose melody to me holds all the beauty of life.

I could hardly wait to meet the beavers. I had always loved the looks of beavers — their round, furry shape, suggesting their gentle temperament; their endearing waddle; their inquisitive noses adorned with long whiskers; and that curious broad paddle of a tail.

I thought that I would have to contain my eagerness until late spring, for during the cold season beavers do not often venture forth from their elaborately constructed dwellings. But to my surprise, I saw the season's first beaver while the pond was still frozen over. He was swimming beneath a thin sheet of ice, trailing bubbles that were caught under the frozen surface and marked his path like a string of pearls. He reached a point near the bank where the ice was melted. His head emerged; and after carefully reconnoitering the neighborhood for possible dangers, he gained the shore and waddled up to a spot where perennial moss provided him with a comfortable hassock.

He was medium sized, as beavers go, being about four feet long and weighing perhaps fifty pounds. But his compact, chunky body conveyed an impression of great muscular strength beneath the soft, furry coat. In my imagination, I pictured the beaver's prehistoric ancestors, the Castoroides, who weighed as much as eight hundred pounds. What splendid, powerful animals they must have been!

There were also others. As soon as we learned to tell them apart individually, we began naming them. Greenbrier and Whiskers were the senior members of the clan, and nearly every spring we happily counted some young ones, among them Fuzzy Face, Fluffy, Goldy, and Brownie. But it took a long time before the cautious beavers were convinced that it was safe to come near us.

After my first encounter with the beaver swimming under the ice, beavers rarely appeared in daytime. At night, I could occasionally see them swimming, but whenever they sensed my presence, they signaled danger by slapping their broad tails on the water and quickly dived out of sight. In the hope of observing them, I once sat quietly at the water's edge for an entire spring night, but the reward for my vigil was only the sound of distant gnawing and a rash of mosquito bites.

Gradually the beavers lost some of their shyness. Nearly every day I broke off some poplar branches, an acknowledged delicacy for beavers, and left them at the dam. Whiskers and Greenbrier came regularly toward evening to nibble on them. Greenbrier was still a little shy, and often stayed back if he saw me too close to the poplars. But Whiskers was getting quite chummy and would contentedly sit beside me after her meal to comb out her thick fur. At those times, I would talk to her gently. She listened gravely, now and then answering with a soft whine.

Despite his shyness, Greenbrier allowed me to watch him at work. One of his projects was a dam near the outflow of the pond to raise the water level. The other was a large beaver lodge near the lake shore.

He was very busy. Every evening he went out to cut down trees and to transport materials to the building site. In his mouth he carried sticks, diving on the way to gather a big armload of mud. Then, rising to his hind feet, he stalked up the steep side of the lodge he was building, carrying a big bundle of mud and sticks. He looked like a little man struggling to get up the stairs with an outsized grocery bag.

Sometimes he had a log too big to carry, and he shoved and tugged at it until he got it up the side of his building. His manner suggested that he had a firm plan in mind and knew exactly what he was doing. His effort was unhurried but persistent. Like an experienced craftsman, he seemed to be working at a comfortable, natural pace, stopping occasionally for a short breather or a snack, but always going right back to the job.

Meanwhile Whiskers was getting fatter at such a rate that I could no longer attribute her growing girth solely to the poplar feasts. I began to suspect that Greenbrier had something to do with it.

One day she stopped coming for her daily dinner. For a whole week I worried about her. At last she came back. No longer did she look like a furry blimp. She had regained her former shape, which by contrast seemed almost svelte, if that term can ever be applied to a beaver. Her breasts, the upper set located between her arms like those of a woman, were full of milk and pink nipples peeked out through her fur. Her manner seemed changed, too — reflecting what I took to be her joy in motherhood.

I resolved to find the beaver kittens, and hoped that Whiskers would not mind a respectful visit. The next day I sat down on the root of a big cedar just across from the lodge and waited. Half an hour later, Whiskers came from upstream and disappeared into the lodge. From inside I heard the mewing of the beaver kittens. Then, with the water swirling about the entrance, two baby beavers popped out. They swam around a little, awkwardly, tipping from side to side, their fur fluffy and buoyant. They looked less than a foot long, with tiny paddle tails. Soon the babies went back in, mewing excitedly.

Day after day, I came back to watch, always sitting quietly, reading with a small pile of poplar twigs at my feet. Sometimes I came at noon, to find Greenbrier at work. When he saw me, he swam swiftly back and forth, circled, and sometimes slapped his tail. I kept very still. Greenbrier began to calm down. When a week had passed, I could come to the lodge, sit down slowly, and not trigger Greenbrier's slap. Whiskers, of course, knew me too well to become alarmed and accepted my presence here as she did at the dam.

One night four babies came out. Water stirred around the lodge, and bubbles rose. With a "bloop-bloop," a baby appeared, floated along, and dived gracefully with a preliminary tip-up just like his parents. He came to the poplar, whining and trying to eat leaves. Three others appeared. Dark tails. Golden faces. One of them was a blonde with dark honey fur. They were about a month old then, still awkward and hesitant in their movements. They ate clumsily, holding the poplar twigs in delicate hands, tussling over disputed sticks with vexed whines. Sometimes one would drop his twig, then examine his empty hands in a puzzled manner.

One July afternoon Whiskers sat near me, companionably grooming her fur and talking to me from time to time with a low murmur. Greenbrier was not in sight. Giving a final pat to her fur and a scratch to her eyebrows, Whiskers ambled down the bank and eased herself into the water. Just then ripples appeared above the underwater door of the lodge, and the baby beavers popped out — one, two, three, four — and swam purposefully toward their mother. But her present mood was impatient, and she made a quick dive to avoid them. They promptly dived in around her, coming up in a roil of water and clinging to her fur. Evidently Whiskers had had a hard day, and any human mother could have identified with her vexation at the whining group. My own reaction was one of sympathy mixed with wonder at how she would solve her problem. It occurred to me that a few harsh words and a slap or two might go far. But Whiskers had other plans. Taking a long, thoughtful look my way, she turned her back on me and the kittens and swam calmly away.

I expected the kittens to follow her, but they did not. Flipping their tails, circling and diving, they began to frolic in their home pool. The sun was still bright. The swamp was very green. A Maryland yellowthroat sang lightheartedly among the laurel, while downstream a family of young flickers whined and squeaked, commenting on the world outside their hole, which they were exploring that day for the very first time.

What will Greenbrier say? I wondered. Much more cautious than his mate, he might be disturbed at finding me alone with his youngsters. I did not have long to wonder. Greenbrier came plowing rapidly downstream, and seeing me there near his young ones, swam back and forth in the yellow afternoon light, his fur glinting as he dipped underwater after each mighty slap of his tail. He was disturbed indeed and indicated his wrath by the most potent means at his command. I did not know whether he was mad at me for being there or at his mate for leaving the children in such risky hands.

At the first crack of his tail, two of the youngsters dived into the lodge. The other two, playing farther away, continued to be absorbed in their game of wrestling, each trying to push the other over backward into the water. Greenbrier circled again and again, giving a vigorous slap at each turn. The two disobedient ones paid no attention. Whenever his frantic swimming brought him close to me, I spoke softly to him. Otherwise, I kept myself strictly a part of the cedar root with which I tried to blend. Inwardly, I was as upset as Greenbrier, but for a different reason. I was contributing to the worries of a devoted father, and I felt guilty. I would have slunk away, but feeling that any action on my part would only aggravate Greenbrier's alarm, I merely tried to shrink smaller and kept on muttering in a voice I hoped might reassure.

Coming back close to me he stared up intently, sniffing the air, his tail quiet. For at least a minute we looked each other in the eye. Then Greenbrier turned, swam over to the log which is one boundary of the pool, dived under, and paddled calmly on upstream leaving me alone with his youngsters.

I felt responsible for four precious lives. The red sun was just an hour from setting. The horned owl might fly by at any time and try to carry off one of the kits. Would the babies, naive and vulnerable, be easy prey? My muscles tensed; I was prepared to throw myself across the water to shield the babies if an owl came by.

On one of these nights, a horned owl did come, sweeping low along the creek toward the east, silent as death. He passed over the beavers and alighted on a dead tree not far down the stream. From there he watched me and perhaps decided I was too big to tackle. He flew away. When the sun went down, the moon was already high, shining through the cedars beyond the lodge. Its light gleamed on little circles and wavelets churned up by the playing beaver babies. A bat flew overhead with tiny cries. Mosquitoes hummed. Should I go home before the parents came back? No. A baby-sitter does not leave her post.

Whiskers came just then, and her young ones hurried with eager cries to meet her. Swimming straight for the lodge, the mother led the four. She tipped up, dived under, and they followed, leaving a glitter of bubbles in their wake. From inside the lodge came a chorus of moans and whines, and soft mewings, as the babies settled down to eat. As the sounds became softer, I rose up, stiff from my long vigil, and splashed back through the swamp toward home. The dark was sparked with fireflies and alive with singing toads. A whippoorwill called. I felt that a great honor had been conferred upon me by Greenbrier and Whiskers in entrusting me with their children.

Whiskers has taught me much about child-rearing. She showed me that the devotion of motherhood need not extinguish independence. There can be gaiety at playtime, and the traditional picture of a mother holding a baby in her arms. There is watchful care, and providing of food; but Whiskers retains her dignity, stands up for her rights as an individual, and maintains discipline while teaching good beaver manners.

I could hardly stay away from the beaver lodge. Almost every day I waded out to watch the little beavers playing. One of their favorite games was climbing up steep banks. At first their balance was very precarious, and if one beaver kit accidentally bumped against another, they'd both topple over and fall into the water together with a loud plop.

One of the kits, Fuzzy Face, became sick. He grew visibly weaker and sometimes stayed huddled in one place for hours. His condition apparently encouraged a predator to take a bite of him. We found him one day atop the lodge, his tail bitten through and bleeding, and his body wasted to the bones. He let Cavit come right up to him and pet him.

We didn't know how to help him. Who could advise us on beavers? I called Fred Ulmer, the curator of mammals at the Philadelphia Zoo.

"It could be almost anything," he said, "perhaps some kind of infection. I really don't know what you could do."

"Would it help if we kept him in a cage where the others couldn't pick on him? Give him plenty of food?"

"Yes, that might help. They may be ostracizing him because of his sickness — driving him out of the lodge — a measure to shield others from disease. At least you could protect him so he can feed undisturbed."

Grey clouds hovered, making dark come early, and we felt the chill of rain in the air as we searched for Fuzzy Face. We had prepared a special feast to restore his strength: dog food, fresh strawberries, and fresh-cut poplar boughs.

"Maybe he's there among the reeds," Cavit said. We looked through the reeds, moving slowly along the shore. We peered into clumps of steeplebush, buttonbush, and blueberries and among the tangles of greenbrier vines. Then at the falls, I saw him, his face wedged into the sticks of the dam as if making a last effort to reach shelter. Fuzzy Face was dead.

We buried the little beaver behind the barn. For my younger children, it was a lesson in death, which is also a part of nature. For me, it was grief at the loss of someone very dear and a reminder that all of us living ones are highly perishable and should be cherished while there is time.

In my fourth spring at Unexpected, I busied myself during most of May planting millet, buckwheat, soybeans, and sunflowers — plants that make excellent wildlife food. All around me was a glorious riot of birds. Tree swallows were swarming around the birdhouses we had set up. Orioles were feeding high up in the treetops and the sun was flashing on the male oriole's brilliant plumage. Wood thrushes, tanagers, and ovenbirds sang.

As always in spring, motherhood was rampant. Everywhere at the refuge animals were being born or hatched. From April till the end of June, I could hardly stroll along the paths I had cut through the woods without coming upon heartening evidence of new life.

I remember one particular occasion when my attention was caught by the amusing sight of a quail pursuing a rather bulky blonde raccoon. Apparently the raccoon had disturbed the bird in the underbrush, and now the irate bird stalked after her, scolding incessantly. The raccoon did not seem overly alarmed and waddled on, stopping occasionally to look back at the bird. Whenever the raccoon halted, the quail advanced menacingly toward her. The raccoon expressed her disdainful unconcern by turning her back and resuming her walk.

Some sixty feet from this encounter, the raccoon climbed up the lower part of a big gum tree by the lake and disappeared into a hole in the trunk.

It was seven in the morning. I sat and waited, watching the sun rise through the mist and feeling the air grow warm. It was just as my wet seat began to ache and my feet grew numb that I again saw the raccoon in the hole. She looked at me from time to time, peered up when a plane passed overhead, licked her fur, and dozed. Right behind me was a swampy section where gnarled old gum trees and huge swamp maples made a fine living place for raccoons. I thought this raccoon was on her way home, and, seeing me, had ducked into the hollow gum to hide till I went away. But by ten o'clock she was still there, her furry back filling up the doorway. Occasionally she stretched and yawned, or looked out blinking at the bright sun.

Starting home for lunch, I waded nearer the tree to get a good look. The furry back stirred, the raccoon drew in, and then I saw two lop-eared kittens in the hole with her. It was a mother raccoon, and the hole was her nesting den. Seating myself on a log ten feet away, I sketched the kittens while they played. Their mother nursed them and groomed them with her tongue. Once she left by the back door. I couldn't see where she went. Returning, she halted just outside the tree and gave a wild, ringing call before entering, a strange, piercing sound I had never before heard. She entered her nest, picked up one of her babies, and stepped silently out the back door. Carrying him high, with his tiny tail just trailing the water, she waded away, not looking back. The other one, left alone, whimpered loudly. His voice was squeaky as he gave forth heartbroken, screechy kitten wails. After fifteen minutes his cries gradually subsided; his head drooped and he fell asleep. The mother came back soon and took him away. Once she stopped to get a better grip on his scruff but she never looked back.

Only then did I realize the tragedy I had caused. Because of me, the mother had taken away her youngsters and left her house desolate. Now I understood the meaning of that curious piercing cry — so different from the contented whicker of the raccoons' usual conversation. I had heard the anguished lament of an exiled mother.

Though shaken by remorse, I could not contain my curiosity about the abandoned raccoon house. I looked inside the dim hollow and found it lined with soft shreds of cedar bark. The hole itself had been filled up with sticks and leaves until the floor was level with the bottom of the entrance. That was how I had been able to see the babies inside.

Shortly afterward, as I sat near the dam to watch Whiskers, I saw another raccoon. Whiskers sat quietly, combing her fur, when the raccoon came out of the thicket right behind her and came forward to eat the food I had put on the dam for raccoons. She was much more cautious than the beavers and never came close to me.

The raccoon and the beaver were quite curious about each other and often approached within two feet to sniff. Neither seemed afraid of the other, and they ate peacefully in each other's company. Since the raccoon cared nothing for poplar and the beaver did not fancy the raccoon's fare, there was no competition over food.

Perhaps I had been naive in expecting the surrounding towns to be delighted at having an animal haven in their midst. While most people subscribe to the principle that kindness to animals is a good thing, they rarely connect this idea with action of any sort. When I tried to explain that loving concern for animals entails practical responsibility for their survival and welfare, I generally met with uncomprehending indifference.

A handful of people, however, seemed downright hostile to the notion of an animal refuge. In some strange, perhaps subconscious way, they feared any kind of animal and were uneasy about animals settling anywhere in the neighborhood. A few farmers were incensed that I might harbor creatures who would raid their fields. For a while, the only real appreciation of our efforts came from poachers, who considered an animal refuge an ideal hunting ground, the idea of shooting in a sanctuary being about par for the prevailing level of sportsmanship.

The first of many incidents occurred soon after we had posted the land with hundreds of signs proclaiming the terrain as a refuge. Within a week, some of the signs had been torn down or defaced by hunters furious at being deprived of their accustomed shooting grounds. The wooden backings on which we had mounted the signs had been hacked to pieces.

I felt my scalp prickle.

"What will we do?" I asked.

"Put them right back," said Cavit, his jaw set.

Fortunately, we had a supply of spare signs. One by one we replaced the mangled posters along the road, working late into the dusk.

Suddenly headlights glared at us and a car pulled up. This was what I had dreaded. But when it came, I was calm.

The sullen hunter in the car did not take it in good grace when he saw us posting our land.

"Trying to keep it all to yourself, eh?" he sneered, leaning out of the car. "A private game preserve!"

I tried to explain the difference between a game preserve for hunting and a true animal refuge. But I failed to get the point across. Compassion for the hunted was simply not within the hunter's range of sympathy and comprehension. Spinning his wheels on the dirt road, he whipped his car around and roared off. I had an uneasy feeling that we had not seen the last of him.

"Let's notify the local game warden," Cavit suggested. "Maybe he can help us guard the place. I suppose that's part of his duties."

Responding to our phone call, the warden came to see us. He was a pleasant, well-mannered young man who explained politely that he could do nothing to protect the refuge.

"It's my job to see that there's no poaching out of season," he told us. "And I have to make sure hunting licenses are in order. But if anyone trespasses on your land, that's for the police to handle. You'd have to make a complaint, and sign a warrant for arrest."

"But aren't you here to protect the animals?" we asked innocently.

"Against illegal taking," he said. "I love to hunt myself. It's the good old American tradition, you know."

I felt like saying, "So is shooting Indians," but kept it in.

We were on our own. Public authorities were evidently unwilling to extend themselves in our behalf, and even the state conservation officers regarded our venture with apparent indifference.

Not until later did I learn why this was so. The state wildlife agencies depend on the sale of hunting licenses for much of their revenue. This tends to pervert their mission. Often they end up by encouraging hunting rather than wildlife conservation. They are pushed further in this direction by political pressure from gun clubs, gun dealers, and gun manufacturers. Since there is not enough public land to accommodate the hordes of licensed hunters, the authorities tend to look the other way when hunters encroach on private property.

All this raises the question as to the real purpose of the various national and state wildlife agencies. Do they exist to protect animals or to provide animals for hunters to kill? The issue gains political significance from the fact that every one of us is required to subsidize hunting through our taxes. Obviously, there is a fiscal inequity here to which any taxpayer may rightly object.

Every year, during hunting season, Cavit and I patrol the refuge constantly, Cavit taking his annual vacation at that time to perform this guard duty. Time and again we have confronted hunters within our borders, and while most of them left peaceably, quite a few were rather unpleasant about it.

One evening, Cavit and I spotted a hunter right beneath one of our *No Hunting* signs. To our surprise, the hunter immediately took the offensive: "Get away from here," he ordered. "You're spoiling my shot. This is private land. Do you know whose land this is?"

"I know whose land this is," Cavit said. "Mine. And I'm patrolling it. What's your name?"

"None of your business," the hunter replied, in defiance of a law that stipulates that trespassing hunters must identify themselves when challenged by a landowner.

There was a tense silence.

The hunter said slowly: "There *could* be an accidental shooting, you know. Or someone could touch a match to your place."

Then he retreated down the road toward the boundary of the refuge, but not before he had ostentatiously cocked his gun.

Soon afterward we had more tangible tokens of a hunter's displeasure. Returning to the cabin after a week's absence, we immediately noticed a broken window. As we came closer we saw that the door was peppered with bullets.

"They shot off the lock!" Cavit called from the porch. As we pushed the door open, a shower of glass fell about our feet. The house was a shambles, the furniture kicked over, the glassware broken, and my father's paintings ripped by shot. His animal pictures had been used as targets.

Cavit and I intensified our patrols, crisscrossing our woods. It was our second autumn at the refuge. The gum leaves were turning red, acorns falling from their cups, and duck tracks coming from the pond clear up to the steps in front of the cabin. The duck tracks were intermingled with those of squirrels and quail. I couldn't make a gun fit into this picture, and refused to carry one.

My only defense was faith. But my faith was a straw. When I pictured invading gunners, and me meeting them unarmed and helpless, I shrank. I prayed, "Father, forgive them, for they know not what they do." But did I really feel it? And if I could forgive anything done to myself or Cavit, could I forgive their murderous intentions toward the animals?

Rather than condemn hunters, I tried to understand them. I tried to talk with them, to learn their reasons and their feelings. If I could approach them with understanding rather than fear or hostility, I felt, perhaps I could help them change their attitudes.

Our own attitude also changed. Cavit decided not to carry a gun on patrol. After thinking about it, we reached the conclusion that people who don't believe in violence should not carry weapons. Sure, it was risky to meet the trespassers unarmed, but Cavit and I were willing to back our principles with our lives.

When we met hunters on our land we drew them into conversation, and, if they seemed at all responsive, invited them into our home.

A surprising number of hunters turned out to be decent, pleasant men. We gradually came to realize that the majority of hunters are not vicious moral morons, but are good people tragically misled by outmoded tradition and commercial propaganda. Most so-called "outdoors" magazines glorify hunting with a kind of "tough-guy" sentimentality that appeals to men's egos. As a result, these otherwise decent people come to feel that they owe it to themselves to go out and kill something.

We got along quite well with some of the hunters we asked in, but when the talk turned to hunting, all too often their views and ours seemed to go past each other without ever touching on common ground.

Time and again we hear hunters say, "Why not shoot animals? That's what they're for."

I counter this with another question: "What are *you for*?" But this only draws blank stares. The idea that a creature has the right to exist for his own sake and to enjoy his life seems to be incomprehensible to many people. They cannot find it within themselves to respect another creature's right to live — regardless of "what he is for." That makes it hard to argue against murder.

Fortunately, public awareness of the needs of fellow creatures is steadily growing. Preservationist ideas are now getting wider attention than ever before. This, I believe, is preparing the soil for more intensive education work on behalf of animals and for suitable political expression of such concern.

As part of my own contribution toward this educative effort I have frequently spoken to audiences of all kinds, including children's groups. And it is in my contact with children that I find the most encouraging sign of all.

Nearly without exception, children have a natural fondness and genuine sympathy for animals and appreciation of an animal's beauty and joy of living. To me, this confirms that man does not have an inborn urge to kill, as is often claimed by those who take a pessimistic view of such related phenomena as hunting, warfare, and wanton cruelty.

Lately we have had less trouble with trespassers than before. Apparently, our constant patrolling has finally convinced the hunters that we are both vigilant and uncompromising. But while we have succeeded in reducing encroachment, we have no control over hunters who virtually ring the refuge, camping just beyond our boundary. The animals, of course, do not know where the boundary lies.

When I read the sad statistics of the long and cruel war man wages on his fellow creatures, I long for ways to atone for all the unknown suffering. My mind searches for the individual fate behind the numbers, wishing that my sympathy could make what is happening less terrible. When I speak of hunting, my memories are of crippled animals staggering into the refuge, bleeding from their wounds. In my own mind I cannot reduce the anguish and tragedy of countless creatures to a set of statistics.

For life and death is always individual. Statistics deny and obscure this fact. There is no common denominator of existence. For life and death, the operative number is always one. That, perhaps, is what is meant by saying that a human being has a soul. I am sure animals do, too.

I am the Woman

Joan Dobbie

I am the woman who
tore the bird
away from the cat

swaddled it lightly
in terry cloth

paced up and down
the street with it
not knowing what to do next

but then felt it move
shift in her hand
shuffle and flutter

I am the woman
who opened a bundle
and saw a bird rise

Milk and Honey
Aileen La Tourette

Some time ago I had to undergo a minor operation, minor in a dual sense of the word. It was a tonsillectomy that I required, something ordinarily endured in childhood when it may be uncomfortable, trying, even terrifying to a degree; but not, I assure you, the horrific trauma it becomes when performed on the mature. After the operation, I lost my voice. I felt far worse than that mean phrase communicates. I felt as if my voice had been amputated. I even heard it, as those who lose limbs are said to feel them in a phantom reconstruction. My voice was everywhere and nowhere. It existed only in my head.

My distress became extreme. I slept not at all. I seemed to hear my ghostly voice all the better at night, when all other voices were silent. I lay, moonlight striping my white hospital sheets, for I was moved to a private room, whether in my own interests or those of my fellow patients, listening, trying vainly to move my lips in tune with the sounds I heard, an arcane exercise that I can only describe as a ghostly inverse of lip-reading.

White on white, moonlight on crisp hospital cotton, changed daily (much to my distress, as I was used to enjoying a nest-like accumulation of crumbs, books, newspapers and other debris on my mattress at home), and the pale medium-like accompaniment of my detached voice — these were the color scheme of my anemic hours. Friends came to visit me at first, then began to slacken the pace of their visits.

I lay on what I began to imagine was indeed my ice floe and drifted into a stupor which might have led me into the ultimate silence, had it not been for Gemma.

Gemma was the woman next door. We had a doorstep relationship, which had all the subtle shadings such relationships hold if left alone to flower in their native habitat, and not brought inside to be bribed and tamed with tea or even with gin. They are a special sort of meeting and must be respected as such.

Gemma understood this. She tiptoed into my room, looking abashed, as if she half-expected the frost of my white, weary kingdom to chill her, too. I wept at the sight of her. My Beatrice had come, had brought me what I so desperately needed, a human voice rooted in a human throat and a human life.

We spoke a great deal about death. I was obsessed with it. Thanks to Gemma, I realized that I equated death with silence and hence had placed myself beyond the pale, as it were, from the moment my voice had fled. Half-seriously, using the pencil and paper which had replaced my phantom voice in her presence, I informed her that I had no intention of allowing myself to be booked into heaven, whatever my eventual fate. There were no animals in heaven, it was well known. Animals have no souls. Hence I would not suffer an eternity there.

She frowned. "Surely you don't believe that," she exclaimed. Before I could answer, she went on, and before I knew it, she had bidden me rise from my sickbed and follow her into another world indeed, not the one I had half-seriously anticipated, but the world of the story, which one must become a child to enter. I stretched out my hand as I closed my eyes, and we were off.

"Streets flowing with milk and honey," she began, patiently. "That indicates the presence of cows and bees for a start, does it not?"

I opened my eyes, thinking an answer was required. She nodded at me to close them again, and resumed.

"Anyway, I can tell you that there are animals in heaven, with the irrefutable evidence of an eyewitness. I have been there, you see.

"I, too, had dreaded the eventuality of heaven as it was presented to me. It sounded, quite simply, too white. A pale, gleaming, sterile place, rather like a modern kitchen without food or drink or mess of any sort, without a cat to brush your ankles, whining for food or purring like the casserole you lift the lid to sniff every few minutes for the sheer pleasure of it. White inimical textures, everything gleaming like tusks or formica, a synthetic gleam, an infinite pretense. The Emperor's new clothes come to life, but forever; for to protest against the glacial perfection of it, to fail to appreciate it, would be to mark yourself out as a sinner and not a saint. A conspiracy of silence, a unanimity of boredom in which misery lacked even company.

"I would protest. I would refuse and refute the empty glory. I would throw myself down and shriek with frustration. I would heave myself against the padded walls and keep up my tantrums until they were forced to remove me to the lakes of fire. There I would at least have warmth, light, color and noise.

"I died. It was stupid of me, really. Not even an original death. I was quite livid with anger, which was advantageous to me in carrying out my plan. I arrived at the celestial gates determined to confront the concierge with my rage.

"To my immense astonishment, this personage turned out to be not a self-important St. Peter or an angel bristling with pin-feathers, but a great hairy ape amiably combing her armpits with a flashy comb set with what, in the circumstances, I could only assume to be real rubies. I was waved in with all the insouciance of a drugged parking-lot attendant, and in I went.

"Heaven, my dear friend, is entirely populated by animals. It is we humans who have no souls. Once you consider the proposition, it begins to make sense, doesn't it? Of course, you begin to mutter to yourself, of course! Another of those lies told according to the classical inverted design, like Adam's rib. Your brain is accustomed to simply turning the proposition presented on its head. This one simply slipped by undetected. Adam came head first from Eve's womb, where else? The first sin of our race was not the silly apple which she pushed on him in traditional maternal fashion, adding perhaps that it was good for him, would keep his bowels open, etc.; but the lie. Adam's lie. We are of course all sprung from the incestuous union of these two, something which, as Freud almost guessed, we all darkly suspect. As to the deleterious genetic effects of incest, well, that we must judge for ourselves.

"I correct my theology on one point: the sin is not the lie, but the envy that produces the lie. Adam envies his mother, and lies as a consequence. His pride will not permit him to drop (like an apple) from her womb; she must arrive from his rib. Is pride, then, the sin, or are pride and envy twins? Never mind. Enough scholasticism. We humans envy animals something they have which we have not; souls. Therefore we lie, and exclude them from our country club in the sky, our heaven.

"'But why,' I ask the ape who admitted me, when she turns up again, 'are there no people here?'

"'Oh,' she beams in return, affectionately combing my cowlick, 'we do hope you'll be the first to stay.'

"With that she linked her arm through mine and skipped me away to tour the sanctuary.

"Others had come then, I mused, and gone away again. Was there perhaps a catch, some unpleasantness to evolve from the delight I saw and felt? I could only wait and see. It had also occurred to me that there might be some few advantages to be gained from my position as the only human being in heaven.

"The old notion of spellbound idleness crumbled before my eyes. Energy is eternal delight — and vice versa. Heaven was a place of bustle and change. It was the most creative place I have ever seen, a teeming hive of activity, all pursued — this was the secret — for its own sake, which is to say, for love. The very grapes grew for love, the wine fermented for love. I can hardly describe the sensation except to say that it was close, very close, to what happens on earth, with the sole difference of love. I cannot make it more exact or specific than that.

"Heaven is more down-to-earth than earth, that's the funny thing. Every action was practical, with a visionary practicality, without the impractical division we make on earth between work and play, between vision and realization. All such divisions had disappeared, and the memory of them was fading fast.

"The animals spent a good deal of time watching the planet earth with a sublimely compassionate detached perplexity. They sent legions of guardian animals, of the sort we name dogs, cats, 'domestic' breeds, downwards to try and help the human race. It was pitiful to witness the treatment meted out to these voluntarily mute creatures, who simply, silently, loved. Only the knowledge that they would be received back in paradise kept them going through successive abandonments, ill-treatments, deprivations and insults of all sorts.

"Sometimes they watched the antics of earth, nestling close to each other and chomping bits of fruit like children at a horror movie, squealing and hiding their eyes during the worst episodes. Sometimes they turned away from the spectacle and went to exorcise its ghastliness with a bath in a fresh spring or a session of gardening. Sometimes, of course, they sighed over human romance, or smiled over human joy. And sometimes they howled and hooted with laughter over the follies and fads of the human circus.

"How could we have assumed that God was of our species? Or of any species? I began, slowly, to understand certain things that had been murky before. Certain images came back to me. The Golden Calf, for instance. And half-digested bits of information; for example, the number of animals rescued from the flood, as opposed to the number of people. . . and: consider the lilies. Even plants could be held up to us as models.

"As, of course, they are. Buddhists come closer to recognizing their exemplars in the universe than we do. Only one thing was missing in heaven, with all the richness of the insight that began to come my way, to flood my being. I began to wonder whether it was the lack of that one thing that had driven others of my race from heaven's precincts. I could not share my craving with the animals. There was something that divided us irrevocably, after all. There were no books in heaven, not even Shakespeare or a Gideon Bible rattling around somewhere. I looked.

"Had I not stumbled upon a fatal flaw in the great design? I was intercepted while searching, blindly, for something I might read, and gently interrogated as to the cause of my agitation. When I explained, I was met with a smile. My tutor began to talk, somewhat irrelevantly I thought, about trees and paper, and the striking coincidence of the fact that human beings used these classicists, these poets, for raw material on which to produce their own works. Indeed, the animals had worked out that eventually all the millions of humans with typewriters might produce a living tree.

"Heaven was a library, an orchard of books. The trees were hung with fictions, inscribed on their leaves, all different but consistent to just the degree necessary to keep the warmth of familiarity. I could spend eternity curled up in a tree.

"But first I had further discoveries to make, far too many to list. Ostriches, for example, were mystics of the school and persuasion of Blake, whom they greatly admired (for animals, while on earth, devour the contents of our books without even opening the covers. They are engaged in so doing during the day, as they drowse or graze, as we think). Infinity in a grain of sand was their total preoccupation.

"Bats were the mother-figures of the upper air, forever offering their adorable little breasts. After much trepidation, I tasted this elixir and found it delicious, as was the sensation of being folded in the sable wings of a bat-mother, and listening to the vibrations of her singular lullaby.

"Rats were, of course, scientifically-minded, forever suggesting, tactfully, ways in which the human race might improve itself while allowing the humans to believe the ideas so presented were their own.

"I had thought to dominate this divine menagerie! Instead I fell into a stupor of depression and panic. How had I allowed myself to be so deceived? I was patted and fêted by my animal friends. Homesick, they sympathized. They understood.

"No, I protested. Homesick, for a place of degradation?

"I missed my friends, they suggested.

"Not a bit of it, I stoutly returned. On the contrary. Not one of my former acquaintances would, or could, comprehend what I now knew. I wished rather to relinquish my human skin, my human identity, to defect, as it were, to the better side.

"Yes, they said hurriedly, it was a temptation to which humans were prone, conversion, but —

"Not a temptation, I persisted. It was evolution. They looked somewhat embarrassed at this. A few of them turned aside to whistle or hum in their characteristic ways. I realized too late that evolution was not a notion that could appeal to them as anything but the supreme delusion of the human mind, in the circumstances.

"I apologized. I had decided, I continued, determined to make up for my error by making good my resolve, which species I wished to join.

"They looked up, silent; rather downcast, I thought. Then again, selection meant exclusion. If I joined one, I could not join all. Hence, perhaps, the rationale for their sorrow.

"I had settled on the zebra. There was no killing or being killed in heaven, I might add. Hunting was pure sport. Food was simply there, as I have explained. Meat was never missed; the taste for it had been extinguished from my palate. It had become unimaginable that one might ingest flesh. The prime disadvantage of zebrahood, then, was irrelevant here. On the other hand, they retained their air of delicacy, though no longer actually delicate of ankle or of heart. They preserved a slight air of graceful fragility, a faint air of invalidism, which would suit my bookish proclivities very well indeed.

"I presented my case with wit and brevity, or so I thought. My audience, by now sizeable, did not laugh when laughter was indicated. I thought I was demonstrating a praiseworthy honesty in describing my laziness. They frowned heavily, seemed distracted by some communal sorrow, which irritated me.

"I fell silent. Then I realized that the sadness in their faces was the sadness of farewell. We were parting.

"'What have I done,' I exclaimed, 'to be banished to hell?' For I presumed that was my destination.

"'You have banished yourself,' they replied. 'There is no hell except of your making, as you know, if you allow yourself to know; just as there is no heaven, except the one that you yourself create. You have made a hell by your betrayal of your own kind. You have lost your soul. All of you have lost your souls in the same manner.' They shook their heads, baffled. 'Not one of you has ever wished to return and attempt to instruct your fellows. Not one. There are no ghosts, no voices from beyond the grave, simply because no human has ever consented to become a ghost, to haunt a friend or relative with warnings or visions or greetings.

"'Now you must go,' they finished. 'Back, of course. To try to learn to love your own kind and so develop a soul. Good luck,' they said. You can do it,' they said, trying to put confidence into their broken, defeated voices. 'We shall be there to assist you, remember —'

"The orchestral insects played me out with a mock-triumphal piece meant to boost my spirits, but — "

But . . .

IV.

Creating the new world in the process of dismantling the old . . .

A Letter to
the City Council

Theresa Corrigan

*In 1987, at the height of pit bull hysteria, the Sacramento City Council
began considering a proposal to ban or severely restrict pit bulls. Because I
count a number of pit bulls as part of my immediate family and friends and
have always known them to be gentle and timid animals, I was incensed at
the proposed discrimination.*

*One night when a friend who was working to defeat the proposal showed
me the city staff report for the ordinance, I rather sardonically remarked that
having worked for years at the Sacramento Rape Crisis Center, I thought
human males were certainly a greater threat; maybe we should have an
ordinance for them. We all laughed, since such a proposal is not unusual
among women who've worked with victims of male violence, but is not
usually spoken aloud in the world. It was this common, and, to many,
unspeakable suggestion that led to the following satire.*

*I sent a copy to each Council member and to the newspaper at the
university where I teach. From the Council members I heard nothing; from
the audience of* The Hornet *I received everything from praise to death
threats. The article seemed to touch a nerve far deeper than I intended. Total
strangers came up to me — some (mostly women) to thank me and tell me
they had put up copies of the article on their office walls and refrigerators,
others (mostly men) to let me know I should be "strung up," "tied and
quartered," or "hog-tied."*

The City Council is currently considering the passage of an
ordinance essentially banning pit bulls from the city of
Sacramento based on a report of seven deaths or serious injuries to
humans caused by pit bulls in the past four years in the Sacramento
area (from a staff report to the City Council 8/27/87). While this

figure obviously raises concerns, Sacramento humans face a considerably more formidable threat which should take precedence for action by the Council. During the same period of time, human males have been responsible for at least 2,056 serious injuries or deaths to other humans (based on conviction statistics from the State Department of Justice Bureau of Criminal Statistics). In light of the low rate of convictions for violent crimes, we can assume that this figure may represent as few as 10 percent of the actual crimes committed. (And we cannot begin to speculate on the number of serious injuries or deaths inflicted on pit bulls by human males, since these crimes usually go not only unreported but uninvestigated by appropriate authorities.) In addition, serious injuries and deaths caused by men have more than doubled in the past two years. It is apparent that human males pose a much greater threat to the Sacramento community than do pit bulls.

Even if we consider crime rates, men are responsible for a higher percentage of serious injuries to humans than pit bulls: pit bulls have been attributed with 78 percent of all serious dog bites, while men have committed 89 percent of all physical and sexual assaults and murders.

Therefore, we can only conclude that we need an ordinance controlling human male behavior more than one governing pit bulls. Since all the preliminary work has been done on the pit bull ordinance, we can borrow its language in constructing a new ordinance for men. The following makes use of this language:

What accounts for man's antisocial behavior? Humans are social animals highly attuned to reading facial and posture signals from both other humans and animals. They can communicate their own intentions and can read the moods and intentions of others. However, men have been bred historically for fighting. As such, they display genetically based physical and behavioral characteristics which reflect their heritage and which are often different from the characteristics of other humans. Most humans fight only when necessary to protect food, territory, or a mate or when provoked by the flight of a potential prey. However, men will attack with no provocation and once engaged, will fight until they physically cannot continue. Therefore, a gender specific ordinance requiring special precautions for humans that are innately dangerous would allow greater protection for public health and safety without relying on individual, case by case complaints.

The newly proposed ordinance shall incorporate the following provisions:

1. Any woman wishing to keep a man must pay a $500 licensing fee. Only those men who are properly licensed on the effective date of the ordinance may remain in the city. They will be subject to registration, to be completed within 60 days after the ordinance takes effect. No new men may be brought into the city after the effective date and newborn males must be removed from the city within eight weeks of birth.

2. For the purpose of this ordinance, man is defined as any human who cannot establish his femaleness.

3. All registered men must be maintained in conformity with the following conditions:

a. Confined securely indoors (no open doors, windows, screens, etc.) or outside in an enclosure.

b. Must be under the control of a female adult. May not be chained to trees, posts, etc.

c. Warning signs, "Human male on premises," required.

d. Must carry $500,000 liability insurance coverage.

4. Harboring an unregistered man or harboring a registered man in violation of the ordinance conditions is a misdemeanor with a minimum $500 fine and a possible jail sentence up to thirty (30) days.

5. A man's registration may be suspended or revoked, subject to appeal, if he is not maintained as required, if the liability insurance lapses, or if the man engages in any behavior which falls within our definition of "vicious," including an unprovoked attack which requires any defensive action by a person or animal to prevent bodily injury or property damage (including injury to another male). Upon revocation or suspension, the man must be removed from the city within ten (10) days.

Questions of constitutionality may be raised by such an ordinance based on issues of vagueness and equal protection, but such challenges can be effectively answered. Vagueness is clearly not a real problem. It is certainly easier to determine the gender of a human male than the breed of any number of dogs that generally fit the description of pit bull. As to the equal protection issue, the general rule is that legislation is presumed to be valid and will be sustained if the classification drawn by the statute is rationally related to a legitimate state interest. It is certainly in the city's interest to regulate its most dangerous menace.

Although this proposed ordinance may sound harsh and perhaps even discriminatory, if we can save the life of one innocent women or child, it will have been worth the inconvenience it may cause to some.

I urge you to reconsider your priorities, to recognize that the human male is the truly vicious animal, and to support an ordinance that would get to the root of the problem.

Sincerely,
Theresa Corrigan

The Arrogant Eye and Animal Experimentation
Carol J. Adams

The Bible says that all of nature (including woman) exists for man. Man is invited to subdue the earth and have dominion over every living thing on it, all of which is said to exist "to you" "for meat." Woman is created to be man's helper. This captures in myth Western Civilization's primary answer to the philosophical question of man's place in nature: everything that is is resource for man's exploitation. With this world view, men see with arrogant eyes which organize everything seen with reference to themselves and their own interests. — Marilyn Frye

What distinguishes man from woman is his access to representation, to cultural symbolization, the power of naming, in which he uses women, along with all the other silent animals, as symbols, as objects for representation. — Susanne Kappeler

Current animal rights scholarship generally fails to acknowledge the locus of its discussion: it is talking in and about a patriarchy; the people whose conduct it discusses are people who are constituting themselves as subjects in a culture suffused with human male cultural symbolization. Nor have feminists fully addressed the implications of the androcentric nature of science for the other animals. Animal experimentation is part of a patriarchal culture in which science, like masculinity, is "tough, rigorous, impersonal, competitive and unemotional," as Sandra Harding writes in *The Science Question in Feminism.*

John Berger first argued in "Why Look at Animals?" that we have transformed animals into spectacles, and so restricted our interactions with animals that they have disappeared from our lives as independent beings, diminished to representations of human fantasies regarding what is exotic, wild, or sentimental. In "Why Look at Women?" Susanne Kappeler shows how in this respect women are interchangeable with the other animals. Her insights into the way in which the dominant subjectivity in our culture — men's — is constructed through objectifying others provide a framework for exploring the feminist implications of the oppression of other animals. In particular, the rituals associated with the vivisection of the other animals and animal experimentation reveal a fundamental way in which twentieth-century patriarchal culture looks at animals. Within patriarchal culture, constituting oneself as a subject involves having an object who is looked at. By its reliance on the object status of the other animals, non-human animal experimentation provides one means for achieving subjectivity as it is constructed within a patriarchy.

Problem I: The Arrogant Eye: The Human Male Gaze

In a world ordered by sexual imbalance, pleasure in looking has been split between active/[human] male and passive/[human] female. The determining [human] male gaze projects its phantasy onto the [human] female figure which is styled accordingly. In their traditional exhibitionist role women are simultaneously looked at and displayed, with their appearance coded for strong visual and erotic impact so that they can be said to connote *to-be-looked-at-ness.*
— Laura Mulvey

The history of representation is the history of the [human] male gender representing itself to itself — the power of naming is men's. Representation is not so much the means of representing an object through imitation (matching contents) as a means of self-representation through authorship: the expression of subjectivity. Culture, as we know it, is patriarchy's self-image.
— Susanne Kappeler

In patriarchal culture, gaze is an essential aspect of subjectivity — the act of looking is an aspect of being self-identified, active, assertive, of knowing who one is. We are a visually oriented species, but the ways in which we look are socially constructed. One is not assertive in our culture, which so values assertiveness, without being assertive over; one knows who one is by defining oneself against others. "Subjectivity as envisaged in patriarchal culture is attainable but through oppression and objectification: subject status equals supremacy over an other, not intersubjectivity. Only then does it produce the feeling of pleasure, the feeling of life. How can the subject be sure that he is high if no one is low, how can he know he is free if no one is bound?" writes Kappeler. This formula allows for no reciprocity, no "intersubjectivity" as Kappeler calls it. Being a subject requires an object; while our species is capable of a great range of behavior, the cultural relationship paradigmatic in the West is one of subject to object. This paradigmatic relationship is typified by what can be called the human male gaze, arising as it does within a patriarchal culture, and exemplified as it is by the way men look at women. In this paradigmatic gaze, it is what the object does for the gazer and what the gazer does with the object that is important; the object's own intrinsic subjectivity is irrelevant in this relationship.

A primary means of making a subject into an object — of objectifying a being — is through depictions, representations. Representation enables conceptualizations in which the subject-object dichotomy recurs; looking at representations provides the gazer with pleasure while simultaneously reinforcing the distance between subject and object as unbridgeable. We learn within a patriarchal culture that the subject feels himself *to be* by the response he perceives in himself to looking at objects arranged for his viewing. This "arrogant eye" is an aspect of what constitutes human male subjects over against human female objects, and contributes also to constituting scientific subjects over the other animals. And because both men and women assimilate patriarchal culture, the human male gaze is exhibited by both when looking at other animals. The practice of animal experimentation is both enabled and reinforced by the unquestioned, culturally established *to-be-looked-at-ness* of animals.

Problem II: Animal Experimentation

The [human] male gender's project of constituting [human] male subjectivity is a serious business that has nothing to do with fictional and playful fantasy. It is the means by which the [human] male subject convinces himself that he is real. . . . He feels the more real, the less real the Other, the less of a subject the Other, the less alive the Other. And the reality he creates for himself through his cultural self-representation is the Authorized Version of reality, the dominant reality for all of us.
— Susanne Kappeler

We cannot know how the other animals subjectively experience looking, and we seldom make the inquiry: particularly in animal experiments the environment is constructed so that the only look is that of subject to object, and the object's look is contained, restricted, eliminated. It is remarkable how many experiments fetishize the animals' eyes in a way that guarantees that the animals will be injured or blinded and thus physically unable to return the experimenter's look. The long-established Draize test, often used in testing cosmetics and chemical products, involves dripping concentrated solutions of these products into rabbits' eyes. An article in *The Animals' Agenda* quotes a former animal care trainee at the Gillette testing laboratory in Rockville, Maryland: "I was walking through the eye room and saw one technician grab a rabbit who had pus draining out of his swollen eye. He forced the eye open to examine it under bright light. I've heard rabbits scream before, but never like that." In the name "eye room," the arrogant eye achieves an eponymous existence. And perhaps it is because of the importance of sight to us that the Draize test has become so effective a rallying point for animal rights activists.

Consider Helen, a female monkey, whose visual cortex was removed. Helen can scan her surroundings but she is unable to identify what she sees. The title of her experimenter's report, "Seeing and Nothingness" — an obvious reference to Sartre's *Being and Nothingness* — makes clear the ontological nature of the human male gaze: Seeing is Being. I see an object, therefore I am a subject. The patriarchal subject is turning subjects into non-seeing objects, thus robbing them of the notion of subjectivity and being.

But as Susanne Kappeler observes the important feature is not blindness *per se*, but the subject's attempt to turn the "object" into "a non-seeing one — i.e. to rob them of *his* notion of subjectivity and being. But of course, whether blinded or with averted gaze, the animal or the woman still remains a subject" — in reality.

Besides imputing an ontological crisis which accompanies a disabled gaze — not seeing is not being — "Seeing and Nothingness" hauntingly, and no doubt inadvertently, indicts the animal experimentation it enacts. Once her visual cortex was destroyed, Helen was dependent on interaction with others to help her relearn what it was she saw. After making this fact clear, the experimenter, Nicholas Humphrey, reports that because he had to finish his thesis, "she was left to her own devices for about ten months — such devices, that is, as she could manage in a small cage." When Humphrey describes her later opportunity to walk in the open air, he calls it "the experience of three-dimensional space," conceding that life in a cage is not fully real. Helen's object status is confirmed not only by the impunity with which she can be deprived of sight but also by the restriction to a less than real life in a cage.

Kappeler argues: "Viewing and self-expression are themselves actions in the world, actions performed by the culture's legitimated subjects. In the structure of representation, the act of perception, of viewing and of self-expression, is predominant and overlays the represented actions of a (potentially) represented agent." The way most people learn about animal experimentation — scientist to scientist, animal supporters to their constituency — is through representations and reports. The denial of access of most lay people to scientific laboratories reinforces the dependence on representations and reports, visual and verbal texts, to communicate the details of the encounter between the arrogant human eye and the other animals. Photographs and videotapes are ineluctably a part of much experimentation these days, reinforcing the subject-object dichotomy enacted by the experiments themselves. A particularly notorious example comes from the videotapes stolen in 1984 from Dr. Thomas Gennarelli's Head Injury Clinical Research Center at the University of Pennsylvania — a laboratory widely considered as one of the best in the country. (We do not know how extreme this example is because most videotapes of animal experiments are as closely guarded as the laboratories themselves.) The following dialogue is described by a reporter for the *Philadelphia Daily News*:

> The tapes show injured monkeys tied to wooden baby
> highchairs, drooling from the mouths, arms and legs
> flapping uncontrollably. Researchers twist their heads
> from one side to the other and clap hands to see if they
> respond. In one scene, a dark-haired woman supports a
> monkey while its [*sic*] arms and legs dangle.
> "She's on TV holding her monkey," a male off-camera
> voice jokes. "Say cheese."
> Again a male voice says, "Better hope the anti-
> vivisectionists don't get a hold of this," while a woman
> tries to get a monkey to move its [*sic*] arms. Another voice
> says, "He [*sic*] has the punk look." The monkey, which has
> been shaved from the middle of the chest to the top of
> the head, has electrodes taped all over its [*sic*] body, and
> has a red scar in the middle of its [*sic*] head, extending
> from the back of the skull to its [*sic*] forehead.
> "Show his [*sic*] part to the camera," a man says. — *The
> Animals' Agenda*

Note the composition of this representation: the human being
filmed with the animal is female, reconfirming the cultural role of
the human male gaze which looks at women and animals. "Say
cheese," she is told, for she is posing as well. As with photographic
representations of women in which they are silenced objects who
stimulate banal discussion between men, the voices in this portion
of the videotape are men's; the woman, like the monkey, is silenced,
and she follows orders given by an off-camera male director.
Through such representations women's and animals' object status is
both reinforced and shown to be similar.

When Kappeler discusses how representations enable the viewer
of them to feel real, she posits that "he feels the more real, the less
real the Other, the less of a subject the Other, the less alive the Other."
What she describes is the situation of animals in scientific
experimentation as well as their fates.

(1) *the less real the Other.* Animals are defined as not having feelings,
not suffering. Because they don't write or talk to us in languages we
understand or admit as language, we presume to know their

intellectual capacity: they don't have any. Yet, if animals weren't like humans nothing that applies to humans could be gained by studying them. This is the crux of the problem in justifying animal experimentation. (And note that Mighty Mouse, Mickey Mouse, the Church Mice, and Templeton the Rat notwithstanding, according to the federal Animal Welfare Act, mice and rats are not even "animals.")

(2) *the less of a subject the Other*: The animal experimented upon cannot be a subject, an actor, only an object called the "subject" of the experiment. The animal does not have interests, does not have legal rights. The animals are called "models," "tools," ("suckers" in the Gennarelli tapes), "it."

(3) *the less alive the Other*: The modus operandi of many experiments is to measure what is fatal. The LD50 test, an acronym for Lethal Dose 50 percent, announces in its unabbreviated title that it must seek the death of animals. According to Andrew N. Rowan, the LD50 test involves calculating the lethal dose of a substance "as the amount that would kill half the group of animals to which it is administered." Many experiments involve long phases of slow dying before euthanasia intervenes. This is a time period during experimentation that could be called precisely the "less alive" period. The less alive period is an important time for observation by experimenters. Peter Singer, in *Animal Liberation*, demonstrates how the less alive period is observed:

> Anthony Hopkins of the Institute of Neurology, London, poisoned twelve adult and three infant baboons by injecting them with lead in varying doses for periods up to one year. Because earlier experiments on cats had shown that absorption of lead is more complete through the lungs, the doses were injected directly into the trachea, or windpipe, of each baboon, which was then held in an upright position so that the poison could "trickle" into its [*sic*] lungs. Before death occurred, loss of weight was "striking," five of the twelve adults losing 40 percent or more of their initial weight. Eight baboons had convulsive fits, thirty-four convulsive fits being observed, although "it is likely that others occurred when no observer was present."

In one baboon, seizures began with "twitching around the right eye, spreading to the rest of the right side of the face. During the next fifteen seconds the right arm became involved, and then seizures became generalized." Seizures were "occasionally preceded by a cry" and were sometimes "precipitated by a sudden movement of the animal as it [*sic*] tried to avoid transfer from one cage to another or whilst reaching up to take a banana." Other symptoms included bloody diarrhea, pneumonia, inflamed and bloody intestines, and liver degeneration. One baboon became so weak it [*sic*] could not stand up, and its [*sic*] left fingers could not grasp orange segments. For three weeks before it [*sic*] died this baboon was partially blind; "it [*sic*] groped for proffered fruit and on occasions appeared not to see it." [Again, damage to vision which eliminates reciprocating gaze.] Five of the baboons died in seizures; seven were found dead in their cages; the remaining three were "sacrificed."

Singer reports other examples of experiments calculated to make animals less alive including ones that "'terminally deprived' 256 young rats of food and water." This less alive period terminates with the animals' deaths, one way or another — if the animals do not die in the course of the experiment, they are put to death.

Problem III: The Dominant Reality

Among the whole gamut of coercive structures in patriarchal capitalism, the scenario of vision, the representational structure imposed on them, isolates a partial "content," framing part of a phenomenon, so as to exclude possibilities of analysing the larger network of structures in which it is embedded. — Susanne Kappeler

The use of animals in experiments, according to Henry Foster, founder of the Charles River Breeding Laboratory, is all "for the benefit of mankind. If you don't use animals, you don't do research." — Troy Soos

The dominant reality is this: we believe in animal experimentation. Though we may be saddened by the information that animals are experimented upon, we optimistically have faith that the experimenters are not inflicting cruel suffering, or at least not unnecessarily. We filter information about animal injuries through our belief that human deaths may be the consequence if these experiments don't occur and the knowledge they could yield is not obtained. Scientists can be irresponsible towards animal rights because they are focused on a "higher" right, the rights of humans to survive. These rights we accept as being in opposition.

Yet, animals experimenters have not been required or even requested by funding agencies or federal law to use alternatives to animal experimentation (simulators, computer models, cell cultures, living human tissue testing or clinical and epidemiological studies). They have not even been asked by those in authority to try an alternative and prove it has failed. Certainly the substitutes would not so well confirm the status of animals as objects.

Animal researchers say they give the public what it needs. Yet what their research focuses on often is "protection" from something we are doing to ourselves or remedying the results of what we have done. It is common knowledge now that next to smoking, animal oppression through the eating of meat and dairy products is linked to many of the major human diseases (heart attacks, breast and colon cancer) which appear in industrialized culture. Experiments continue on what causes cancer while the consumption of known cancer-producing agents also continues, the focus kept narrowly on the supposed need for scientific experimentation which protects us (making us objects as well), excluding any questioning of the dominant reality that causes both our object status and our need for protection. The Authorized Version of reality disempowers both consumers and animals.

Problem IV: Strangers and Other Victims
Under his aesthetic gaze any woman, known or unknown, turns into the "stranger," that object of no interest except for its capacity to stimulate the subject's feeling of life. — Susanne Kappeler

Animals must be kept as "strangers" to permit experimentation.

We could rephrase Kappeler to say, "Under his scientific gaze, any animal, known or unknown, turns into the 'stranger', *the material:* that object of no interest except for its capacity to be a medium for the subject's sense of knowledge." Strangers are less likely to arouse emotional attachment; strangers already exist within a framework of distancing. They are marginalized beings. The outcry over dogs and cats used for experimentation may be explained because they are defined as pets, not as strangers. The drive for legislation against getting animals from pounds for experiments arises to protect these pets. According to Rowan, the humane shelters view the "forced surrender" of cats and dogs to animal experimenters as threatening their "basic structure, namely, a suffering-free sanctuary for animals."

The Charles River Breeding Laboratory provides "micropigs," "macropigs" and "minipigs" and expects that the increased use of pigs instead of dogs will decrease the outcry against animal experimentation since "everybody eats them," i.e. pigs have already been rendered strangers through our consumption of their kind.

Animals must be strangers to confirm the myth of scientific objectivity. As Kappeler writes of literature, "The claim to universality stems from the fact of the disinterestedness with which the subject regards the represented object." The other animals, like women, are points of exchange between two or more subjects. According to Kappeler, pornography occurs when the pornographer speaks to another subject, the consumer of the pornographic material, about a woman who is an object, a point of exchange between them. Animal experimentation similarly involves one scientist speaking to another scientist about the animal, their point of exchange.

Problem V: The Collapse of Categories

The centrality of visual objectification to both [human] male sexual arousal and [human] male models of knowledge and verifications requires further study.
— Catherine MacKinnon

Frequently pornography employs language that celebrates the collapse of the categories of "women" and "animals." We hear of "beaver hunters" who bag a woman, a seductive pig, and the "woman-breaking" tradition of late nineteenth-century pornography which was built on horse-breaking images. In her analysis of this type of pornography, Coral Lansbury finds parallels with the then-current medical treatment of women:

> Women are subdued and held by straps so they can be mounted and flogged more easily, and they always end as grateful victims, trained to enjoy the whip and the straps, proud to provide pleasure for their masters. There is an uneasy similarity between the devices made to hold women for sexual pleasure and those tables and chairs, replete with stirrups and straps, which made women ready for the surgeon's knife.

In protesting the vivisection of the other animals, nineteenth-century women revolted "against a world of [human] male sexual authority." Further, Lansbury argues, "continually animals were seen as surrogates for women who read their own misery into the vivisector's victims." The anti-vivisection movement of the late nineteenth century was predominantly composed of women who saw themselves as the referent in vivisectionists' activities.

The rage these women felt toward vivisection of other animals might have been because they were separated by a vast psychological distance from medical doctors' activities; they were viewed as holding childlike opinions about animals; they were seen as being close kin to the animals themselves; they saw symbols of their own suffering in animal victims. The "absent referent" in the vivisection of other animals was for these women hardly absent — they saw themselves similarly positioned. As Alice Park wrote with alarm to *The Vegetarian Magazine*: "A physician who will deliberately vivisect helpless, harmless, little animals will just as deliberately vivisect women or any human being he can find to experiment on." Concerned by the increasing role "the medical trust" was exercising in the United States, she encouraged women to "drop all worry about the ballot for a few weeks and get out your 'hatchet' to smash all fond hopes these AMA physicians have to eventually rule our nation."

The permeability of categories remains for us today: we frequently read of studies determining that a high proportion of gynecological surgeries performed in the United States are unnecessary. Cesarean deliveries have skyrocketed for women. Andrea Dworkin, in

Pornography: Men Possessing Women, and Gena Corea, in The Mother
Machine, argue the patriarchal source of the epidemic of cesarean
section in the U.S. Interestingly, cesarean deliveries have become, as
well, the standard way to "produce" the most commonly used
laboratory animals. The Charles River Breeding Laboratory
emphasizes that their animals are "Cesarean-Derived," assuring
animal experimenters that they are thereby receiving "pure" strains.

Problem VI: Knowledge
In characterizing scientific and objective thought as
masculine, the very activity by which the knower can
acquire knowledge is also genderized. The relation
specified between knower and known is one of distance
and separation. It is that between a subject and an object
radically divided. — Evelyn Fox Keller

It is clear that the *pursuit* of knowledge in our society is gendered
to begin with. The originating structure which determines both the
sorts of experiments to be undertaken and the kind of quantifiable
knowledge to be gained is a patriarchal one. Animal experimentation rigidly upholds cultural sex-role presumptions. Because
pregnancies are undesirable in many experiments, researchers using
mice rely on "70 males for every 30 females," according to Troy Soos,
writing in The Animals' Agenda. Other experiments look at female
animals precisely for their femaleness. Carolyn Merchant reports
that in England in the 1630's William Harvey "dissected large
numbers of King Charles' does just after coition with bucks." Modern
experimenters can place an order for pregnant animals with the
Charles River Breeding Laboratory. Not only is the control of
females reified in the act of the experiment itself, but so also are the
categories of "maleness" and "femaleness" as the subjects under
study. A fixation on femaleness moves smoothly from the realm of
representation to the realm of experimentation.

Men's distance from women, from their own parenting ability and
their capacity to feel for others, determines experiments such as
Henry Harlow's in which baby monkeys are denied maternal care.
Harlow has described the restricted environment he constructed to
insure the denial of all affection to the baby monkeys. This
environment of non-feeling mirrors the standard for scientific ideas:

reason rules, and feelings are controlled. Norma Benney caustically noted that these experiments proved "what most women know and certainly every mother knows, namely, that young ones need the love of their mother."

Although other animals can be experimented upon only because they are not human, if they weren't like humans nothing would be gained for humans by studying them. But what precisely is gained? How can pain be measured, quantified, interpreted, especially if chronic pain changes an animal's response? How is the knowledge applied once gained? Once the dilemma (animals are different from us; animals are like us) is acknowledged, it attaches itself to the rationale of the animal experiments: Animals are different from us so we can . . . , animals are like us so we conclude. . . . The wedge of differentiation between humans and other animals, which can never be precisely located, is both necessary for and undercuts the premise of scientific knowledge.

That the observer cannot but influence the experiment by the very watching reinforces yet again our awareness of how a patriarchal subject constitutes himself. It is a fact that experiments are often repeated or so designed that they produce results that are not even arguably useful. For instance, although the practical shortcomings of the Draize test are widely admitted, its use is scarcely modified or curtailed. Where experimenters' behavior is so obviously ritual rather than purposive, we must consider the question of agency and sadism.

Problem VII: Agents and Sadism

We are told that animal experimentation is not sadism. But what mental gymnastics are required to consider what in fact happens to other animals without imputing any human, let alone malignant, agency? The argument is made that experimenters are the products of conditioning in which their peers and superiors reinforce the legitimacy of painful experiments on animals. Experimenters do not see themselves as agents of pain, cruelty, etc., because they do not see themselves as agents. Routine and ritual insulate them from their activities. By viewing animals as tools toward their research ends, they render the transitive verb intransitive; they eliminate agency.

Kappeler writes, "Representation foregrounds content. . . and obscures the agent of representation." Science foregrounds knowledge, and obscures the role of the scientist, the agent of scientific experimentation. An experiment on an animal is like representation because neither is "really" happening. It is not happening because the agent is not willing it to happen to be hurtful. Kappeler reminds us to look at the role of the subject: all else arises out of the subject's need to confirm his subjectivity. How else, really, to explain the repetition of experiments? Repetition, Kappler suggests, is an essential aspect of pornography, of constructing the subject in patriarchy — "there is a plot: the cultural archeplot of power."

Sandra Harding implicates the capitalist and patriarchal structure of science. She sees a division of labor involving a select group of white decision-making men dictating the activities of a larger group of less powerful men and women who essentially become scientific technicians: "Because the priorities conceptualized by white males often create ambivalences about the social value of particular projects, research priorities may differ from those of their private lives outside science. Who would *choose* a career goal of building bombs, torturing animals, or manufacturing machines that will put one's sisters and brothers out of work?" While the division of labor and the control of power reinforce the structure of white men's control and posit an absence of agency at the technician level, the arrogant eye is not without a role also. Direct observation of animal "torture" by notable scientists and the fact that scientists achieve notability by their *direct* involvement in animal experimentation (viz. Pavlov, Harlow, Seligman) confirms the presence of agency. They need to be able to say "*I* observed 'y' reaction by these animals after we had done 'x' to them." Scientific knowledge depends on "quantifiable" information; in the case of animal experimentation this requires close observation. Enter the gaze of the arrogant eye, both as an action and a rationale. And that human male gaze involves, to some degree, agency: "*I* am watching *it*."

Theresa Corrigan has remarked on the similarity between the conceptual framework suggested here and Mary Daly's description of the Sado-Ritual Syndrome in her book, *Gyn/Ecology*. A fascinating case can be made that inevitably a Sado-Ritual Syndrome which targets women will also theoretically undergird the intertwined oppression of animals. Many of the components of the Sado-Ritual Syndrome described by Daly are evident in animal experiments as well as other forms of oppressing animals, such as eating meat and wearing animal skins: absence of agency, obsessive repetition, token torturers, otherwise unacceptable behavior taken as normal, and scholarly legitimation.

Once the formula for knowledge is understood as shaky if not bankrupt ("animals are not like us so we can. . ., animals are like us so we conclude. . ."), then the two sides to this formula can be disengaged one from the other. The actions of the former do not always neatly lead to the conclusions of the latter. In breaking the premise of the cause and effect of the experiment, in stripping animal experiments of the legitimacy they gain as gendered scientific knowledge, in questioning the premise of "animals are like us so we conclude. . .," then we are free to look specifically at the phrase, "animals are not like us so we can. . . ." This leads to scrutinizing the agency of the experimenters. What exactly are they doing? We do not have the absence of sadistic violence, we have the refusal to acknowledge agency.

Problem VIII: Consumption

Representations are not just a matter of mirrors, reflections, keyholes. Somebody is making them, and somebody is looking at them, through a complex array of means and conventions. — Susanne Kappeler

Animal experiments reify us as consumers, objects who consume, rather than subjects who decide about the ethics of consumption. This concept explains the testing on animals of cosmetics which promote the "feminine" look, as well as experiments to define what our proper food is — meat? food coloring? with what levels of toxins? In addition, we become consumers of animal experiments: we hear about them without thinking. News reports discussing advances in cancer research or AIDS research usually name the animals used — "a study of rats" or "a study of monkeys." We consume the information, congratulating ourselves, if we are healthy, that science proceeds, helping us to protect ourselves from illness. But it is also because we are consumers that many scientific experiments continue. Because we (some of us) consume meat and smoke cigarettes we have scientific experiments on animals to discover cures for the resulting cancer; because we (some of us) use cosmetics, cleansers, etc., product testing on animals continues. If we restructured consumption, we would eliminate the need for many animal experiments. But this is not the point, of course. Animal experimentation is not only a means to an end — a way by which we can hope to continue consuming without changing habits of harmful consumption; animal experimentation is both socially and economically an end in itself. How many people earn their living experimenting on animals? How many people earn their living supplying animals to be experimented on? The Charles River Breeding Laboratory (1-800-LAB-RATS) had sales of $45 million in 1983. How many people earn their living supplying food, cages and transportation for "lab" animals? What percentage of university budgets is raised from grants funding animal experiments?

Problem IX: What's the Difference?
Meat is like pornography: before it was someone's fun,
it was someone's life. — Melinda Vadas

Ron Martin, producer of a live sex show in New York, was asked if he does not think that he degrades women for profit. His reply: "I know I do. So does the *New York Times*. I have one girl who felt degraded every time she stepped outside. She came here because she was constantly getting hit up by men anyway, so why not get paid? Is working here any more degrading than walking down the street?" Some pornographers say, What's the difference between us and the *New York Times*? Animal experimenters say, What's the difference between what we are doing and what you are doing? You eat animals, don't you? Aren't you wearing leather? You benefit from what we do, so why shouldn't we experiment on animals? The subject status imputed to our acts as consumers of information, meat, and other animal products veils the subject status of the experimenters. Animal oppression thus becomes the legitimating force for the continuance of the system. Neither science nor art stand apart from culture: patriarchal culture is deeply implicated in both. It has been by and large white middle-class and upper-class men who have created scientific theorems, ethics, and the ground rules for animal experimentation. They have created these out of the perspective by which they approach the world: as subjects surveying an object world. Non-human animal experimentation is not an isolated case of animal oppression nor is it unrelated to human male dominance. Animal experimentation is inherent in the way men have made themselves subjects in the world by making others objects. Thus the human male gaze — the arrogant eye of patriarchy — constructs animal experiments.

Sources

Thanks for the support and suggestions of Carol Barash, Melinda Vadas, Nancy Tuana, Marie Fortune, Susanne Kappeler, Theresa Corrigan and Stephanie Hoppe as I worked on this issue.

Adams, Carol J. "The Rape of Animals, The Butchering of Women." *Critical Matrix: Princeton Working Papers in Women's Studies*, Special Issue I (Spring 1988).

"Animal Abuse at Gillette Labs Exposed — International Boycott Called." *The Animals' Agenda* (456 Monroe Turnpike, Monroe, CT. 06468.) December 1986.

Benney, Norma. "All of One Flesh: The Rights of Animals." In *Reclaim the Earth: Women Speak Out for Life on Earth*, edited by Leonie Caldecott and Stephanie Leland. London: The Women's Press, 1983.

Berger, John. "Why Look at Animals?" In *About Looking*. New York: Pantheon, 1980.

Corea, Gena. *The Mother Machine: Reproductive Technologies from Artificial Insemination to Artificial Wombs*. New York: Harper & Row, 1985.

Daly, Mary. *Gyn/Ecology: The Metaethics of Radical Feminism*. Boston: Beacon Press, 1978.

Dworkin, Andrea. *Pornography: Men Possessing Women*. New York: Perigee Books, 1981.

French, R.D. *Antivivisection and Medical Science in Victorian Society*. Princeton: Princeton University Press, 1975.

Frye, Marilyn. *The Politics of Reality: Essays in Feminist Theory*. Trumansburg, New York: The Crossing Press, 1983.

Harding, Sandra. *The Science Question in Feminism*. Ithaca, New York: Cornell University, 1986. (Harding's source for the cultural stereotype of science is M. Rossiter's *Women Scientists in America*.) Used by permission of the publisher, Cornell University Press.

Humphrey, Nicholas. "Seeing and Nothingness." *New Scientist*, March 30, 1972.

Kalechofsky, Roberta. "Metaphors of Nature: Vivisection and Pornography — The Manichean Machine." *On The Issues* 14 (1988).

Kappeler, Susanne. *The Pornography of Representation*. Minneapolis: University of Minnesota Press, 1986. (First published in Britain by Polity Press); and personal communication, October 31, 1988.

Keller, Evelyn Fox. *Reflections on Gender and Science*. New Haven: Yale University Press, 1985.

Lansbury, Coral. *The Old Brown Dog: Women, Workers and Vivisection in Edwardian England*. Madison, Wisconsin: University of Wisconsin Press, 1985.

MacKinnon, Catherine. "A Feminist/Political Approach: 'Pleasure Under Patriarchy.'" In *Theories of Human Sexuality*, edited by James H. Greer and William T. O'Donohue. New York: Plenum, 1987.

Merchant, Carolyn. *The Death of Nature: Women, Ecology, and the Scientific Revolution*. New York: Harper & Row, 1980.

Mulvey, Laura. "Visual Pleasure and Narrative Cinema." *Screen* 16, no.3 (1975).

Park, Alice. In *The Vegetarian Magazine* 14, no. 5 (1910).

Rowan, Andrew N. *Of Mice, Models, and Men: A Critical Evaluation of Animal Research*. Albany, New York: State University of New York Press, 1984.

Singer, Peter. *Animal Liberation*. New York: New York Review Books, 1975; used by permission of author.

Soos, Troy. "Charles River Breeding Labs." *The Animals' Agenda* December 1986.

Ware, Michael D. "The ALF Strikes: Animal Liberators Come to North America." *The Animals' Agenda* July/August 1984.

Animal Liberation
Sally Roesch Wagner

Standing on the screened-in porch, I laughed at the sounds of Pinky the cat chasing her tail in the leaves outside. Suddenly I heard a desperate high-pitched "chit-chit-chit" and ran outside. Rounding the corner of the house, I saw a little gray tail. "Oh, it's just another mouse," I thought, slowing down. Getting closer, I saw that the tail was too big for a mouse. "Oh, thank god, it's a rat." But wait. The body was wrong somehow. The tail was a little too bushy. "Oh shit, Pinky, it's a baby squirrel," I said out loud, feeling suddenly sick to my stomach. I ran toward the cat and chased her away. Seeing that the poor squirrel was going to die anyway, I walked slowly back inside, fighting back tears. I tried to call my daughter, who knows about animals, to find out what I should do, but she wasn't home. I started to dial another animal-identified friend, but stopped myself after three digits, thinking, "This is insane." Suddenly I was face-to-face with a contradiction that I didn't want to look at: my animal politics are rotten.

I have a very patriarchal pecking order of importance when it comes to the members of other animal nations, based on their functional value to me. Mice don't matter. Rats should be killed. Squirrels deserve to live, especially cute little baby ones. This belief that I have the right to decide who shall live and who shall die based on whether or not they bring me pleasure or problem is a reflex. Learned, of course, through several thousand years of Judeo-Christian culture. Animals, argued the early church fathers, have no souls. "It should seem," wrote Normal Pearson in a January 1891 article published by *The Nineteenth Century*, "as if the primitive Christians, by laying so much stress upon a future life, in contradistinction to *this* life, and placing the lower creatures out of the pale of hope, placed them at the same time out of the pale of sympathy, and thus laid the foundation for this utter disregard of animals in the light of our fellow-creatures."

Not all groups of humans are so "humancentric." I could have been born a Native American (pre-white influence) and learned the reflexive body-knowledge that all living things have an integrity in and of themselves. Or I could have been a Buddhist, my belief in ahimsa requiring a code of moral ethics towards animals. But I was raised a Congregationalist, taught to "do unto others as you would have them do unto you," a sweet, banal sentiment which Christians can practice or pay lip service to.

I divide up the animal world in another, deadlier way: animals are edible and non-edible. When Pinky made me squeamish by killing the baby squirrel, I had just finished eating a bowl of turkey soup for lunch, soup I'd made myself, dismantling the turkey carcass to make it. I tore off its legs and wings, broke the torso in half, humming to the radio the whole time. No reaction. But a baby squirrel in pain made me sick. Like driving past the massive, smelly feed lot on my way to Los Angeles on I-5, which used to turn me into a vegetarian for at least an hour.

There's no way I can justify eating "dead animals," as nineteenth-century vegetarians called meat eating. It's a serious contradiction in my life, as smoking cigarettes was before I quit. Smoking is a physical addiction with no redeeming social or physical value. To justify doing it, I was reduced to quoting the *National Enquirer* article about the man who gave up smoking and started eating a box of toothpicks every day, which killed him. Better to die of tobacco than toothpicks, I'd say. There's really no defense for smoking. Nor is there for eating meat. In both cases, the political arguments for stopping the behavior are compelling.

Smoking seriously injures us, our children (born and unborn) and those around us. Meat-eating is obviously fatal to the animal eaten and causes cancer and heart-disease (for starters) in the eater. Even within a human framework, meat-eating is politically irresponsible in a world where people are starving. There would be plenty of food in the world for everyone, animals and humans, if we equally allocated the world's resources and raised only vegetables, not animals for slaughter.

But how far do I need to go? I'm convinced about cattle, sheep and pigs; we shouldn't eat them. But what about fish? Fowl? Dairy products, since they are the result of exploiting animals? Fertilized eggs, since they're undeveloped fowl, or unfertilized ones, which means keeping chickens for our use?

As soon as I get these questions out of my mouth, I see what they are: resistance to consciousness. They are the speculation of the uninvolved, those who choose not to be part of changing the world. Lenin taught me that you create the new world in the process of dismantling the old. I've taken the first step of no longer eating red meat, and it's becoming clearer to me about eating fish and fowl. One contradiction at a time. As I can afford to emotionally invest more of myself in animals, knowing that I am no longer basing my life on their destruction, I will be better able to undo my pecking order of animal importance.

I have to take on faith and through hard listening many truths that don't come easy to a person separated for years from her ability to "see" animals. I must open up to feelings that hurt; feelings beyond defensiveness, trivialization — in short, beyond power. For the oppressor, the process of liberation always involves a major shift away from the accepted mode of thought. More than that, it precipitates a personality change, for when we incorporate these transformational ideas into practice, we become different human beings.

I've been thinking about what happened to derail me from being a child with a healthy caring about animals to someone with intellectual indifference, how I learned not to feel as I grew up. What I'm finding is a process of cultural deadening similar to the one men describe as the way they learned emotional detachment from women.

I drag up memories of a time when I cared. Sobbing through the spring dehorning, town kid come to the farm for a day, watching the blood spurting from the head of cattle whose eyes were wild with fear and pain. Screaming for someone to stop it, laughed at by "wiser" adults, covering my ears to shut out the unnatural bellowing that signaled the branding that followed.

Another vignette: glancing out the side window of our car and seeing a group of boys stoning a cat. I felt sick inside. My reflexive "Stop them!" was ignored. Another: watching my father "break" a horse to the saddle. Bridled and snubbed to a post, the horse kicks each time my father hits her on the rump with a blanket. Her reflex makes her fall to her knees, because my father has tied three of her legs together.

The men talk at leisure, spit tobacco, laugh at my pleas to stop.

At some point I shut down. It cost too much to feel into animals' pain; my body rebelled at the bottled-up outrage I was storing. I experienced the isolation of powerful, unshared feelings overlaid by my powerlessness to stop such horror. Going back to the place before these feelings stopped is like opening the door of a packed closet. The childhood reactions sit in their original packaging, and unwrapping their memory releases pain still as fresh as when I boxed it. But I'm changed; the adult woman I am *can* do something to stop the cruel treatment of animals. I begin circulating petitions, and I stop eating red meat. I worry about "coming out" as a vegetarian-in-training to my father, who has raised Hereford cattle all his eighty-odd years. He too has shifted, confessing that he eats little beef anymore.

I bring my new consciousness to the place I most intensely live, my research into nineteenth-century radical reform movements. Could there have been people concerned about animal rights a hundred years ago? Digging hard, I am amazed to find not isolated individuals, but a massive, organized movement, with newsletters and journals, separate organizations reflecting different issues of concern and perspectives.

The American Humane Education Society distributed copies of *Black Beauty* by the thousands in the 1880's and sponsored an essay contest in 1891 on the question: "In the interests of humanity, should vivisection be permitted, and if so, under what restrictions and limitations?" The Harvard University Medical School judged the "pro" arguments. The American Anti-Vivisection Society chose the prize-winning essay opposing the practice of animal experimentation, which quoted numerous anti-vivisection physicians who argued that "operations have been performed on thousands of animals every year for centuries, and nothing whatever has been learned from this wholesale vivisection." Worse than nothing, "the opening of animals has done more to perpetuate error than to confirm the just views taken from the study of anatomy," various authorities contended.

My growing vegetarianism is strengthened by the founder and Chief of Staff of the Salvation Army, who convinces me from the grave that "a vegetarian diet of wheat, oatmeal and other grains, lentils, peas, beans, nuts and similar food is more than ten times as economical as a flesh diet" and "is favorable to robust health and strength" since "the digestive organs of man are not well adapted for the use of flesh." Writing in the 1890's, Chief William Booth was certain that "the great increase in cancer during the last hundred years has been caused by the great increase in the use of animal food."

There are animal liberationists who simply want better treatment for animals, while continuing to objectify them, like the noted abolitionist Lydia Maria Child, who said in 1865, "There are not many people who are conscientious about being kind in their relations with human beings; and therefore it is not surprising that still fewer should be considerate about humanity to animals. . . .The fact that they cannot speak to tell of what they suffer makes the sad expression of their great patient eyes the more touching to any compassionate heart." Nathaniel P. Rogers, also an abolitionist, believed that approach didn't go far enough. "We hear it spoken of as a man's *duty to be kind* to the brutes — but never of the brute's right to just treatment. But why has not a brute rights, as well as man? What is the foundation of human rights, that is not foundation for animal rights also?. . .The horse has rights. The dog. The cat, and the *rat* even. Real rights. And these rights are sacred. They are not to be invaded."

Rogers and Child were both abolitionists, which seems not chance, and Child directly draws the connection between the treatment of animals and that of slaves:

> Fugitive slaves, looking out mournfully and wearily upon a cold, unsympathizing world, have often reminded me of overworked and absued oxen; for though slaves were endowed by their Creator with the gift of speech, their oppressors have made them afraid to use it to complain of their wrongs. In fact, they have been in a more trying situation than abused oxen, for they have been induced by fear to use their gift of speech in professions of contentment with their bondage. Therefore, those who have been slaves know how to sympathize with the dumb creatures of God; and they, more than others, ought to have compassion on them. The great and good Toussaint l'Ouverture was always kind to the animals under his care, and I consider it by no means the smallest of his merits.

Ingrid Newkirk, co-founder of People for the Ethical Treatment of Animals (PETA), believes there is a parallel between the anti-slavery movement in the United States and her organization's work to liberate animals. My research says she's on the money.

For one thing, animal liberationists follow the tried-and-true method of raising consciousness used by the abolitionists. Graphic pictures of the brutal enforcement of power and prejudice are shocking us out of our sneering trivialization of animal oppression in 1988 as effectively as it broke through the "I don't want to get involved" indifference of our foreparents one hundred fifty years ago. First, the strategy of social change goes, you get people to identify and connect with the oppressed. Once they identify with the oppressed, their next step is action.

Lydia Maria Child won thousands of converts to the abolitionist cause with this 1833 description of the kidnapping of Africans into slavery:

> Husbands are torn from their wives, children from their parents, while the air is filled with the shrieks and lamentations of the bereaved. Sometimes they are brought from a remote country; obliged to wander over mountains and through deserts; chained together in herds; driven by the whip; scorched by a tropical sun; compelled to carry heavy bales of merchandise; suffering with hunger and thirst; worn down with fatigue; and often leaving their bones to whiten in the desert. . . . In some places. . . they become the prey of wild beasts, more merciful than white men.

A recent PETA News publication describes the torture of food animals:

> The stockyard workers proceeded to beat and kick her in the face, ribs and back. They used the customary electric prods in her ear to try to get her out of the truck, but she still did not move. The workers then tied a rope around her head, tied the other end to a post in the ground and drove the truck away. She was dragged along the floor of the truck and fell to the ground, land-

ing with both hind legs and her pelvis broken. . . . She lay in the hot sun crying out for the first three hours. Periodically, when she urinated or defecated, she used her front legs to drag herself along the gravel roadway to a clean spot. She also tried to crawl to a shaded area but could not move far enough. . . . The stockyard employees would not allow her any drinking water.

Public reaction to the animal rights literature is predictable. Truth about injustice demands changes, uncomfortable and hard ones. Those benefiting from oppression lose in the short run when justice is instituted. And so people often turn on the bearer of the bad news. Tirades against "fanatics," "lunatics," "reckless incendiaries" and "firebrands" follow animal rights activists just as they greeted the enemies of slavery. Many newspapers exulted over the mobs which violently broke up abolition meetings; one paper in 1835 warned that "Hereafter, the leaders of the Abolitionists will be treated with less forbearing than they have been heretofore. The people will consider them as out of the pale of the legal and conventional protection which society affords to honest and well-meaning members. They will be treated as robbers and pirates, and the enemy of humankind." Those who demanded an immediate, unconditional end to slavery, seen as the enemies of humankind? Yes, indeed.

This newspaper wasn't from the Southern slavery press; it was a respected New York journal which represented the feelings of a large majority of the North. Mobs that attacked abolitionists were typically made up of "gentlemen of property and standing," pillars of the community and church members. The right of private property, even when the property was human beings, had precedence over the right to life, liberty and the pursuit of happiness. Churches, almost without exception at this time, ignored or actively supported the institution of slavery, quoting the Old Testament's approval of slavery as justification. These gentlemen were the great-grandfathers, probably, of some of the respected scientists and scholars who today attack as "robbers and terrorists" members of the Animal Liberation Front who free lab animals and destroy the means of torturing them.

We as a society don't see the torture death of lab animals as murder, any more than most whites saw the killing of slaves as murder. Oppression always rests its power on prejudice. Definitions of the oppressed are surprisingly similar. Blacks, children, women, animals: all have been defined as less important, less intelligent, and incapable of taking care of themselves, therefore requiring a master who is the legal, god-given superior of his lesser counterpart. Those who defy this pecking order break not only man's law, but are seen as challenging the divine order of the universe as well.

While no form of oppression has been ended, there's been some recognition of most systems of injustice. Animals are one of the remaining frontiers of patriarchal power; we're just beginning culturally to question the system of human chauvinism. Men still prove their physical prowess by killing animals, and the great sportsmen of the National Rifle Association grab their guns with castration anxiety every time someone threatens to take them away, or control their use. Men still prove their economic prowess by draping their willing women with the skins of dead animals. More sophisticated corporate executives, who wouldn't be caught dead with deer horns above their mantels, maximize their farming, medical, cosmetic and household product profits off the bodies of animals. As corporate farming buries the family farm, the brutality becomes more detached and horrific.

In the grand pecking order of white-christian-capitalist-patriarchy, god is at the top and animals are at the bottom. And just as god has the right to do anything to humans that he wants, and men have the right to do anything to women that they want, and adults to children, everyone lords it over animals. When the California legislature was debating the marital rape law in 1979, Senator Bob Wilson quipped, "If you can't rape your own wife, who can you rape?" Indeed. If you can't exploit animals, who can you exploit? But as each group claims their right to equality and self-determination and as each of us fights for the rights of others, the hierarchy crumbles.

Most of us who claim to be "civilized" people believe, in the depths of our culturally created souls, that we're more important than animals, and that animals exist for us. And so we shampoo our hair oblivious to the number of rabbits who were blinded, tortured and eventually killed to ensure that the soap we use won't irritate our eyes. Never mind that experts are questioning the validity of toxicology and medical research on animals when the results are extrapolated to humans. Never mind that non-animal testing methods have been developed, using computers and cell-culture and organ-culture systems. Never mind that animal tests are not legally required for cosmetics and household products. We still believe that the conductors of the underground railroad who break into laboratories, liberate test animals and deliver them to safety are going too far. Even if we sympathize with their goals, we oppose their righteous anger and militancy. Our reaction is like that of the liberal clergyman Dr. William Ellery Channing, who opposed slavery, but accused the abolitionists of having "fallen into the common error of enthusiasts — that of exaggerating their object, of feeling as if no evil existed but that which they opposed, and as if no guilt could be compared with that of countenancing or upholding it." To which Lydia Maria Child countered, "the simple fact is, anti-slavery societies are the steam, and they [those who believed like Channing] are the passengers in the cars. They may not like the puffing and blowing, the cinders and the jolting; but the powerful agency carries them onward."

The animal liberation movement is the "powerful agency" that is carrying us forward into a paradigm shift. And a paradigm shift will occur. We view the demand for an immediate end to animal testing as just as utopian as our nineteenth-century counterparts saw the abolitionist demand for immediate unconditional emancipation of slaves. It was a worthwhile goal, some agreed, but slavery simply couldn't be abolished overnight, there was too much at stake. We are as hooked economically on the exploitation of animals as they were (North and South) on the exploitation of black labor; we can't envision how the drugs we're dependent upon can be tested without appropriating animal labor.

Our foreparents didn't find a way to end slavery until they decided it was wrong, and it finally took a war to convince them. Similarly, once we decide that the exploitation of animals is wrong, we'll turn to the existing alternatives to animal experimentation. The hard part is never the creation of new ways of doing things; the real struggle is accepting that we need them. To get to the point of saying, individually and as a society, "I won't have my existence (food, health, clothing and recreation) rest upon the exploitation and killing of animals," requires shifting the whole way we see the world. Animal rights groups are forcing us and guiding us in making that shift.

Contributors' Notes

Carol Adams, with a grant from The Culture and Animals Foundation, is finishing a book, *Against the Texts of Meat*, which explores how a patriarchal culture authorizes meat-eating.

Jean Anaporte-Easton's poetry has appeared in anthologies and magazines. She presently teaches writing at Butler University in Indianapolis, IN.

Gloria Anzaldúa is a Chicana *tejana* lesbian-feminist poet and fiction writer. She is co-editor of *This Bridge Called My Back: Writings by Radical Women of Color*.

Margaret Atwood was born in Ottawa, Canada, in 1939, and grew up in Ontario, Quebec and Toronto. She is the author of more than twenty volumes of poetry, fiction and nonfiction.

Becky Birtha is the author of two collections of short stories, *For Nights Like This One: Stories of Loving Women*, and *Lovers' Choice*. She writes that connections with animals are rare in her life.

Hope Sawyer Buyukmihci was born in Lorraine, NY, in 1913. She founded the Unexpected Wildlife Refuge in Newfield, NJ, in 1961, and she has lived there ever since, writing, drawing and working for animal rights.

Anne Cameron is the author of numerous books, screenplays, poems and stories. She lives in British Columbia.

Sally Carrighar lived much of her adult life in California, where she began writing about wildlife in 1937, starting with her study of the animal community around Beetle Rock at Sequoia National Park.

Shirley Graves Cochrane is a teacher, editor and writer in Washington, D.C. Her story "Rescue" is based on memories of her grandmother and of a stay on a hard-scrabble farm in the Virginia foothills.

Joan Dobbie was born in 1946 and grew up in New York State. She lives now with a houseful of animals and children in Eugene, OR, where she is a graduate student in creative writing, teaches poetry and Hatha Yoga, and makes clay sculpture.

Judy Grahn is a founding mother and shaper of lesbian-feminism and the author of numerous books. She has spent fifteen years developing the magical language-scape of her latest novel, *Mundane's World*, where all characters — plants, animals and humans — have equal standing.

Karen Kidd was born in San Francisco and has lived in New York and the Southwest. She now lives with one woman, two dogs, two cats, one parakeet, and spirits of many. . . including Queen Jane, still whispering and whispering at her.

Natalie Kusz recently moved to Minnesota after living in Alaska for twenty years. Her publications include pieces in *Iowa Woman* and *The Threepenny Review*.

Aileen La Tourette was born in New Jersey in 1946. She has lived in England for twenty years, where she has published several novels as well as radio and theater plays and short fiction.

Ursula K. Le Guin grew up in California, partly in the Napa Valley, which is associated with the site of her book *Always Coming Home* as well of "May's Lion," a story in which, she says, she began to see how to write the connections of history and dream that are at the heart of the book.

Cris Mazza's fiction has been published in numerous literary magazines. Her first book, *Animal Acts*, a story collection, will be released in early 1989. She lives in San Diego, CA, where she breeds, trains and shows Shetland Sheepdogs.

Patricia Monaghan grew up in Alaska, where she fished and hunted for her food, and gained a strong, but unsentimental, awareness of animal — and for that matter vegetable — life. She recently moved to Chicago where she teaches writing at an inner-city literacy program.

Rochelle Natt has published poetry and short stories in many literary magazines and anthologies. She has won the Branden Memorial Award and is a finalist in the 1989 Eve of St. Agnes Award.

Juanita M. Sanchez is a native New Mexican of Indian/Spanish ancestry. She is a machinist, union shop steward, and Curandera. She lives in a small brown house with two dogs and two cats.

Nan Sherman works as a staff consultant for the Women's Center at Council House in Los Angeles. She has had numerous poems published in literary magazines and anthologies.

Mary TallMountain, of Koyukon Athabascan Russian Celtic origin, was born in Alaska Territory in 1918. Her poetry has appeared in numerous anthologies and a collection, *There is No Word for Goodbye*. She has in progress a novel set in Alaska, devoted like much of her other work to social insights.

Sally Roesch Wagner is an activist/historian who specializes in 19th-century radical reform movements and performs as the vegetarian suffragist Matilda Joslyn Gage.

Dorothy Wood was born in Kansas City, MO, the day after Thanksgiving, in 1910 and worked most of her life in advertising. She died in Anaheim, CA, in 1988.

zana lives in a rural lesbian community, choosing to enjoy wild animals rather than keep domesticated ones. she's disabled, jewish, a writer and artist.

About the Editors

Theresa Corrigan's life has always been a montage of furred, feathered and finned friends — from earliest memories of a farm near Philadelphia where she lived with her family of three humans, thirty-five cats (all named and known), Smoky Dog, chickens, cows and countless "saved" rabbits, mice and birds to her current household of nine cats, four dogs and dozens of fish. Neighbors call her "the weird cat lady on the corner" and vagabond animals know her as a reliable meal ticket.

She teaches Women's Studies at California State University, Sacramento, owns and operates Lioness Books, the local feminist bookstore, and writes. She also volunteers at the PAWS animal shelter and counts among her friends a baboon, a lioness, a baby elephant and several bears. It was Sweet William, an old black bear, who first encouraged her to work on this anthology.

Stephanie T. Hoppe was born in San Francisco in 1947 and grew up in the coastal hill country of Northern California, where her family has lived for five generations. Through her work as a lawyer involved in natural resource protection, she came to see the starting place for achieving a right relation with the world and its varied inhabitants lies elsewhere: in the mind, with cultural assumptions. Here she found a connection with her early ambitions to be a writer: work at the very edge of fiction, with the forms and conventions that underlie fiction and reality alike. *The Windrider*, a sf/fantasy novel re-visioning myths of the American West, was published in 1985.

She now lives in Mendocino County with her husband and a black cat, Vanessa, who has, sleeping and waking, put in long hours overseeing this as earlier books, as well as the world in general.

Books from Cleis Press

AIDS: The Women edited by Ines Rieder and Patricia Ruppelt. ISBN: 0-939416-20-4 24.95 cloth; ISBN: 0-939416-21-2 9.95 paper.

A Lesbian Love Advisor by Celeste West. ISBN: 0-939416-27-1 21.95 cloth; ISBN: 0-939416-26-3 9.95 paper.

Different Daughters: A Book by Mothers of Lesbians edited by Louise Rafkin. ISBN: 0-939416-12-3 21.95 cloth; ISBN: 0-939416-13-1 8.95 paper.

Don't: A Woman's Word by Elly Danica. ISBN: 0-939416-23-9 21.95 cloth; ISBN: 0-939416-22-0 8.95 paper.

Fight Back! Feminist Resistance to Male Violence edited by Frédérique Delacoste & Felice Newman. ISBN: 0-939416-01-8 13.95 paper.

Long Way Home: The Odyssey of a Lesbian Mother & Her Children by Jeanne Jullion. ISBN: 0-939416-05-0 8.95 paper.

On Women Artists: Poems 1975-1980 by Alexandra Grilikhes. ISBN: 0-939416-00-X 4.95 paper.

Peggy Deery by Nell McCafferty. ISBN: 0-939416-29-8 21.95 cloth; ISBN: 0-939416-28-X 9.95 paper.

Sex Work: Writings by Women in the Sex Industry edited by Frédérique Delacoste and Priscilla Alexander. ISBN: 0-939416-10-7 24.95 cloth; ISBN: 0-939416-11-5 10.95 paper.

The Absence of the Dead Is Their Way of Appearing by Mary Winfrey Trautmann. ISBN: 0-939416-04-2 8.95 paper.

The Little School: Tales of Disappearance & Survival in Argentina by Alicia Partnoy. ISBN: 0-939416-08-5 15.95 cloth; ISBN: 0-939416-07-7 8.95 paper.

The One You Call Sister: New Women's Fiction edited by Paula Martinac. ISBN: 0-939416-30-1 24.95 cloth; ISBN: 0-939416031-X 9.95 paper.

The Shape of Red: Insider/Outsider Reflections by Ruth Hubbard and Margaret Randall. ISBN: 0-939416-19-0 24.95 cloth; ISBN: 0-939416-18-2 9.95 paper.

Unholy Alliances: New Women's Fiction edited by Louise Rafkin. ISBN: 0-939416-14-X 21.95 cloth; ISBN: 0-939416-15-8 9.95 paper.

Voices in the Night: Women Speaking About Incest edited by Toni A.H. McNaron & Yarrow Morgan. ISBN: 0-939416-02-6 9.95 paper.

With a Fly's Eye, Whale's Wit and Woman's Heart: Relationships Between Animals and Women edited by Theresa Corrigan & Stephanie T. Hoppe. ISBN: 0-939416-24-7 24.95 cloth; ISBN: 0-939416-25-5 9.95 paper.

With the Power of Each Breath: A Disabled Women's Anthology edited by Susan Browne, Debra Connors & Nanci Stern. ISBN: 0-939416-09-3 24.95 cloth; ISBN: 0-939416-06-9 10.95 paper.

Woman-Centered Pregnancy & Birth by the Federation of Feminist Women's Health Centers. ISBN: 0-939416-03-4 11.95 paper.

You Can't Drown the Fire: Latin American Women Writing in Exile edited by Alicia Partnoy. ISBN: 0-939416-16-6 21.95 cloth; ISBN: 0-939416-17-4 9.95 paper.

Since 1980, Cleis Press has published progressive books by women. We welcome your order and will ship your books as quickly as possible. Order from: Cleis Press, PO Box 8933, Pittsburgh PA 15221. Individual orders must be prepaid. Please add shipping (1.50 for the first book; .75 for each additional book). PA residents add sales tax. MasterCard and Visa orders welcome — include account number, exp. date, and signature. Payment in US dollars only.